Steep Trails

THE JOHN MUIR LIBRARY

The Story of My Boyhood and Youth
A Thousand-Mile Walk to the Gulf
My First Summer in the Sierra
The Cruise of the Corwin
The Yosemite
The Mountains of California
Travels in Alaska
Our National Parks
Steep Trails

JOHN MUIR

Steep Trails

SIERRA CLUB BOOKS · SAN FRANCISCO

The Sierra Club, founded in 1892 by John Muir, has devoted itself to the study and protection of the earth's scenic and ecological resources—mountains, wetlands, woodlands, wild shores and rivers, deserts and plains. The publishing program of the Sierra Club offers books to the public as a nonprofit educational service in the hope that they may enlarge the public's understanding of the Club's basic concerns. The point of view expressed in each book, however, does not necessarily represent that of the Club. The Sierra Club has some sixty chapters coast to coast, in Canada, Hawaii, and Alaska. For information about how you may participate in its programs to preserve wilderness and the quality of life, please address inquiries to Sierra Club, 730 Polk Street, San Francisco, CA 94109.

Library of Congress Cataloging-in-Publication Data
Muir, John, 1838–1914.
    Steep trails / John Muir.
        p.   cm.
    Originally published: Boston : Houghton Mifflin, 1918.
    Includes index.
    ISBN 0-87156-535-8 : $10.00
        1. West (U.S.)—Description and travel—1860–1880.   2. Shasta, Mount (Calif.)   3. Forests and forestry—West (U.S.)   I. Title.
F594.M95   1994
917.8—dc20   93-25661
                                                            CIP

Production by Susan Ristow
Book design and illustration by Michael McCurdy
Composition by Wilsted & Taylor

Printed in the United States of America on acid-free paper containing a minimum of 50% recovered waste paper of which at least 10% of the fiber content is post-consumer waste.

10   9   8   7   6   5   4   3   2   1

Contents

Foreword by Edward Hoagland   vii

Editor's Note by William Frederic Badè   xvi

1. Wild Wool   1

2. A Geologist's Winter Walk   12

3. Summer Days at Mount Shasta   20

4. A Perilous Night on Shasta's Summit   40

5. Shasta Rambles and Modoc Memories   58

6. The City of the Saints   75

7. A Great Storm in Utah   81

8. Bathing in Salt Lake   86

9. Mormon Lilies   90

10. The San Gabriel Valley   97

11. The San Gabriel Mountains   103

12. Nevada Farms   110

13. Nevada Forests 117

14. Nevada's Timber Belt 124

15. Glacial Phenomena in Nevada 131

16. Nevada's Dead Towns 139

17. Puget Sound 146

18. The Forests of Washington 162

19. People and Towns of Puget Sound 177

20. An Ascent of Mount Rainier 186

21. The Physical and Climatic Characteristics of Oregon 193

22. The Forests of Oregon and Their Inhabitants 213

23. The Rivers of Oregon 234

24. The Grand Cañon of the Colorado 248

Index 273

Foreword

Up in the thin air, the "upness" near the heavens in the High Sierra or on snowy Mount Shasta or Alaska's Stikine River glaciers, John Muir went clambering after revelation with strong lungs and long legs. Tidewater Florida and the Arizona desert didn't please him quite as much, though we have his diaries, belatedly put into books, from all over. Many people kept diaries in Muir's day (1838–1914), but his rough scribblings from the field were not just a keepsake. Ranging much of the continent's high terrain, he began to have the idea of speaking to the nation on behalf of wild nature, both in order to try to protect what he loved and to evangelize. Romanticism is "spilled religion," as Alfred North Whitehead suggested, and Muir was certainly a romantic. He didn't believe in a precise locus for God in church or prayer, but, rather, spilled his enthusiasm over massifs and rivers, creeks and foothills, flowery meadows and granite talus slides. To believe in God we have the evidence of our ears and eyes, and Muir possessed a vaulting energy to pursue enlightenment in this way, like a kind of human tuning fork. As no one else in literature, up and up and *up* he climbed.

Making books out of his exaltation was harder for him. He was 56 before *The Mountains of California*, his first, came out. At half that age he had finished climbing out of the brutalized, benighted boyhood his fundamentalist father had imposed on him in Scotland, where he was born, then after the age of eleven, on two hardscrabble Wisconsin farms. He had meanwhile acquired the beginnings of a sophisticated education in two and a half years at the university in Madison, had proven himself an ingenious and talented machinist while working as a craftsman in a couple of factories, and had wrestled with his conscience over whether to serve in the Civil War, dodging off instead to Canada for two years. Neither Yankee patriotism nor his father's hellfire Presbyterianism now had much hold on him. "John Muir, Earth-planet, Universe" was the heading (and address) he gave to his journal of his *Thousand-Mile Walk to the Gulf*, from Louisville to Florida, in 1867, at the age of 29.

The ebullient book by that name was not actually published until two years after his death, however, long after he had become a famous public figure and literary man. He didn't dictate even the first draft of *The Story of My Boyhood and Youth* until 1908, when he was 69 and his wife, Louie, was dead and a private stenographer had been provided to him almost against his will by his powerful, somewhat coercive friend, E. H. Harriman, the Southern Pacific railroad magnate, while Muir was mewed up at Harriman's vacation home on Klamath Lake in Oregon. *My First Summer in the Sierra*, celebrating his earliest rambles in 1869 through the colossal landscape that afterwards became his spiritual home, did not appear until 1911—though quite unchanged from his battered blue notebooks of forty years before, says his biographer, Frederick Turner. And *Travels in Alaska*, which surely could have been still more resplendent with descriptions and epiphanies if Muir had given himself more time to finish it before he died, also was put together from old journals, dating to 1879, and published in 1915.

Muir had to huff and puff a bit to produce his books. He wanted them to count politically and spiritually, and some of them do show it in occasionally labored, high-flown passages, proselytizing for the wilderness. For that reason *Steep Trails*, which was assembled by his literary executor, William Frederic Badè, ranks among his best because it consists of newspaper and magazine pieces dashed off in a feeling of gaiety and spontaneity after a series of strenuous, exuberant hikes. The travelogue aspect, after all these years, adds a piquant, present-tense dimension, as if we too—readers of the *San Francisco Bulletin* in 1877—could take a jaunt by sea to Santa Monica to visit "the handsome, conceited little town of Los Angeles," population 15,000, and "the Pasadena Colony . . . scarce three years old, but . . . growing rapidly, like a pet tree . . . sixty families, mostly drawn from the better class of vagabond pioneers." The wilderness is only "checkered" with these "brusque little bits of civilization" and "quack climates" that draw pitiful invalids "already on the verge of the grave," and "the city held me but a short time, for the San Gabriel Mountains were in sight, advertising themselves grandly along the northern sky."

Washington Territory, in 1889, has just been made a state, and Seattle, with 20,000 citizens, is four days' steamer voyage north of San Francisco. Muir, who is by now a connoisseur of trees twelve feet thick and imposing mountains, exults in the new wonders of primeval Oregon and Puget Sound. He climbs Mount Rainier, having fifteen years earlier indulged in a stormy, rapturous, dangerous, lengthy love affair with Mount Shasta, which we are also privy to. In the tall-timber big woods, the loggers' clothing "is full of rosin and never wears out. A little of everything in the woods is stuck fast to [it] and their trousers grow constantly thicker with age." Their faces, however, have a tired, haggard look, "doubtful in color . . . and all the fresh, leafy, outreaching branches of the mind seem to have been withered and killed with fatigue, leaving their lives little more than dry lumber."

Foreword

His pictures of people are apt and mixed, not skewed toward the beamish or jubilant, as his landscapes sometimes are. In a Nevada ghost town, where the gold-mining fever burned hot and out, "only one man remains—a lone bachelor with one suspender." Nevada's frontier farms and mountains, which he explored during three summers and a three-thousand-mile horseback ride, evoke his intelligent, detailed enthusiasm. As on the Shasta trips, he was in the midst of what for him were the sanguine, energetic 1870s, when he was seasoned but just turning 40. In Utah, where he rambled as extensively, most of the Mormon women "have a weary, repressed look, as if for the sake of their religion they were patiently carrying burdens heavier than they were well able to bear. But, strange as it may seem . . . the many wives of one man, instead of being repelled from one another by jealousy, appear to be drawn all the closer together, as if the real marriage existed between the wives." In short, a pioneering feminism.

In the nooks of the mountains are individuals who are gophering not for ore but after veins of water—a spring which, loosed, will make them rich. Yet Muir pauses to ask whether people can "be brought to see that possibly Nature may have other uses even for *rich* soil besides the feeding of human beings." "Even the sky," he remarks elsewhere in astonishment, "is not safe from scath."

"All this good world," a phrase from his Nevada saunterings, sums up the spirit of *Steep Trails*—its "blessed" ouzels, his favorite bird, and the elegantly tasseled foxtail pine, "extravagantly picturesque," which vies with the sequoia for the position of favorite tree. In Mormon country he swims in the famous salt waves, getting "myself into right lusty relationship with the brave old lake," and climbs to witness "snow flowers" falling onto alpine lilies. In the

Foreword

Cascade Mountains east of Seattle he admires Snoqualmie Falls, 240 feet high and braided at the top but plunging "in numberless comet-shaped masses" to a deep pool misting "a beautiful rose color." Up the "foodful" Columbia River in Oregon run countless millions of salmon, "plump and smooth like loaves of bread." Perhaps because he had grown up on Fountain Lake in central Wisconsin, the word "fountain" often recurs as he explores the head of watercourses, glaciers, valleys, the wellsprings of great rivers.

Muir, although pausing to discuss economic and social matters, is so emotional and above all enthusiastic a traveler that readers who don't believe in distilled happiness may be bored by him. The special high points were what he was after. "We too must write Bibles," Emerson had said; and this is part of what Muir was attempting. Yet, like Henry Thoreau at Walden Pond, he was capable of the much humbler, playful gambit of standing on his head (at the Grand Canyon and in Alaska) to revivify a panorama of colors and because we "become new creatures with bodies inverted." Earlier, when life needed no revivifying, the informality and juicy joy of his pieces is sometimes enhanced, as in Tenaya Canyon in 1873 or on Shasta's summit in May the next year, by sheer, sharp gratitude that, after a giddy misstep or miscalculation, he is still alive.

By the time of his Grand Canyon essay of 1902, Muir had become a distinguished figure, charter member of the National Institute of Arts and Letters, recipient of a Harvard honorary degree, founding president of the Sierra Club. He had previously toured the same region with the National Forest Commission, in the company of Gifford Pinchot, later recognized as the most influential forester who ever lived; and Muir's own magisterial account, published not as a free-lance newspaper "letter" but as a paean

Foreword

commissioned by *Century* magazine, helped to preserve the Canyon for the public in a near-pristine state. Already, the Santa Fe Railroad was carrying tourists to the rim, as the Southern Pacific ferried them close to Yosemite and the Northern Pacific brought them to Yellowstone Park. Muir, an accomplished lobbyist, was about to meet President Theodore Roosevelt and hike with him in Yosemite Valley and then embark on a grand tour of Europe, Siberia, Manchuria, India, New Zealand. His rhapsodies about Douglas firs and sugar pines—the uniquely confident pleasure he took in proclaiming, after swimming in Utah's Salt Lake and before climbing the Oquirrh Range, "Now I shall have another baptism. I will bathe in the high sky"—had gradually made him famous.

A driven man, like Thoreau, Audubon, George Catlin, Meriwether Lewis and many another naturalist or explorer (think of nineteenth-century Africa's berserk collection), Muir had converted himself from beaten child to espouser of high-country joy. At best, in such larks as "Wild Wool," his mind is acrobatic and humorous as well as evangelical. "The mole, living always in the dark and in the dirt, is yet as clean as the otter or the wave-washed seal," he remarks, while characterizing "the love-work of Nature." And in the San Gabriel Mountains he spares and sympathizes with a rattlesnake he has discovered coiled between his feet, because "there was a bashful look in his eye, and a withdrawing, deprecating kink in his neck that showed plainly as words could tell that he would not strike." Within a forest in Nevada, the sight of piñon nuts reminds him how, inside, insect grubs, "happy fellows," are fattening "until their wings are grown and they are ready to launch out into the free ocean of air and light."

American conservation did not begin with Muir. George Washington, for instance, in a letter to a friend in 1797 had said,

Foreword

"We ruin the lands that are already cleared and either cut down more wood, if we have it, or emigrate into the western country. . . . A half, a third, or even a fourth of what land we mangle, well wrought and properly dressed, would produce more than the whole under our system of management, yet such is the force of habit that we cannot depart from it. . . ." But Muir's writing has survived for a century because he was not afraid to wear his heart on his sleeve. He was a mountainman, yet a pacifist, a politician and yet selfless. He didn't hunt or fish in the wilderness, sell trees or snag nuggets, and thus in a sense he has only been freshened for us by the passage of time. Snow and ice are "the jewelry of winter," he suggests, and that's why we roam outdoors too.

"Divine with the jewelry of winter" is his phrase for Mount Tissiack. Having suffered from his father's rogue form of Christianity, he is not enamored of Judeo-Christian doctrine, particularly that which specifies in *Genesis* that men should subdue and rule over all other creatures. "I have never yet happened upon a trace of evidence that . . . any one animal was ever made for another as much as it was made for itself. Not that Nature manifests any such thing as selfish isolation. In the making of every animal the presence of every other animal has been recognized. Indeed, every atom in creation may be said to be acquainted with and married to every other," he adds. Wild versus domestic sheep are his subject, and he argues that although "we eat wild oysters alive with great directness . . . leaving scarce a second . . . between the shell and the lip . . . we take wild sheep home and subject them to the many extended processes of husbandry, and finish by boiling them in a pot . . . which completes all sheep improvements as far as man is concerned."

Fire and brimstone again, compared to a wolf's simple culling. Few of us would wish to nibble dried breadballs and camp out for weeks in our clothes, as Muir did, and his prose, like his treks, can seem excessive. But its piquant personality and lucent affirmation are irrepressible. "Wild with delight" is a frequent phrase—delight being synchronous with whatever is wild—and his phenomenal hiking feats were surely propelled more by this pursuit than by his scientific curiosity as a botanist and geologist or the various compulsions which may have resulted from the whippings of his childhood. It is easy enough to understand the atavism of going into woods with a gun after "game" or the more placid satisfaction of lying in warm sunshine on a lawn, but Muir was after the goodness of life at its root, in rocks and ice and trees and sky. There was no money or protein, no Darwinian or egotistical self-aggrandizement, in gazing jubilantly at a granite cliff and the changing cloud shapes in a brilliant sky.

Muir was an elegaic impressionist whose subject matter is mostly gone. Like Kit Carson and Jim Bridger, he can have no real rivals in a posthumous world. Yet in re-reading him, I've grown fonder, more respectful of his durability, and have visited his house in Martinez, California, which is now a petroleum-storage town. This tall, olive-colored, cupola-topped, seventeen-room Victorian grandee's home is on the former property of the Strentzel family, who in their heyday as fruitgrowers, when he married their daughter, owned twenty-six hundred acres. His grave, like that of Thoreau in Concord, Massachusetts, is a subsidiary one in a family plot dominated by the headstones of a previous generation: in Muir's case, his rich father-in-law, John Strentzel, in Thoreau's, by Henry's paterfamilias, John Thoreau, because both these writers were men of the woods, not exactly burghers.

Foreword

The "scribble den" upstairs, where Muir labored once he had been provided with a settled home, is, however, maintained by the National Park Service as a proper Muirian mess. No bourgeois Strentzel influence here. Writing came hard to Muir, as did romance (he married past 40), city walking, and bookish learning. His words didn't ring as internationally as Thoreau's, or delve as trenchantly into how he thought people themselves ought to live. Yet one obvious difficulty Muir had was just the stretch, the range of what he hugged. From Arizona to Alaska, from sea level to 14,000 feet, he fell repeatedly in love. At rock bottom, love was what he was about.

Take his hymn to Mount Shasta, a volcanic cone built way up into the blue over the course of eons by molten lava. Then its surface had been remodeled by "a down-crawling mantle of ice" upon this "fountain of smouldering fire." And nowadays, in "the blessed wilderness" of Strawberry Meadows, there springs "an outburst of organic life . . . the air stirred into one universal hum with rejoicing insects, a milky way of wings and petals . . . a foam of plant bloom and bees. . . . The deeps of the sky are mottled with singing wings of every color . . . enameling the light."

Amen.

Edward Hoagland
1994

Editor's Note

The papers brought together in this volume have, in a general way, been arranged in chronological sequence. They span a period of twenty-nine years of Muir's life, during which they appeared as letters and articles, for the most part in publications of limited and local circulation. The Utah and Nevada sketches, and the two San Gabriel papers, were contributed, in the form of letters, to the *San Francisco Evening Bulletin* toward the end of the seventies. Written in the field, they preserve the freshness of the author's first impressions of those regions. Much of the material in the chapters on Mount Shasta first took similar shape in 1874. Subsequently it was rewritten and much expanded for inclusion in *Picturesque California, and the Region West of the Rocky Mountains*, which Muir began to edit in 1888. In the same work appeared the description of Washington and Oregon. The charming little essay "Wild Wool" was written for the *Overland Monthly* in 1875. "A Geologist's Winter Walk" is an extract from a letter to a friend, who, appreciating its fine literary quality, took the responsibility of sending it to the *Overland Monthly* without the author's knowledge. The concluding chapter on "The Grand Cañon of the Colorado" was published in the *Century Magazine* in 1902, and exhibits Muir's powers of description at their maturity.

Some of these papers were revised by the author during the later years of his life, and these revisions are a part of the form in which they now appear. The chapters on Mount Shasta, Oregon, and Washington will be found to contain occasional sentences and a few paragraphs that were included, more or less verbatim, in *The*

Editor's Note

Mountains of California and *Our National Parks*. Being an important part of their present context, these paragraphs could not be omitted without impairing the unity of the author's descriptions.

The editor feels confident that this volume will meet, in every way, the high expectations of Muir's readers. The recital of his experiences during a stormy night on the summit of Mount Shasta will take rank among the most thrilling of his records of adventure. His observations on the dead towns of Nevada, and on the Indians gathering their harvest of pine-nuts, recall a phase of Western life that has left few traces in American literature. Many, too, will read with pensive interest the author's glowing description of what was one time called the New Northwest. Almost inconceivably great have been the changes wrought in that region during the past generation. Henceforth the landscapes that Muir saw there will live in good part only in his writings, for fire, axe, plough, and gunpowder have made away with the supposedly boundless forest wildernesses and their teeming life.

William Frederic Badè
1918

Steep Trails

1

Wild Wool

MORAL improvers have calls to preach. I have a friend who has a call to plough, and woe to the daisy sod or azalea thicket that falls under the savage redemption of his keen steel shares. Not content with the so-called subjugation of every terrestrial bog, rock, and moorland, he would fain discover some method of reclamation applicable to the ocean and the sky, that in due calendar time they might be brought to bud and blossom as the rose. Our efforts are of no avail when we seek to turn his attention to wild roses, or to the fact that both ocean and sky are already about as rosy as possible— the one with stars, the other with dulse, and foam, and wild light. The practical developments of his culture are orchards and clover-fields wearing a smiling, benevolent aspect, truly excellent in their way, though a near view discloses something barbarous in them all. Wildness charms not my friend, charm it never so wisely: and whatsoever may be the character of his heaven, his earth seems only a chaos of agricultural possibilities calling for grubbing-hoes and manures.

Sometimes I venture to approach him with a plea for wildness, when he good-naturedly shakes a big mellow apple in my face, reiterating his favorite aphorism, "Culture is an orchard apple; Nature is a crab." Not all culture, however, is equally destructive and inappreciative. Azure skies and crystal waters find loving recognition, and few there be who would welcome the axe among mountain pines, or would care to apply any correction to the tones and costumes of mountain waterfalls. Nevertheless, the barbarous notion is almost universally entertained by civilized man, that there is in all the manufactures of Nature something essentially coarse which can and must be eradicated by human culture. I was, therefore, delighted in finding that the wild wool growing upon mountain sheep in the neighborhood of Mount Shasta was much finer than the average grades of cultivated wool. This *fine* discovery was made some three months ago,[1] while hunting among the Shasta sheep between Shasta and Lower Klamath Lake. Three fleeces were obtained—one that belonged to a large ram about four years old, another to a ewe about the same age, and another to a yearling lamb. After parting their beautiful wool on the side and many places along the back, shoulders, and hips, and examining it closely with my lens, I shouted: "Well done for wildness! Wild wool is finer than tame!"

My companions stooped down and examined the fleeces for themselves, pulling out tufts and ringlets, spinning them between their fingers, and measuring the length of the staple, each in turn paying tribute to wildness. It *was* finer, and no mistake; finer than Spanish Merino. Wild wool *is* finer than tame.

"Here," said I, "is an argument for fine wildness that needs no explanation. Not that such arguments are by any means rare, for all wildness is finer than tameness, but because fine wool is appreciable by everybody alike—from the most speculative president of national wool-growers' associations all the way down to the gudewife spinning by her ingleside."

[1]This essay was written early in 1875. [Editor.]

Wild Wool

Nature is a good mother, and sees well to the clothing of her many bairns—birds with smoothly imbricated feathers, beetles with shining jackets, and bears with shaggy furs. In the tropical south, where the sun warms like a fire, they are allowed to go thinly clad; but in the snowy northland she takes care to clothe warmly. The squirrel has socks and mittens, and a tail broad enough for a blanket; the grouse is densely feathered down to the ends of his toes; and the wild sheep, besides his undergarment of fine wool, has a thick overcoat of hair that sheds off both the snow and the rain. Other provisions and adaptations in the dresses of animals, relating less to climate than to the more mechanical circumstances of life, are made with the same consummate skill that characterizes all the love-work of Nature. Land, water, and air, jagged rocks, muddy ground, sand-beds, forests, underbrush, grassy plains, etc., are considered in all their possible combinations while the clothing of her beautiful wildlings is preparing. No matter what the circumstances of their lives may be, she never allows them to go dirty or ragged. The mole, living always in the dark and in the dirt, is yet as clean as the otter or the wave-washed seal; and our wild sheep, wading in snow, roaming through bushes, and leaping among jagged storm-beaten cliffs, wears a dress so exquisitely adapted to its mountain life that it is always found as unruffled and stainless as a bird.

On leaving the Shasta hunting-grounds I selected a few specimen tufts, and brought them away with a view to making more leisurely examinations; but, owing to the imperfectness of the instruments at my command, the results thus far obtained must be regarded only as rough approximations.

As already stated, the clothing of our wild sheep is composed of fine wool and coarse hair. The hairs are from about two to four inches long, mostly of a dull bluish-gray color, though varying somewhat with the seasons. In general characteristics they are closely related to the hairs of the deer and antelope, being light, spongy, and elastic, with a highly polished surface, and though somewhat ridged and spiraled, like wool, they do not manifest the slightest tendency to felt or become taggy. A hair two and a half inches long, which is perhaps near the average length, will stretch about one fourth of an inch before breaking. The diameter decreases rapidly both at the top and bottom, but is maintained throughout the greater portion of the length with a fair degree of regularity. The slender tapering point in which the hairs terminate is nearly black: but, owing to its fineness as compared with the main trunk, the quantity of blackness is not sufficient to affect greatly the general color. The number of hairs growing upon a square inch is about ten thousand; the number of wool fibers is about twenty-five thousand, or two and a half times that of the hairs. The wool fibers are white and glossy, and beautifully spired into ringlets. The average length of the staple is about an inch and a half. A fiber of this length, when growing undisturbed down among the hairs, measures about an inch; hence the degree of curliness may easily be inferred. I regret exceedingly that my instruments do not enable me to measure the diameter of the fibers, in order that their degrees of fineness might be definitely compared with each other and with the finest of the domestic breeds; but that the three wild fleeces under consideration are considerably finer than the average grades of Merino shipped from San Francisco is, I think, unquestionable.

When the fleece is parted and looked into with a good lens, the skin appears of a beautiful pale-yellow color, and the delicate wool fibers are seen growing up among the strong hairs, like grass among stalks of corn, every individual fiber being protected about as specially and effectively as if inclosed in a separate husk. Wild wool is too fine to stand by itself, the fibers being about as frail and invisible as the floating threads of spiders, while the hairs against which they lean stand erect like hazel wands; but, notwithstanding their great dissimilarity in size and appearance, the wool and hair are forms of the same thing, modified in just that way and to just that degree that renders them most perfectly subservient to the well-being of the sheep. Furthermore, it will be observed that these wild modifications are entirely distinct from those which are brought chancingly into existence through the accidents and caprices of culture; the former being inventions of God for the attainment of definite ends. Like the modifications of limbs—the fin for swimming, the wing for flying, the foot for walking—so the fine wool for warmth, the hair for additional warmth and to protect the wool, and both together for a fabric to wear well in mountain roughness and wash well in mountain storms.

The effects of human culture upon wild wool are analogous to those produced upon wild roses. In the one case there is an abnormal development of petals at the expense of the stamens, in the other an abnormal development of wool at the expense of the hair. Garden roses frequently exhibit stamens in which the transmutation to petals may be observed in various stages of accomplishment, and analogously the fleeces of tame sheep occasionally contain a few wild hairs that are undergoing transmutation to wool. Even wild wool presents here and there a fiber that appears to be in a state of change. In the course of my examinations of the wild fleeces mentioned above, three fibers were found that were wool at one end and hair at the other. This, however, does not necessarily imply imperfection, or any process of change similar to that caused by human culture. Water-lilies contain parts variously developed into stamens at one end, petals at the other, as the constant and normal condition. These half wool, half hair fibers may therefore subserve some fixed requirement essential to the perfection of the whole, or they may simply be the fine boundary-lines where an exact balance between the wool and the hair is attained.

I have been offering samples of mountain wool to my friends, demanding in return that the fineness of wildness be fairly recognized and confessed, but the returns are deplorably tame. The first question asked is, "Now truly, wild sheep, wild sheep, have you any wool?" while they peer curiously down among the hairs through lenses and spectacles. "Yes, wild sheep, you *have* wool; but Mary's lamb had more. In the name of use, how many wild sheep, think you, would be required to furnish wool sufficient for a pair of socks?" I endeavor to point out the irrelevancy of the latter question, arguing that wild wool was not made for man but for sheep, and that, however deficient as clothing for other animals, it is just the thing for the brave mountain-dweller that wears it. Plain, however, as all this appears, the quantity question rises again and again in all its commonplace tameness. For in my experience it seems well-nigh impossible to obtain a hearing on behalf of Nature from any other standpoint than that of human use. Domestic flocks yield more flannel per sheep than the wild, therefore it is claimed that culture has improved upon wildness; and so it has as far as flannel is concerned, but all to the contrary as far as a sheep's dress is concerned. If every wild sheep inhabiting the Sierra were to put on tame wool, probably only a few would survive the dangers of a single season. With their fine limbs muffled and buried beneath a tangle of hairless wool, they would become short-winded, and fall an easy prey to the strong mountain wolves. In descending precipices they would be thrown out of balance and killed, by their taggy wool catching upon sharp points of rocks. Disease would also be brought on by the dirt which always finds a lodgment in tame wool, and by the draggled and water-soaked condition into which it falls during stormy weather.

No dogma taught by the present civilization seems to form so insuperable an obstacle in the way of a right understanding of the relations which culture sustains to wildness as that which regards the world as made especially for the uses of man. Every animal, plant, and crystal controverts it in the plainest terms. Yet it is taught from century to century as something ever new and precious, and in the resulting darkness the enormous conceit is allowed to go unchallenged.

I have never yet happened upon a trace of evidence that seemed to show that any one animal was ever made for another as much as it was made for itself. Not that Nature manifests any such thing as selfish isolation. In the making of every animal the presence of every other animal has been recognized. Indeed, every atom in creation may be said to be acquainted with and married to every other, but with universal union there is a division sufficient in degree for the purposes of the most intense individuality; no matter, therefore, what may be the note which any creature forms in the song of existence, it is made first for itself, then more and more remotely for all the world and worlds.

Were it not for the exercise of individualizing cares on the part of Nature, the universe would be felted together like a fleece of tame wool. But we are governed more than we know, and most when we are wildest. Plants, animals, and stars are all kept in place, bridled along appointed ways, *with* one another, and *through the midst* of one another—killing and being killed, eating and being eaten, in harmonious proportions and quantities. And it is right that we should thus reciprocally make use of one another, rob, cook, and consume, to the utmost of our healthy abilities and desires. Stars attract one another as they are able, and harmony results. Wild lambs eat as many wild flowers as they can find or desire, and men and wolves eat the lambs to just the same extent.

This consumption of one another in its various modifications is a kind of culture varying with the degree of directness with which it is carried out, but we should be careful not to ascribe to such culture any improving qualities upon those on whom it is brought to bear. The water-ouzel plucks moss from the river-bank to build its nest, but it does not improve the moss by plucking it. We pluck feathers from birds, and less directly wool from wild sheep, for the manufacture of clothing and cradle-nests, without improving the wool for the sheep, or the feathers for the bird that wore them. When a hawk pounces upon a linnet and proceeds to pull out its feathers, preparatory to making a meal, the hawk may be said to be cultivating the linnet, and he certainly does effect an improvement as far as hawk-food is concerned; but what of the songster? He ceases to be a linnet as soon as he is snatched from the woodland choir; and when, hawklike, we snatch the wild sheep from its native rock, and, instead of eating and wearing it at once, carry it home, and breed the hair out of its wool and the bones out of its body, it ceases to be a sheep.

Wild Wool

These breeding and plucking processes are similarly improving as regards the secondary uses aimed at; and, although the one requires but a few minutes for its accomplishment, the other many years or centuries, they are essentially alike. We eat wild oysters alive with great directness, waiting for no cultivation, and leaving scarce a second of distance between the shell and the lip; but we take wild sheep home and subject them to the many extended processes of husbandry, and finish by boiling them in a pot—a process which completes all sheep improvements as far as man is concerned. It will be seen, therefore, that wild wool and tame wool— wild sheep and tame sheep—are terms not properly comparable, nor are they in any correct sense to be considered as bearing any antagonism toward each other; they are different things, planned and accomplished for wholly different purposes.

Illustrative examples bearing upon this interesting subject may be multiplied indefinitely, for they abound everywhere in the plant and animal kingdoms wherever culture has reached. Recurring for a moment to apples. The beauty and completeness of a wild apple tree living its own life in the woods is heartily acknowledged by all those who have been so happy as to form its acquaintance. The fine wild piquancy of its fruit is unrivaled, but in the great question of quantity as human food wild apples are found wanting. Man, therefore, takes the tree from the woods, manures and prunes and grafts, plans and guesses, adds a little of this and that, selects and rejects, until apples of every conceivable size and softness are produced, like nut-galls in response to the irritating punctures of insects. Orchard apples are to me the most eloquent words that culture has ever spoken, but they reflect no imperfection upon Nature's spicy crab. Every cultivated apple is a crab, not improved, *but cooked*, variously softened and swelled out in the process, mellowed, sweetened, spiced, and rendered pulpy and foodful, but as utterly unfit for the uses of nature as a meadowlark killed and plucked and roasted. Give to Nature every cultured apple—codling, pippin, russet—and every sheep so laboriously compounded—muffled Southdowns, hairy Cotswolds, wrinkled Merinos—and she would throw the one to her caterpillars, the other to her wolves.

It is now some thirty-six hundred years since Jacob kissed his mother and set out across the plains of Padan-aram to begin his experiments upon the flocks of his uncle, Laban; and, notwithstanding the high degree of excellence he attained as a wool-grower, and the innumerable painstaking efforts subsequently made by individuals and associations in all kinds of pastures and climates, we still seem to be as far from definite and satisfactory results as we ever were. In one breed the wool is apt to wither and crinkle like hay on a sun-beaten hillside. In another, it is lodged and matted together like the lush tangled grass of a manured meadow. In one the staple is deficient in length, in another in fineness; while in all there is a constant tendency toward disease, rendering various washings and dippings indispensable to prevent its falling out. The problem of the quality and quantity of the carcass seems to be as doubtful and as far removed from a satisfactory solution as that of the wool. Desirable breeds blundered upon by long series of groping experiments are often found to be unstable and subject to disease—bots, foot-rot, blind-staggers, etc.—causing infinite trouble, both among breeders and manufacturers. Would it not be well, therefore, for some one to go back as far as possible and take a fresh start?

Wild Wool

The source or sources whence the various breeds were derived is not positively known, but there can be hardly any doubt of their being descendants of the four or five wild species so generally distributed throughout the mountainous portions of the globe, the marked differences between the wild and domestic species being readily accounted for by the known variability of the animal, and by the long series of painstaking selection to which all its characteristics have been subjected. No other animal seems to yield so submissively to the manipulations of culture. Jacob controlled the color of his flocks merely by causing them to stare at objects of the desired hue; and possibly Merinos may have caught their wrinkles from the perplexed brows of their breeders. The California species (*Ovis montana*)[1] is a noble animal, weighing when full-grown some three hundred and fifty pounds, and is well worthy the attention of wool-growers as a point from which to make a new departure, for pure wildness is the one great want, both of men and of sheep.

[1]The wild sheep of California are now classified as *Ovis nelsoni*. Whether those of the Shasta region belonged to the latter species, or to the bighorn species of Oregon, Idaho, and Washington, is still an unsettled question. [Editor.]

2

A Geologist's Winter Walk[1]

AFTER reaching Turlock, I sped afoot over the stubble fields and through miles of brown hemizonia and purple erigeron, to Hopeton, conscious of little more than that the town was behind and beneath me, and the mountains above and before me; on through the oaks and chaparral of the foothills to Coulterville; and then ascended the first great mountain step upon which grows the sugar pine. Here I slackened pace, for I drank the spicy, resiny wind, and beneath the arms of this noble tree I felt that I was safely home. Never did pine trees seem so dear. How sweet was their breath and their song, and how grandly they winnowed the sky! I tingled my fingers among their tassels, and rustled my feet among their brown needles and burrs, and was exhilarated and joyful beyond all I can write.

When I reached Yosemite, all the rocks seemed talkative, and more telling and lovable than ever. They are dear friends, and seemed to have warm blood gushing through their granite flesh; and I love them with a love intensified by long and close companionship. After I had bathed in the bright river, sauntered over the meadows, conversed with the domes, and played with the pines, I still felt blurred and weary, as if tainted in some way with the sky of your streets. I determined, therefore, to run out for a while to say

[1]An excerpt from a letter to a friend, written in 1873. [Editor.]

A Geologist's Winter Walk

my prayers in the higher mountain temples. "The days are sunful," I said, "and, though now winter, no great danger need be encountered, and no sudden storm will block my return, if I am watchful."

The morning after this decision, I started up the cañon of Tenaya, caring little about the quantity of bread I carried; for, I thought, a fast and a storm and a difficult cañon were just the medicine I needed. When I passed Mirror Lake, I scarcely noticed it, for I was absorbed in the great Tissiack—her crown a mile away in the hushed azure; her purple granite drapery flowing in soft and graceful folds down to my feet, embroidered gloriously around with deep, shadowy forest. I have gazed on Tissiack a thousand times—in days of solemn storms, and when her form shone divine with the jewelry of winter, or was veiled in living clouds; and I have heard her voice of winds, and snowy, tuneful waters when floods were falling; yet never did her soul reveal itself more impressively than now. I hung about her skirts, lingering timidly, until the higher mountains and glaciers compelled me to push up the cañon.

This cañon is accessible only to mountaineers, and I was anxious to carry my barometer and clinometer through it, to obtain sections and altitudes, so I chose it as the most attractive highway. After I had passed the tall groves that stretch a mile above Mirror Lake, and scrambled around the Tenaya Fall, which is just at the head of the lake groves, I crept through the dense and spiny chaparral that plushes the roots of the mountains here for miles in warm green, and was ascending a precipitous rock-front, smoothed by glacial action, when I suddenly fell—for the first time since I touched foot to Sierra rocks. After several somersaults, I became insensible from the shock, and when consciousness returned I found myself wedged among short, stiff bushes, trembling as if cold, not injured in the slightest.

Judging by the sun, I could not have been insensible very long; probably not a minute, possibly an hour; and I could not remember what made me fall, or where I had fallen from; but I saw that if I had rolled a little further, my mountain-climbing would have been finished, for just beyond the bushes the cañon wall steepened and I might have fallen to the bottom. "There," said I, addressing my feet, to whose separate skill I had learned to trust night and day on any mountain, "that is what you get by intercourse with stupid town stairs, and dead pavements." I felt degraded and worthless. I had not yet reached the most difficult portion of the cañon, but I determined to guide my humbled body over the most nerve-trying places I could find; for I was now awake, and felt confident that the last of the town fog had been shaken from both head and feet.

I camped at the mouth of a narrow gorge which is cut into the bottom of the main cañon, determined to take earnest exercise next day. No plushy boughs did my ill-behaved bones enjoy that night, nor did my bumped head get a spicy cedar plume pillow mixed with flowers. I slept on a naked boulder, and when I awoke all my nervous trembling was gone.

The gorged portion of the cañon, in which I spent all the next day, is about a mile and a half in length; and I passed the time in tracing the action of the forces that determined this peculiar bottom gorge, which is an abrupt, ragged-walled, narrow-throated cañon, formed in the bottom of the wide-mouthed, smooth, and beveled main cañon. I will not stop now to tell you more; some day you may see it, like a shadowy line, from Cloud's Rest. In high water, the stream occupies all the bottom of the gorge, surging and chafing in glorious power from wall to wall. But the sound of the grinding was low as I entered the gorge, scarcely hoping to be able to pass through its entire length. By cool efforts, along glassy, ice-worn slopes, I reached the upper end in a little over a day, but was compelled to pass the second night in the gorge, and in the moon-light I wrote you this short pencil-letter in my notebook:—

The moon is looking down into the cañon, and how marvelously the great rocks kindle to her light! Every dome, and brow, and swelling boss touched by her white rays, glows as if lighted with snow. I am now only a mile from last night's camp; and have been climb-ing and sketching all day in this difficult but instructive gorge. It is formed in the bottom of the main cañon, among the roots of Cloud's Rest. It begins at the filled-up lake-basin where I camped last night, and ends a few hundred yards above, in another basin of the same kind. The walls everywhere are craggy and vertical, and in some places they overlean. It is only from twenty to sixty feet wide, and not, though black and broken enough, the thin, crooked mouth of some mysterious abyss; but it was eroded, for in many places I saw its solid, seamless floor.

I am sitting on a big stone, against which the stream divides, and goes brawling by in rapids on both sides; half of my rock is white in the light, half in shadow. As I look from the opening jaws of this shadowy gorge, South Dome is immediately in front—high in the stars, her face turned from the moon, with the rest of her body gloriously muffled in waved folds of granite. On the left, sculptured from the main Cloud's Rest ridge, are three magnificent rocks, sisters of the great South Dome. On the right is the massive, moonlit front of Mount Watkins, and between, low down in the furthest distance, is Sentinel Dome, girdled and darkened with forest. In the near foreground Tenaya Creek is singing against boulders that are white with snow and moonbeams. Now look back twenty yards, and you will see a waterfall fair as a spirit; the moonlight just touches it, bringing it into relief against a dark background of shadow. A little to the left, and a dozen steps this side of the fall, a flickering light marks my camp—and a precious camp it is. A huge, glacier-polished slab, falling from the smooth, glossy flank of Cloud's Rest, happened to settle on edge against the wall of the gorge. I did not know that this slab was glacier-polished until I lighted my fire. Judge of my delight. I think it was sent here by an earthquake. It is about twelve feet square. I wish I could take it home[1] for a hearthstone. Beneath this slab is the only place in this torrent-swept gorge where I could find sand sufficient for a bed.

I expected to sleep on the boulders, for I spent most of the afternoon on the slippery wall of the cañon, endeavoring to get around this difficult part of the gorge, and was compelled to hasten down here for water before dark. I shall sleep soundly on this sand; half of it is mica.

---

[1]Muir at this time was making Yosemite Valley his home. [Editor.]

A Geologist's Winter Walk

Here, wonderful to behold, are a few green stems of prickly rubus, and a tiny grass. They are here to meet us. Ay, even here in this darksome gorge, "frightened and tormented" with raging torrents and choking avalanches of snow. Can it be? As if rubus and the grass leaf were not enough of God's tender prattle words of love, which we so much need in these mighty temples of power, yonder in the "benmost bore" are two blessed adiantums. Listen to them! How wholly infused with God is this one big word of love that we call the world! Good-night. Do you see the fire-glow on my ice-smoothed slab, and on my two ferns and the rubus and grass panicles? And do you hear how sweet a sleep-song the fall and cascades are singing?

The water-ground chips and knots that I found fastened between the rocks kept my fire alive all through the night. Next morning I rose nerved and ready for another day of sketching and noting, and any form of climbing. I escaped from the gorge about noon, after accomplishing some of the most delicate feats of mountaineering I ever attempted; and here the cañon is all broadly open again—the floor luxuriantly forested with pine, and spruce, and silver fir, and brown-trunked librocedrus. The walls rise in Yosemite forms, and Tenaya Creek comes down seven hundred feet in a white brush of foam. This is a little Yosemite Valley. It is about two thousand feet above the level of the main Yosemite, and about twenty-four hundred below Lake Tenaya.

I found the lake frozen, and the ice was so clear and unruffled that the surrounding mountains and the groves that look down upon it were reflected almost as perfectly as I ever beheld them in the calm evening mirrors of summer. At a little distance, it was difficult to believe the lake frozen at all; and when I walked out on it, cautiously stamping at short intervals to test the strength of the ice, I seemed to walk mysteriously, without adequate faith, on the surface of the water. The ice was so transparent that I could see through it the beautifully wave-rippled, sandy bottom, and the scales of mica glinting back the down-pouring light. When I knelt down with my face close to the ice, through which the sunbeams were pouring, I was delighted to discover myriads of Tyndall's six-rayed water flowers, magnificently colored.

A grand old mountain mansion is this Tenaya region! In the glacier period it was a *mer de glace*, far grander than the *mer de glace* of Switzerland, which is only about half a mile broad. The Tenaya *mer de glace* was not less than two miles broad, late in the glacier epoch, when all the principal dividing crests were bare; and its depth was not less than fifteen hundred feet. Ice-streams from Mounts Lyell and Dana, and all the mountains between, and from the nearer Cathedral Peak, flowed hither, welded into one, and worked together. After eroding this Tenaya Lake basin, and all the splendidly sculptured rocks and mountains that surround and adorn it, and the great Tenaya Cañon, with its wealth of all that makes mountains sublime, they were welded with the vast South, Lyell, and Illilouette glaciers on one side, and with those of Hoffman on the other—thus forming a portion of a yet grander *mer de glace* in Yosemite Valley.

I reached the Tenaya Cañon, on my way home, by coming in from the northeast, rambling down over the shoulders of Mount Watkins, touching bottom a mile above Mirror Lake. From thence home was but a saunter in the moonlight.

A Geologist's Winter Walk

After resting one day, and the weather continuing calm, I ran up over the left shoulder of South Dome and down in front of its grand split face to make some measurements, completed my work, climbed to the right shoulder, struck off along the ridge for Cloud's Rest, and reached the topmost heave of her sunny wave in ample time to see the sunset.

Cloud's Rest is a thousand feet higher than Tissiack. It is a wavelike crest upon a ridge, which begins at Yosemite with Tissiack, and runs continuously eastward to the thicket of peaks and crests around Lake Tenaya. This lofty granite wall is bent this way and that by the restless and weariless action of glaciers just as if it had been made of dough. But the grand circumference of mountains and forests are coming from far and near, densing into one close assemblage; for the sun, their god and father, with love ineffable, is glowing a sunset farewell. Not one of all the assembled rocks or trees seemed remote. How impressively their faces shone with responsive love!

I ran home in the moonlight with firm strides; for the sun-love made me strong. Down through the junipers; down through the firs; now in jet shadows, now in white light; over sandy moraines and bare, clanking rocks; past the huge ghost of South Dome rising weird through the firs; past the glorious fall of Nevada, the groves of Illilouette; through the pines of the valley; beneath the bright crystal sky blazing with stars. All of this mountain wealth in one day!—one of the rich ripe days that enlarge one's life; so much of the sun upon one side of it, so much of the moon and stars on the other.

3

Summer Days at Mount Shasta

MOUNT SHASTA rises in solitary grandeur from the edge of a comparatively low and lightly sculptured lava plain near the northern extremity of the Sierra, and maintains a far more impressive and commanding individuality than any other mountain within the limits of California. Go where you may, within a radius of from fifty to a hundred miles or more, there stands before you the colossal cone of Shasta, clad in ice and snow, the one grand, unmistakable landmark—the pole-star of the landscape. Far to the southward Mount Whitney lifts its granite summit four or five hundred feet higher than Shasta, but it is nearly snowless during the late summer, and is so feebly individualized that the traveler may search for it in vain among the many rival peaks crowded along the axis of the range to north and south of it, which all alike are crumbling residual masses brought into relief in the degradation of the general mass of the range. The highest point on Mount Shasta, as determined by the State Geological Survey, is 14,440 feet above mean tide. That of Whitney, computed from fewer observations, is about 14,900 feet. But inasmuch as the average elevation of the plain out of which Shasta rises is only about four thousand feet above the sea, while the actual base of the peak of Mount Whitney lies at an elevation of eleven thousand feet, the individual height of the former is about two and a half times as great as that of the latter.

Summer Days at Mount Shasta

Approaching Shasta from the south, one obtains glimpses of its snowy cone here and there through the trees from the tops of hills and ridges; but it is not until Strawberry Valley is reached, where there is a grand out-opening of the forests, that Shasta is seen in all its glory, from base to crown clearly revealed with its wealth of woods and waters and fountain snow, rejoicing in the bright mountain sky, and radiating beauty on all the subject landscape like a sun. Standing in a fringing thicket of purple spiræa in the immediate foreground is a smooth expanse of green meadow with its meandering stream, one of the smaller affluents of the Sacramento; then a zone of dark, close forest, its countless spires of pine and fir rising above one another on the swelling base of the mountain in glorious array; and, over all, the great white cone sweeping far into the thin, keen sky—meadow, forest, and grand icy summit harmoniously blending and making one sublime picture evenly balanced.

The main lines of the landscape are immensely bold and simple, and so regular that it needs all its shaggy wealth of woods and chaparral and its finely tinted ice and snow and brown jutting crags to keep it from looking conventional. In general views of the mountain three distinct zones may be readily defined. The first, which may be called the Chaparral Zone, extends around the base in a magnificent sweep nearly a hundred miles in length on its lower edge, and with a breadth of about seven miles. It is a dense growth of chaparral from three to six or eight feet high, composed chiefly of manzanita, cherry, chincapin, and several species of ceanothus, called deerbrush by the huners, forming, when in full bloom, one of the most glorious flower-beds conceivable. The continuity of this flowery zone is interrupted here and there, especially on the south side of the mountain, by wide swaths of coniferous trees, chiefly the sugar and yellow pines, Douglas spruce, silver fir, and incense cedar, many specimens of which are two hundred feet high and five to seven feet in diameter. Goldenrods, asters, gilias, lilies, and lupines, with many other less conspicuous plants, occur in warm sheltered openings in these lower woods, making charming gardens of wildness where bees and butterflies are at home and many a shy bird and squirrel.

The next higher is the Fir Zone, made up almost exclusively of two species of silver fir. It is from two to three miles wide, has an average elevation above the sea of some six thousand feet on its lower edge and eight thousand on its upper, and is the most regular and best defined of the three.

The Alpine Zone has a rugged, straggling growth of storm-beaten dwarf pines (*Pinus albicaulis*), which forms the upper edge of the timber-line. This species reaches an elevation of about nine thousand feet, but at this height the tops of the trees rise only a few feet into the thin frosty air, and are closely pressed and shorn by wind and snow; yet they hold on bravely and put forth an abundance of beautiful purple flowers and produce cones and seeds. Down towards the edge of the fir belt they stand erect, forming small, well-formed trunks, and are associated with the taller two-leafed and mountain pines and the beautiful Williamson spruce. Bryanthus, a beautiful flowering heathwort, flourishes a few hundred feet above the timber-line, accompanied with kalmia and spiræa. Lichens enliven the faces of the cliffs with their bright colors, and in some of the warmer nooks of the rocks, up to a height of eleven thousand feet, there are a few tufts of dwarf daisies, wallflowers, and penstemons; but, notwithstanding these bloom freely, they make no appreciable show at a distance, and the stretches of rough brown lava beyond the storm-beaten trees seem as bare of vegetation as the great snow-fields and glaciers of the summit.

Shasta is a fire-mountain, an old volcano gradually accumulated and built up into the blue deep of the sky by successive eruptions of ashes and molten lava which, shot high in the air and falling in darkening showers, and flowing from chasms and craters, grew outward and upward like the trunk of a knotty, bulging tree. Not in one grand convulsion was Shasta given birth, nor in any one special period of volcanic storm and stress, though mountains more than a thousand feet in height have been cast up like mole-hills in a night—quick contributions to the wealth of the landscapes, and most emphatic statements, on the part of Nature, of the gigantic character of the power that dwells beneath the dull, dead-looking surface of the earth. But sections cut by the glaciers, displaying some of the internal framework of Shasta, show that comparatively long periods of quiescence intervened between many distinct eruptions, during which the cooling lavas ceased to flow, and took their places as permanent additions to the bulk of the growing mountain. Thus with alternate haste and deliberation eruption succeeded eruption, until Mount Shasta surpassed even its present sublime height.

Then followed a strange contrast. The glacial winter came on. The sky that so often had been darkened with storms of cinders and ashes and lighted by the glare of volcanic fires was filled with crystal snow-flowers, which, loading the cooling mountain, gave birth to glaciers that, uniting edge to edge, at length formed one grand conical glacier—a down-crawling mantle of ice upon a fountain of smouldering fire, crushing and grinding its brown, flinty lavas, and thus degrading and remodeling the entire mountain from summit to base. How much denudation and degradation has been effected we have no means of determining, the porous, crumbling rocks being ill adapted for the reception and preservation of glacial inscriptions.

The summit is now a mass of ruins, and all the finer striations have been effaced from the flanks by post-glacial weathering, while the irregularity of its lavas as regards susceptibility to erosion, and the disturbance caused by inter- and post-glacial eruptions, have obscured or obliterated those heavier characters of the glacial record found so clearly inscribed upon the granite pages of the high Sierra between latitude 36° 30' and 39°. This much, however, is plain: that the summit of the mountain was considerably lowered, and the sides were deeply grooved and fluted while it was a center of dispersal for the glaciers of the circumjacent region. And when at length the glacial period began to draw near its close, the ice mantle was gradually melted off around the base of the mountain, and in receding and breaking up into its present fragmentary condition the irregular heaps and rings of moraine matter were stored upon its flanks on which the forests are growing. The glacial erosion of most of the Shasta lavas gives rise to detritus composed of rough subangular boulders of moderate size and porous gravel and sand, which yields freely to the transporting power of running water. Several centuries ago immense quantities of this lighter material were washed down from the higher slopes by a flood of extraordinary magnitude, caused probably by the sudden melting of the ice and snow during an eruption, giving rise to the deposition of conspicuous delta-like beds around the base. And it is upon these flood-beds of moraine soil, thus suddenly and simultaneously laid down and joined edge to edge, that the flowery chaparral is growing.

Thus, by forces seemingly antagonistic and destructive, Nature accomplishes her beneficent designs—now a flood of fire, now a flood of ice, now a flood of water; and again in the fullness of time an outburst of organic life—forest and garden, with all their wealth of fruit and flowers, the air stirred into one universal hum with rejoicing insects, a milky way of wings and petals, girdling the new-born mountain like a cloud, as if the vivifying sunbeams beating against its sides had broken into a foam of plant-bloom and bees.

But with such grand displays as Nature is making here, how grand are her reservations, bestowed only upon those who devotedly seek them! Beneath the smooth and snowy surface the fountain fires are still aglow, to blaze forth afresh at their appointed times. The glaciers, looking so still and small at a distance, represented by the artist with a patch of white paint laid on by a single stroke of his brush, are still flowing onward, unhalting, with deep crystal currents, sculpturing the mountain with stern, resistless energy. How many caves and fountains that no eye has yet seen lie with all their fine furniture deep down in the darkness, and how many shy wild creatures are at home beneath the grateful lights and shadows of the woods, rejoicing in their fullness of perfect life!

Standing on the edge of the Strawberry Meadows in the sundays of summer, not a foot or feather or leaf seems to stir; and the grand, towering mountain with all its inhabitants appears in rest, calm as a star. Yet how profound is the energy ever in action, and how great is the multitude of claws and teeth, wings and eyes, wide-awake and at work and shining! Going into the blessed wilderness, the blood of the plants throbbing beneath the life-giving sunshine seems to be heard and felt; plant-growth goes on before our eyes, and every tree and bush and flower is seen as a hive of restless industry. The deeps of the sky are mottled with singing wings of every color and tone—clouds of brilliant chrysididae dancing and swirling in joyous rhythm, golden-barred vespidae, butterflies, grating cicadas and jolly rattling grasshoppers—fairly enameling the light, and shaking all the air into music. Happy fellows they are, every one of them, blowing tiny pipe and trumpet, plodding and prancing, at work or at play.

Though winter holds the summit, Shasta in summer is mostly a massy, bossy mound of flowers colored like the alpenglow that flushes the snow. There are miles of wild roses, pink bells of huckleberry and sweet manzanita, every bell a honey-cup, plants that tell of the north and of the south; tall nodding lilies, the crimson sarcodes, rhododendron, cassiope, and blessed linnæa; phlox, calycanthus, plum, cherry, cratægus, spiræa, mints, and clovers in endless variety; ivesia, larkspur, and columbine; golden aplopappus, linosyris,[1] bahia, wyethia, arnica, brodiæa, etc.,—making sheets and beds of light edgings of bloom in lavish abundance for the myriads of the air dependent on their bounty.

The common honey-bees, gone wild in this sweet wilderness, gather tons of honey into the hollows of the trees and rocks, clambering eagerly through bramble and hucklebloom, shaking the clustered bells of the generous manzanita, now humming aloft among polleny willows and firs, now down on the ashy ground

---

[1] An obsolete genus of plants now replaced in the main by *Chrysothamnus* and *Ericameria*. [Editor.]

among small gilias and buttercups, and anon plunging into banks
of snowy cherry and buckthorn. They consider the lilies and roll
into them, pushing their blunt polleny faces against them like ba-
bies on their mother's bosom; and fondly, too, with eternal love
does Mother Nature clasp her small bee-babies and suckle them,
multitudes at once, on her warm Shasta breast. Besides the common honey-bee there are many others here, fine, burly, mossy
fellows, such as were nourished on the mountains many a flowery
century before the advent of the domestic species—bumble-bees,
mason-bees, carpenter-bees, and leaf-cutters. Butterflies, too, and
moths of every size and pattern; some wide-winged like bats, flapping slowly and sailing in easy curves; others like small flying violets
shaking about loosely in short zigzag flights close to the flowers,
feasting in plenty night and day.

Deer in great abundance come to Shasta from the warmer
foothills every spring to feed in the rich, cool pastures, and bring
forth their young in the ceanothus tangles of the chaparral zone,
retiring again before the snowstorms of winter, mostly to the southward and westward of the mountain. In like manner the wild sheep
of the adjacent region seek the lofty inaccessible crags of the summit as the snow melts, and are driven down to the lower spurs and
ridges where there is but little snow, to the north and east of Shasta.

Bears, too, roam this foodful wilderness, feeding on grass,
clover, berries, nuts, ant-eggs, fish, flesh, or fowl,—whatever
comes in their way,—with but little troublesome discrimination.
Sugar and honey they seem to like best of all, and they seek far to
find the sweets; but when hard pushed by hunger they make out to
gnaw a living from the bark of trees and rotten logs, and might
almost live on clean lava alone.

Notwithstanding the California bears have had as yet but little experience with honey-bees, they sometimes succeed in reaching the bountiful stores of these industrious gatherers and enjoy the feast with majestic relish. But most honey-bees in search of a home are wise enough to make choice of a hollow in a living tree far from the ground, whenever such can be found. There they are pretty secure, for though the smaller brown and black bears climb well, they are unable to gnaw their way into strong hives, while compelled to exert themselves to keep from falling and at the same time endure the stings of the bees about the nose and eyes, without having their paws free to brush them off. But woe to the unfortunates who dwell in some prostrate trunk, and to the black bumble-bees discovered in their mossy, mouselike nests in the ground. With powerful teeth and claws these are speedily laid bare, and almost before time is given for a general buzz the bees, old and young, larvæ, honey, stings, nest, and all, are devoured in one ravishing revel.

The antelope may still be found in considerable numbers to the northeastward of Shasta, but the elk, once abundant, have almost entirely gone from the region. The smaller animals, such as the wolf, the various foxes, wildcats, coon, squirrels, and the curious wood rat that builds large brush huts, abound in all the wilder places; and the beaver, otter, mink, etc., may still be found along the sources of the rivers. The blue grouse and mountain quail are plentiful in the woods and the sage-hen on the plains about the northern base of the mountain, while innumerable smaller birds enliven and sweeten every thicket and grove.

There are at least five classes of human inhabitants about the Shasta region: the Indians, now scattered, few in numbers and miserably demoralized, though still offering some rare specimens of savage manhood; miners and prospectors, found mostly to the north and west of the mountain, since the region about its base is overflowed with lava; cattle-raisers, mostly on the open plains to the northeastward and around the Klamath Lakes; hunters and trappers, where the woods and waters are wildest; and farmers, in Shasta Valley on the north side of the mountain, wheat, apples, melons, berries, all the best production of farm and garden growing and ripening there at the foot of the great white cone, which seems at times during changing storms ready to fall upon them— the most sublime farm scenery imaginable.

The Indians of the McCloud River that have come under my observation differ considerably in habits and features from the Diggers and other tribes of the foothills and plains, and also from the Pah Utes and Modocs. They live chiefly on salmon. They seem to be closely related to the Tlingits of Alaska, Washington, and Oregon, and may readily have found their way here by passing from stream to stream in which salmon abound. They have much better features than the Indians of the plains, and are rather wide awake, speculative and ambitious in their way, and garrulous, like the natives of the northern coast.

Before the Modoc War they lived in dread of the Modocs, a tribe living about the Klamath Lake and the Lava Beds, who were in the habit of crossing the low Sierra divide past the base of Shasta on freebooting excursions, stealing wives, fish, and weapons from the Pitts and McClouds. Mothers would hush their children by telling them that the Modocs would catch them.

During my stay at the Government fish-hatching station on the McCloud I was accompanied in my walks along the river-bank by a McCloud boy about ten years of age, a bright, inquisitive fellow, who gave me the Indian names of the birds and plants that we met. The water-ousel he knew well and he seemed to like the sweet singer, which he called "Sussinny." He showed me how strips of the stems of the beautiful maidenhair fern were used to adorn baskets with handsome brown bands, and pointed out several plants good to eat, particularly the large saxifrage growing abundantly along the river-margin. Once I rushed suddenly upon him to see if he would be frightened; but he unflinchingly held his ground, struck a grand heroic attitude, and shouted, "Me no 'fraid; me Modoc!"

Mount Shasta, so far as I have seen, has never been the home of Indians, not even their hunting-ground to any great extent, above the lower slopes of the base. They are said to be afraid of fire-mountains and geyser-basins as being the dwelling-places of dangerously powerful and unmanageable gods. However, it is food and their relations to other tribes that mainly control the movements of Indians; and here their food was mostly on the lower slopes, with nothing except the wild sheep to tempt them higher. Even these were brought within reach without excessive climbing during the storms of winter.

On the north side of Shasta, near Sheep Rock, there is a long cavern, sloping to the northward, nearly a mile in length, thirty or forty feet wide, and fifty feet or more in height, regular in form and direction like a railroad tunnel, and probably formed by the flowing away of a current of lava after the hardening of the surface. At the mouth of this cave, where the light and shelter is good, I found many of the heads and horns of the wild sheep, and the remains of campfires, no doubt those of Indian hunters who in stormy weather had camped there and feasted after the fatigues of the chase. A wild picture that must have formed on a dark night—the glow of the fire, the circle of crouching savages around it seen through the smoke, the dead game, and the weird darkness and half-darkness of the walls of the cavern, a picture of cave-dwellers at home in the stone age!

Interest in hunting in almost universal, so deeply is it rooted as an inherited instinct ever ready to rise and make itself known. Fine scenery may not stir a fiber of mind or body, but how quick and how true is the excitement of the pursuit of game! Then up flames the slumbering volcano of ancient wildness, all that has been done by church and school through centuries of cultivation is for the moment destroyed, and the decent gentleman or devout saint becomes a howling, bloodthirsty, demented savage. It is not long since we all were cave-men and followed game for food as truly as wildcat or wolf, and the long repression of civilization seems to make the rebound to savage love of blood all the more violent. This frenzy, fortunately, does not last long in its most exaggerated form, and after a season of wildness refined gentlemen from cities are not more cruel than hunters and trappers who kill for a living.

Dwelling apart in the depths of the woods are the various kinds of mountaineers,—hunters, prospectors, and the like,—rare men, "queer characters," and well worth knowing. Their cabins are located with reference to game and the ledges to be examined, and are constructed almost as simply as those of the wood rats made of sticks laid across each other without compass or square. But they afford good shelter from storms, and so are "square" with the need of their builders. These men as a class are singularly fine in manners, though their faces may be scarred and rough like the bark of trees. On entering their cabins you will promptly be placed on your good behavior, and, your wants being perceived with quick insight, complete hospitality will be offered for body and mind to the extent of the larder.

These men know the mountains far and near, and their thousand voices, like the leaves of a book. They can tell where the deer may be found at any time of year or day, and what they are doing; and so of all the other furred and feathered people they meet in their walks; and they can send a thought to its mark as well as a bullet. The aims of such people are not always the highest, yet how brave and manly and clean are their lives compared with too many in crowded towns mildewed and dwarfed in disease and crime! How fine a chance is here to begin life anew in the free fountains and sky-lands of Shasta, where it is so easy to live and to die! The future of the hunter is likely to be a good one; no abrupt change about it, only a passing from wilderness to wilderness, from one high place to another.

Now that the railroad has been built up the Sacramento, everybody with money may go to Mount Shasta, the weak as well as the strong, fine-grained, succulent people, whose legs have never ripened, as well as sinewy mountaineers seasoned long in the weather. This, surely, is not the best way of going to the mountains, yet it is better than staying below. Many still small voices will not be heard in the noisy rush and din, suggestive of going to the sky in a chariot of fire or a whirlwind, as one is shot to the Shasta mark in a booming palace-car cartridge; up the rocky cañon, skimming the foaming river, above the level reaches, above the dashing spray— fine exhilarating translation, yet a pity to go so fast in a blur, where so much might be seen and enjoyed.

Summer Days at Mount Shasta

The mountains are fountains not only of rivers and fertile soil, but of men. Therefore we are all, in some sense, mountaineers, and going to the mountains is going home. Yet how many are doomed to toil in town shadows while the white mountains beckon all along the horizon! Up the cañon to Shasta would be a cure for all care. But many on arrival seem at a loss to know what to do with themselves, and seek shelter in the hotel, as if that were the Shasta they had come for. Others never leave the rail, content with the window views, and cling to the comforts of the sleeping-car like blind mice to their mothers. Many are sick and have been dragged to the healing wilderness unwillingly for body-good alone. Were the parts of the human machine detachable like Yankee inventions, how strange would be the gatherings on the mountains of pieces of people out of repair!

How sadly unlike the whole-hearted ongoing of the seeker after gold is this partial, compulsory mountaineering!—as if the mountain treasuries contained nothing better than gold! Up the mountains they go, high-heeled and high-hatted, laden like Christian with mortifications and mortgages of divers sorts and degrees, some suffering from the sting of bad bargains, others exulting in good ones; hunters and fishermen with gun and rod and leggins; blythe and jolly troubadours to whom all Shasta is romance; poets singing their prayers; the weak and the strong, unable or unwilling to bear mental taxation. But, whatever the motive, all will be in some measure benefited. None may wholly escape the good of Nature, however imperfectly exposed to her blessings. The minister will not preach a perfectly flat and sedimentary sermon after climbing a snowy peak; and the fair play and tremendous impartiality of Nature, so tellingly displayed, will surely affect the after pleadings of the lawyer. Fresh air at least will get into everybody, and the cares of mere business will be quenched like the fires of a sinking ship.

Possibly a branch railroad may some time be built to the summit of Mount Shasta like the road on Mount Washington. In the mean time tourists are dropped at Sisson's, about twelve miles from the summit, whence as headquarters they radiate in every direction to the so-called "points of interest"; sauntering about the flowery fringes of the Strawberry Meadows, bathing in the balm of the woods, scrambling, fishing, hunting; riding about Castle Lake, the McCloud River, Soda Springs, Big Spring, deer pastures, and elsewhere. Some demand bears, and make excited inquiries concerning their haunts, how many there might be altogether on the mountain, and whether they are grizzly, brown, or black. Others shout, "Excelsior," and make off at once for the upper snow-fields. Most, however, are content with comparatively level ground and moderate distances, gathering at the hotel every evening laden with trophies—great sheaves of flowers, cones of various trees, cedar and fir branches covered with yellow lichens, and possibly a fish or two, or quail, or grouse.

But the heads of deer, antelope, wild sheep, and bears are conspicuously rare or altogether wanting to tourist collections in the "paradise of hunters." There is a grand comparing of notes and adventures. Most are exhilarated and happy, though complaints may occasionally be heard—"The mountain does not look so very high after all, nor so very white; the snow is in patches like rags spread out to dry," reminding one of Sydney Smith's joke against Jeffrey, "D——n the Solar System; bad light, planets too indistinct." But far the greater number are in good spirits, showing the influence of holiday enjoyment and mountain air. Fresh roses come to cheeks that long have been pale, and sentiment often begins to blossom under the new inspiration.

The Shasta region may be reserved as a national park, with special reference to the preservation of its fine forests and game. This should by all means be done; but, as far as game is concerned, it is in little danger from tourists, notwithstanding many of them carry guns, and are in some sense hunters. Going in noisy groups, and with guns so shining, they are oftentimes confronted by inquisitive Douglas squirrels, and are thus given opportunities for shooting; but the larger animals retire at their approach and seldom are seen. Other gun people, too wise or too lifeless to make much noise, move slowly along the trails and about the open spots of the woods, like benumbed beetles in a snowdrift. Such hunters are themselves hunted by the animals, which in perfect safety follow them out of curiosity.

During the bright days of midsummer the ascent of Shasta is only a long, safe saunter, without fright or nerve-strain, or even serious fatigue, to those in sound health. Setting out from Sisson's on horseback, accompanied by a guide leading a pack-animal with provisions, blankets, and other necessaries, you follow a trail that leads up to the edge of the timber-line, where you camp for the night, eight or ten miles from the hotel, at an elevation of about ten thousand feet. The next day, rising early, you may push on to the summit and return to Sisson's. But it is better to spend more time in the enjoyment of the grand scenery on the summit and about the head of the Whitney Glacier, pass the second night in camp, and return to Sisson's on the third day. Passing around the margin of the meadows and on through the zones of the forest, you will have good opportunities to get ever-changing views of the mountain and its wealth of creatures that bloom and breathe.

The woods differ but little from those that clothe the mountains to the southward, the trees being slightly closer together and generally not quite so large, marking the incipient change from the open sunny forests of the Sierra to the dense damp forests of the northern coast, where a squirrel may travel in the branches of the thick-set trees hundreds of miles without touching the ground. Around the upper belt of the forest you may see gaps where the ground has been cleared by avalanches of snow, thousands of tons in weight, which, descending with grand rush and roar, brush the trees from their paths like so many fragile shrubs or grasses.

At first the ascent is very gradual. The mountain begins to leave the plain in slopes scarcely perceptible, measuring from two to three degrees. These are continued by easy gradations mile after mile all the way to the truncated, crumbling summit, where they attain a steepness of twenty to twenty-five degrees. The grand simplicity of these lines is partially interrupted on the north subordinate cone that rises from the side of the main cone about three thousand feet from the summit. This side cone, past which your way to the summit lies, was active after the breaking-up of the main ice-cap of the glacial period, as shown by the comparatively unwasted crater in which it terminates and by streams of fresh-looking, unglaciated lava that radiate from it as a center.

The main summit is about a mile and a half in diameter from southwest to northeast, and is nearly covered with snow and *névé*, bounded by crumbling peaks and ridges, among which we look in vain for any sure plan of an ancient crater. The extreme summit is situated on the southern end of a narrow ridge that bounds the general summit on the east. Viewed from the north, it appears as an irregular blunt point about ten feet high, and is fast disappearing before the stormy atmospheric action to which it is subjected.

At the base of the eastern ridge, just below the extreme summit, hot sulphurous gases and vapor escape with a hissing, bubbling noise from a fissure in the lava. Some of the many small vents cast up a spray of clear hot water, which falls back repeatedly until wasted in vapor. The steam and spray seem to be produced simply by melting snow coming in the way of the escaping gases, while the gases are evidently derived from the heated interior of the mountain, and may be regarded as the last feeble expression of the mighty power that lifted the entire mass of the mountain from the volcanic depths far below the surface of the plain.

The view from the summit in clear weather extends to an immense distance in every direction. Southeastward, the low volcanic portion of the Sierra is seen like a map, both flanks as well as the crater-dotted axis, as far as Lassen's[1] Butte, a prominent landmark and an old volcano like Shasta, between ten and eleven thousand feet high, and distant about sixty miles. Some of the higher summit peaks near Independence Lake, one hundred and eighty miles away, are at times distinctly visible. Far to the north, in Oregon, the snowy volcanic cones of Mounts Pitt, Jefferson, and the Three Sisters rise in clear relief, like majestic monuments, above the dim dark sea of the northern woods. To the northeast lie the Rhett and Klamath Lakes, the Lava Beds, and a grand display of hill and mountain and gray rocky plains. The Scott, Siskiyou, and

---

[1]An early local name for what is now known as Lassen Peak, or Mt. Lassen. In 1914 its volcanic activity was resumed with spectacular eruptions of ashes, steam, and gas. [Editor.]

Trinity Mountains rise in long, compact waves to the west and southwest, and the valley of the Sacramento and the coast mountains, with their marvelous wealth of woods and waters, are seen; while close around the base of the mountain lie the beautiful Shasta Valley, Strawberry Valley, Huckleberry Valley, and many others, with the headwaters of the Shasta, Sacramento, and McCloud Rivers. Some observers claim to have seen the ocean from the summit of Shasta, but I have not yet been so fortunate.

The Cinder Cone near Lassen's Butte is remarkable as being the scene of the most recent volcanic eruption in the range. It is a symmetrical truncated cone covered with gray cinders and ashes, with a regular crater in which a few pines an inch or two in diameter are growing. It stands between two small lakes which previous to the last eruption, when the cone was built, formed one lake. From near the base of the cone a flood of extremely rough black vesicular lava extends across what was once a portion of the bottom of the lake into the forest of yellow pine.

This lava-flow seems to have been poured out during the same eruption that gave birth to the cone, cutting the lake in two, flowing a little way into the woods and overwhelming the trees in its way, the ends of some of the charred trunks still being visible, projecting from beneath the advanced snout of the flow where it came to rest; while the floor of the forest for miles around is so thickly strewn with loose cinders that walking is very fatiguing. The Pitt River Indians tell of a fearful time of darkness, probably due to this eruption, when the sky was filled with falling cinders which, as they thought, threatened every living creature with destruction, and say that when at length the sun appeared through the gloom it was red like blood.

Summer Days at Mount Shasta

Less recent craters in great numbers dot the adjacent region, some with lakes in their throats, some overgrown with trees, others nearly bare—telling monuments of Nature's mountain fires so often lighted throughout the northern Sierra. And, standing on the top of icy Shasta, the mightiest fire-monument of them all, we can hardly fail to look forward to the blare and glare of its next eruption and wonder whether it is nigh. Elsewhere men have planted gardens and vineyards in the craters of volcanoes quiescent for ages, and almost without warning have been hurled into the sky. More than a thousand years of profound calm have been known to intervene between two violent eruptions. Seventeen centuries intervened between two consecutive eruptions on the island of Ischia. Few volcanoes continue permanently in eruption. Like gigantic geysers, spouting hot stone instead of hot water, they work and sleep, and we have no sure means of knowing whether they are only sleeping or dead.

4

A Perilous Night
on Shasta's Summit

TOWARD the end of summer, after a light, open winter, one may reach the summit of Mount Shasta without passing over much snow, by keeping on the crest of a long narrow ridge, mostly bare, that extends from near the camp-ground at the timber-line. But on my first excursion to the summit the whole mountain, down to its low swelling base, was smoothly laden with loose fresh snow, presenting a most glorious mass of winter mountain scenery, in the midst of which I scrambled and reveled or lay snugly snowbound, enjoying the fertile clouds and the snow-bloom in all their growing, drifting grandeur.

I had walked from Redding, sauntering leisurely from station to station along the old Oregon stage-road, the better to see the rocks and plants, birds and people, by the way, tracing the rushing Sacramento to its fountains around icy Shasta. The first rains had fallen on the lowlands, and the first snows on the mountains, and everything was fresh and bracing, while an abundance of balmy sunshine filled all the noonday hours. It was the calm afterglow that usually succeeds the first storm of the winter. I met many of the birds that had reared their young and spent their summer in the Shasta woods and chaparral. They were then on their way south to their winter homes, leading their young full-fledged and about as large and strong as the parents. Squirrels, dry and elastic after the storms, were busy about their stores of pine nuts, and the latest goldenrods were still in bloom, though it was now past the middle of October. The grand color glow—the autumnal jubilee of ripe leaves—was past prime, but, freshened by the rain, was still making a fine show along the banks of the river and in the ravines and the dells of the smaller streams.

At the salmon-hatching establishment on the McCloud River I halted a week to examine the limestone belt, grandly developed there, to learn what I could of the inhabitants of the river and its banks, and to give time for the fresh snow that I knew had fallen on the mountain to settle somewhat, with a view to making the ascent. A pedestrian on these mountain roads, especially so late in the year, is sure to excite curiosity, and many were the interrogations concerning my ramble. When I said that I was simply taking a walk, and that icy Shasta was my mark, I was invariably admonished that I had come on a dangerous quest. The time was far too late, the snow was too loose and deep to climb, and I should be lost in drifts and slides. When I hinted that new snow was beautiful and storms not so bad as they were called, my advisers shook their heads in token of superior knowledge and declared the ascent of "Shasta Butte" through loose snow impossible. Nevertheless, before noon of the second of November I was in the frosty azure of the utmost summit.

When I arrived at Sisson's everything was quiet. The last of the summer visitors had flitted long before, and the deer and bears also were beginning to seek their winter homes. My barometer and the sighing winds and filmy, half-transparent clouds that dimmed the sunshine gave notice of the approach of another storm, and I was in haste to be off and get myself established somewhere in the midst of it, whether the summit was to be attained or not. Sisson, who is a mountaineer, speedily fitted me out for storm or calm as only a mountaineer could, with warm blankets and a week's provisions so generous in quantity and kind that they easily might have been made to last a month in case of my being closely snowbound. Well I knew the weariness of snow-climbing, and the frosts, and the dangers of mountaineering so late in the year; therefore I could not ask a guide to go with me, even had one been willing. All I wanted was to have blankets and provisions deposited as far up in the timber as the snow would permit a pack-animal to go. There I could build a storm nest and lie warm, and make raids up and around the mountain in accordance with the weather.

Setting out on the afternoon of November first, with Jerome Fay, mountaineer and guide, in charge of the animals, I was soon plodding wearily upward through the muffled winter woods, the snow of course growing steadily deeper and looser, so that we had to break a trail. The animals began to get discouraged, and after night and darkness came on they became entangled in a bed of rough lava, where, breaking through four or five feet of mealy snow, their feet were caught between angular boulders. Here they were in danger of being lost, but after we had removed packs and saddles and assisted their efforts with ropes, they all escaped to the side of a ridge about a thousand feet below the timber-line.

To go farther was out of the question, so we were compelled to camp as best we could. A pitch-pine fire speedily changed the temperature and shed a blaze of light on the wild lava-slope and the straggling storm-bent pines around us. Melted snow answered for coffee, and we had plenty of venison to roast. Toward midnight

A Night on Shasta's Summit

I rolled myself in my blankets, slept an hour and a half, arose and ate more venison, tied two days' provisions to my belt, and set out for the summit, hoping to reach it ere the coming storm should fall. Jerome accompanied me a little distance above camp and indicated the way as well as he could in the darkness. He seemed loath to leave me, but, being reassured that I was at home and required no care, he bade me good-bye and returned to camp, ready to lead his animals down the mountain at daybreak.

After I was above the dwarf pines, it was fine practice pushing up the broad unbroken slopes of snow, alone in the solemn silence of the night. Half the sky was clouded; in the other half the stars sparkled icily in the keen, frosty air; while everywhere the glorious wealth of snow fell away from the summit of the cone in flowing folds, more extensive and continuous than any I had ever seen before. When day dawned the clouds were crawling slowly and becoming more massive, but gave no intimation of immediate danger, and I pushed on faithfully, though holding myself well in hand, ready to return to the timber; for it was easy to see that the storm was not far off. The mountain rides ten thousand feet above the general level of the country, in blank exposure to the deep upper currents of the sky, and no labyrinth of peaks and cañons I had ever been in seemed to me so dangerous as these immense slopes, bare against the sky.

The frost was intense, and drifting snow-dust made breathing at times rather difficult. The snow was as dry as meal, and the finer particles drifted freely, rising high in the air, while the larger portions of the crystals rolled like sand. I frequently sank to my armpits between buried blocks of loose lava, but generally only to my knees. When tired with walking I still wallowed slowly upward on

[43]

all fours. The steepness of the slope—thirty-five degrees in some places—made any kind of progress fatiguing, while small avalanches were being constantly set in motion in the steepest places. But the bracing air and the sublime beauty of the snowy expanse thrilled every nerve and made absolute exhaustion impossible. I seemed to be walking and wallowing in a cloud; but, holding steadily onward, by half-past ten o'clock I had gained the highest summit.

I held my commanding foothold in the sky for two hours, gazing on the glorious landscapes spread maplike around the immense horizon, and tracing the outlines of the ancient lava-streams extending far into the surrounding plains, and the pathways of vanished glaciers of which Shasta had been the center. But, as I had left my coat in camp for the sake of having my limbs free in climbing, I soon was cold. The wind increased in violence, raising the snow in magnificent drifts that were drawn out in the form of wavering banners glowing in the sun. Toward the end of my stay a succession of small clouds struck against the summit rocks like drifting icebergs, darkening the air as they passed, and producing a chill as definite and sudden as if ice-water had been dashed in my face. This is the kind of cloud in which snow-flowers grow, and I turned and fled.

Finding that I was not closely pursued, I ventured to take time on the way down for a visit to the head of the Whitney Glacier and the "Crater Butte." After I reached the end of the main summit ridge the descent was but little more than one continuous soft, mealy, muffled slide, most luxurious and rapid, though the hissing, swishing speed attained was obscured in great part by flying snow-dust—a marked contrast to the boring seal-wallowing upward struggle. I reached camp about an hour before dusk, hollowed a strip of loose ground in the lee of a large block of red lava, where firewood was abundant, rolled myself in my blankets, and went to sleep.

Next morning, having slept little the night before the ascent and being weary with climbing after the excitement was over, I slept late. Then, awaking suddenly, my eyes opened on one of the most beautiful and sublime scenes I ever enjoyed. A boundless wilderness of storm-clouds of different degrees of ripeness were congregated over all the lower landscape for thousands of square miles, colored gray, and purple, and pearl, and deep-glowing white, amid which I seemed to be floating; while the great white cone of the mountain above was all aglow in the free, blazing sunshine. It seemed not so much an ocean as a *land* of clouds— undulating hill and dale, smooth purple plains, and silvery mountains of cumuli, range over range, diversified with peak and dome and hollow fully brought out in light and shade.

I gazed enchanted, but cold gray masses, drifting like dust on a wind-swept plain, began to shut out the light, forerunners of the coming storm I had been so anxiously watching. I made haste to gather as much wood as possible, snugging it as a shelter around my bed. The storm side of my blankets was fastened down with stakes to reduce as much as possible the sifting-in of drift and the danger of being blown away. The precious bread-sack was placed safely as a pillow, and when at length the first flakes fell I was exultingly ready to welcome them. Most of my firewood was more than half rosin and would blaze in the face of the fiercest drifting; the winds could not demolish my bed, and my bread could be made to last indefinitely; while in case of need I had the means of making snowshoes and could retreat or hold my ground as I pleased.

Presently the storm broke forth into full snowy bloom, and the thronging crystals darkened the air. The wind swept past in hissing floods, grinding the snow into meal and sweeping down into the hollows in enormous drifts all the heavier particles, while the finer dust was sifted through the sky, increasing the icy gloom. But my fire glowed bravely as if in glad defiance of the drift to quench it, and, notwithstanding but little trace of my nest could be seen after the snow had leveled and buried it, I was snug and warm, and the passionate uproar produced a glad excitement.

Day after day the storm continued, piling snow on snow in weariless abundance. There were short periods of quiet, when the sun would seem to look eagerly down through rents in the clouds, as if to know how the work was advancing. During these calm intervals I replenished my fire—sometimes without leaving the nest, for fire and woodpile were so near this could easily be done— or busied myself with my notebook, watching the gestures of the trees in taking the snow, examining separate crystals under a lens, and learning the methods of their deposition as an enduring fountain for the streams. Several times, when the storm ceased for a few minutes, a Douglas squirrel came frisking from the foot of a clump of dwarf pines, moving in sudden interrupted spurts over the bossy snow; then, without any apparent guidance, he would dig rapidly into the drift where were buried some grains of barley that the horses had left. The Douglas squirrel does not strictly belong to these upper woods, and I was surprised to see him out in such weather. The mountain sheep also, quite a large flock of them, came to my camp and took shelter beside a clump of matted dwarf pines a little above my nest.

The storm lasted about a week, but before it was ended Sisson became alarmed and sent up the guide with animals to see what had become of me and recover the camp outfit. The news spread that "there was a man on the mountain," and he must surely have perished, and Sisson was blamed for allowing any one to attempt climbing in such weather; while I was as safe as anybody in the lowlands, lying like a squirrel in a warm, fluffy nest, busied about my own affairs and wishing only to be let alone. Later, however, a trail could not have been broken for a horse, and some of the camp furniture would have had to be abandoned. On the fifth day I returned to Sisson's, and from that comfortable base made excursions, as the weather permitted, to the Black Butte, to the foot of the Whitney Glacier, around the base of the mountain, to Rhett and Klamath Lakes, to the Modoc region and elsewhere, developing many interesting scenes and experiences.

But the next spring, on the other side of this eventful winter, I saw and felt still more of the Shasta snow. For then it was my fortune to get into the very heart of a storm, and to be held in it for a long time.

On the 28th of April [1875] I led a party up the mountain for the purpose of making a survey of the summit with reference to the location of the Geodetic monument. On the 30th, accompanied by Jerome Fay, I made another ascent to make some barometrical observations, the day intervening between the two ascents being devoted to establishing a camp on the extreme edge of the timberline. Here, on our red trachyte bed, we obtained two hours of shallow sleep broken for occasional glimpses of the keen, starry night. At two o'clock we rose, breakfasted on a warmed tin-cupful of coffee and a piece of frozen venison broiled on the coals, and started for the summit. Up to this time there was nothing in sight that betokened the approach of a storm; but on gaining the summit, we saw toward Lassen's Butte hundreds of square miles of white cumuli boiling dreamily in the sunshine far beneath us, and causing no alarm.

The slight weariness of the ascent was soon rested away, and our glorious morning in the sky promised nothing but enjoyment. At 9 A.M. the dry thermometer stood at 34° in the shade and rose steadily until at 1 P.M. it stood at 50°, probably influenced somewhat by radiation from the sun-warmed cliffs. A common bumblebee, not at all benumbed, zigzagged vigorously about our heads for a few moments, as if unconscious of the fact that the nearest honey flower was a mile beneath him.

In the mean time clouds were growing down in Shasta Valley—massive swelling cumuli, displaying delicious tones of purple and gray in the hollows of their sun-beaten bosses. Extending gradually southward around on both sides of Shasta, these at length united with the older field towards Lassen's Butte, thus encircling Mount Shasta in one continuous cloud-zone. Rhett and Klamath Lakes were eclipsed beneath clouds scarcely less brilliant than their own silvery disks. The Modoc Lava Beds, many a snow-laden peak far north in Oregon, the Scott and Trinity and Siskiyou Mountains, the peaks of the Sierra, the blue Coast Range, Shasta Valley, the dark forests filling the valley of the Sacramento, all in turn were obscured or buried, leaving the lofty cone on which we stood solitary in the sunshine between two skies—a sky of spotless blue above, a sky of glittering cloud beneath. The creative sun shone glorious on the vast expanse of cloudland; hill and dale, mountain and valley springing into existence responsive to his rays and steadily developing in beauty and individuality. One huge mountain-cone of cloud, corresponding to Mount Shasta in these newborn cloud-ranges, rose close alongside with a visible motion, its firm, polished bosses seeming so near and substantial that we almost fancied we might leap down upon them from where we stood and make our way to the lowlands. No hint was given, by anything in their appearance, of the fleeting character of these most sublime and beautiful cloud mountains. On the contrary they impressed one as being lasting additions to the landscape.

The weather of the springtime and summer, throughout the Sierra in general, is usually varied by slight local rains and dustings of snow, most of which are obviously far too joyous and life-giving to be regarded as storms—single clouds growing in the sunny sky, ripening in an hour, showering the heated landscape, and passing away like a thought, leaving no visible bodily remains to stain the sky. Snowstorms of the same gentle kind abound among the high peaks, but in spring they not unfrequently attain larger proportions, assuming a violence and energy of expression scarcely surpassed by those bred in the depths of winter. Such was the storm now gathering about us.

It began to declare itself shortly after noon, suggesting to us the idea of at once seeking our safe camp in the timber and abandoning the purpose of making an observation of the barometer at 3 P.M.,—two having already been made, at 9 A.M., and 12 P.M., while simultaneous observations were made at Strawberry Valley. Jerome peered at short intervals over the ridge, contemplating the rising clouds with anxious gestures in the rough wind, and at length declared that if we did not make a speedy escape we should be compelled to pass the rest of the day and night on the summit. But anxiety to complete my observations stifled my own instinctive promptings to retreat, and held me to my work. No inexperienced person was depending on me, and I told Jerome that we two mountaineers should be able to make our way down through any storm likely to fall.

Presently thin, fibrous films of cloud began to blow directly over the summit from north to south, drawn out in long fairy webs like carded wool, forming and dissolving as if by magic. The wind twisted them into ringlets and whirled them in a succession of graceful convolutions like the outside sprays of Yosemite Falls in flood-time; then, sailing out into the thin azure over the precipitous brink of the ridge they were drifted together like wreaths of foam on a river. These higher and finer cloud fabrics were evidently produced by the chilling of the air from its own expansion caused by the upward deflection of the wind against the slopes of the mountain. They steadily increased on the north rim of the cone, forming at length a thick, opaque, ill-defined embankment from the icy meshes of which snow-flowers began to fall, alternating with hail. The sky speedily darkened, and just as I had completed my last observation and boxed my instruments ready for the descent, the storm began in serious earnest. At first the cliffs were beaten with hail, every stone of which, as far as I could see, was regular in form, six-sided pyramids with rounded base, rich and sumptuous-looking, and fashioned with loving care, yet seemingly thrown away on those desolate crags down which they went rolling, falling, sliding in a network of curious streams.

A Night on Shasta's Summit

After we had forced our way down the ridge and past the group of hissing fumaroles, the storm became inconceivably violent. The thermometer fell 22° in a few minutes, and soon dropped below zero. The hail gave place to snow, and darkness came on like night. The wind, rising to the highest pitch of violence, boomed and surged amid the desolate crags; lightning-flashes in quick succession cut the gloomy darkness; and the thunders, the most tremendously loud and appalling I ever heard, made an almost continuous roar, stroke following stroke in quick, passionate succession, as though the mountain were being rent to its foundations and the fires of the old volcano were breaking forth again.

Could we at once have begun to descend the snow-slopes leading to the timber, we might have made good our escape, however dark and wild the storm. As it was, we had first to make our way along a dangerous ridge nearly a mile and a half long, flanked in many places by steep ice-slopes at the head of the Whitney Glacier on one side and by shattered precipices on the other. Apprehensive of this coming darkness, I had taken the precaution, when the storm began, to make the most dangerous points clear to my mind, and to mark their relations with reference to the direction of the wind. When, therefore, the darkness came on, and the bewildering drift, I felt confident that we could force our way through it with no other guidance. After passing the "Hot Springs" I halted in the lee of a lava-block to let Jerome, who had fallen a little behind, come up. Here he opened a council in which, under circumstances sufficiently exciting but without evincing any bewilderment, he maintained, in opposition to my views, that it was impossible to proceed. He firmly refused to make the venture to find the camp, while I, aware of the dangers that would necessarily attend our efforts, and conscious of being the cause of his present peril, decided not to leave him.

Our discussions ended, Jerome made a dash from the shelter of the lava-block and began forcing his way back against the wind to the "Hot Springs," wavering and struggling to resist being carried away, as if he were fording a rapid stream. After waiting and watching in vain for some flaw in the storm that might be urged as a new argument in favor of attempting the descent, I was compelled to follow. "Here," said Jerome, as we shivered in the midst of the hissing, sputtering fumaroles, "we shall be safe from frost." "Yes," said I "we can lie in this mud and steam and sludge, warm at least on one side; but how can we protect our lungs from the acid gases, and how, after our clothing is saturated, shall we be able to reach camp without freezing, even after the storm is over? We shall have to wait for sunshine, and when will it come?"

The tempered area to which we had committed ourselves extended over about one fourth of an acre; but it was only about an eighth of an inch in thickness, for the scalding gas-jets were shorn off close to the ground by the oversweeping flood of frosty wind. And how lavishly the snow fell only mountaineers may know. The crisp crystal flowers seemed to touch one another and fairly to thicken the tremendous blast that carried them. This was the bloom-time, the summer of the cloud, and never before have I seen even a mountain cloud flowering so profusely.

When the bloom of the Shasta chaparral is falling, the ground is sometimes covered for hundreds of square miles to a depth of half an inch. But the bloom of this fertile snow-cloud grew and matured and fell to a depth of two feet in a few hours. Some crystals landed with their rays almost perfect, but most of them were worn and broken by striking against one another, or by rolling on the ground. The touch of these snow-flowers in calm weather is infinitely gentle—glinting, swaying, settling silently in the dry mountain air, or massed in flakes soft and downy. To lie out alone in the mountains of a still night and be touched by the first of these small silent messengers from the sky is a memorable experience, and the fineness of that touch none will forget. But the storm-blast laden with crisp, sharp snow seems to crush and bruise and stupefy with its multitude of stings, and compels the bravest to turn and flee.

The snow fell without abatement until an hour or two after what seemed to be the natural darkness of the night. Up to the time the storm first broke on the summit its development was remarkably gentle. There was a deliberate growth of clouds, a weaving of translucent tissue above, then the roar of the wind and the thunder, and the darkening flight of snow. Its subsidence was not less sudden. The clouds broke and vanished, not a crystal was left in the sky, and the stars shone out with pure and tranquil radiance.

During the storm we lay on our backs so as to present as little surface as possible to the wind, and to let the drift pass over us. The mealy snow sifted into the folds of our clothing and in many places reached the skin. We were glad at first to see the snow packing about us, hoping it would deaden the force of the wind, but it soon froze into a stiff, crusty heap as the temperature fell, rather augmenting our novel misery.

When the heat became unendurable, on some spot where steam was escaping through the sludge, we tried to stop it with snow and mud, or shifted a little at a time by shoving with our heels; for to stand in blank exposure to the fearful wind in our frozen-and-broiled condition seemed certain death. The acrid incrustations sublimed from the escaping gases frequently gave way, opening new vents to scald us; and, fearing that if at any time the wind should fall, carbonic acid, which often formed a considerable portion of the gaseous exhalations of volcanoes, might collect in sufficient quantities to cause sleep and death, I warned Jerome against forgetting himself for a single moment, even should his sufferings admit of such a thing.

Accordingly, when during the long, dreary watches of the night we roused from a state of half-consciousness, we called each other by name in a frightened, startled way, each fearing the other might be benumbed or dead. The ordinary sensations of cold give but a faint conception of that which comes on after hard climbing with want of food and sleep in such exposure as this. Life is then seen to be a fire, that now smoulders, now brightens, and may be easily quenched. The weary hours wore away like dim half-forgotten years, so long and eventful they seemed, though we did nothing but suffer. Still the pain was not always of that bitter, intense kind that precludes thought and takes away all capacity for enjoyment. A sort of dreamy stupor came on at times in which we fancied we saw dry, resinous logs suitable for campfires, just as after going days without food men fancy they see bread.

Frozen, blistered, famished, benumbed, our bodies seemed lost to us at times—all dead but the eyes. For the duller and fainter we became the clearer was our vision, though only in momentary glimpses. Then, after the sky cleared, we gazed at the stars, blessed immortals of light, shining with marvelous brightness with long lance rays, near-looking and new-looking, as if never seen before. Again they would look familiar and remind us of star-gazing at home. Oftentimes imagination coming into play would present charming pictures of the warm zone below, mingled with others near and far. Then the bitter wind and the drift would break the blissful vision and dreary pains cover us like clouds. "Are you suffering much?" Jerome would inquire with pitiful faintness. "Yes," I would say, striving to keep my voice brave, "frozen and burned; but never mind, Jerome, the night will wear away at last, and tomorrow we go a-Maying, and what campfires we will make, and what sun-baths we will take!"

The frost grew more and more intense, and we became icy and covered over with a crust of frozen snow, as if we had lain cast away in the drift all winter. In about thirteen hours—every hour like a year—day began to dawn, but it was long ere the summit's rocks were touched by the sun. No clouds were visible from where we lay, yet the morning was dull and blue, and bitterly frosty; and hour after hour passed by while we eagerly watched the pale light stealing down the ridge to the hollow where we lay. But there was not a trace of that warm, flushing sunrise splendor we so long had hoped for.

As the time drew near to make an effort to reach camp, we became concerned to know what strength was left us, and whether or no we could walk; for we had lain flat all this time without once rising to our feet. Mountaineers, however, always find in themselves a reserve of power after great exhaustion. It is a kind of second life, available only in emergencies like this; and, having proved its existence, I had no great fear that either of us would fail, though one of my arms was already benumbed and hung powerless.

At length, after the temperature was somewhat mitigated on this memorable first of May, we arose and began to struggle homeward. Our frozen trousers could scarcely be made to bend at the knee, and we waded the snow with difficulty. The summit ridge was fortunately wind-swept and nearly bare, so we were not compelled to lift our feet high, and on reaching the long home slopes laden with loose snow we made rapid progress, sliding and shuffling and pitching headlong, our feebleness accelerating rather than diminishing our speed. When we had descended some three thousand feet the sunshine warmed our backs and we began to revive. At 10 A.M. we reached the timber and were safe.

Half an hour later we heard Sisson shouting down among the firs, coming with horses to take us to the hotel. After breaking a trail through the snow as far as possible he had tied his animals and walked up. We had been so long without food that we cared but little about eating, but we eagerly drank the coffee he prepared for us. Our feet were frozen, and thawing them was painful, and had to be done very slowly by keeping them buried in soft snow for several hours, which avoided permanent damage. Five thousand feet below the summit we found only three inches of new snow, and at the base of the mountain only a slight shower of rain had fallen, showing how local our storm had been, notwithstanding its terrific fury. Our feet were wrapped in sacking, and we were soon mounted and on our way down into the thick sunshine—"God's Country," as Sisson calls the Chaparral Zone. In two hours' ride the last snow-bank was left behind. Violets appeared along the edges of the trail, and the chaparral was coming into bloom, with young lilies and larkspurs about the open places in rich profusion. How beautiful seemed the golden sunbeams streaming through the woods between the warm brown boles of the cedars and pines! All my friends among the birds and plants seemed like *old* friends, and we felt like speaking to every one of them as we passed, as if we had been a long time away in some far, strange country.

In the afternoon we reached Strawberry Valley and fell asleep. Next morning we seemed to have risen from the dead. My bed-room was flooded with sunshine, and from the window I saw the great white Shasta cone clad in forests and clouds and bearing them loftily in the sky. Everything seemed full and radiant with the freshness and beauty and enthusiasm of youth. Sisson's children came in with flowers and covered my bed, and the storm on the mountain-top vanished like a dream.

5

Shasta Rambles and Modoc Memories

ARCTIC beauty and desolation, with their blessings and dangers, all may be found here, to test the endurance and skill of adventurous climbers; but far better than climbing the mountain is going around its warm, fertile base, enjoying its bounties like a bee circling around a bank of flowers. The distance is about a hundred miles, and will take some of the time we hear so much about—a week or two—but the benefits will compensate for any number of weeks. Perhaps the profession of doing good may be full, but everybody should be kind at least to himself. Take a course of good water and air, and in the eternal youth of Nature you may renew your own. Go quietly, alone; no harm will befall you. Some have strange, morbid fears as soon as they find themselves with Nature, even in the kindest and wildest of her solitudes, like very sick children afraid of their mother—as if God were dead and the devil were king.

One may make the trip on horseback, or in a carriage, even; for a good level road may be found all the way round, by Shasta Valley, Sheep Rock, Elk Flat, Huckleberry Valley, Squaw Valley, following for a considerable portion of the way the old Emigrant Road, which lies along the east disk of the mountain, and is deeply worn by the wagons of the early gold-seekers, many of whom chose this northern route as perhaps being safer and easier, the pass here being only about six thousand feet above sea-level. But it is far better to go afoot. Then you are free to make wide waverings and zigzags away from the roads to visit the great fountain streams of the rivers, the glaciers also, and the wildest retreats in the primeval forests, where the best plants and animals dwell, and where many a flower-bell will ring against your knees, and friendly trees will reach out their fronded branches and touch you as you pass. One blanket will be enough to carry, or you may forego the pleasure and burden altogether, as wood for fires is everywhere abundant. Only a little food will be required. Berries and plums abound in season, and quail and grouse and deer—the magnificent shaggy mule deer as well as the common species.

As you sweep around so grand a center, the mountain itself seems to turn, displaying its riches like the revolving pyramids in jewelers' windows. One glacier after another comes into view, and the outlines of the mountain are ever changing, though all the way around, from whatever point of view, the form is maintained of a grand, simple cone with a gently sloping base and rugged, crumbling ridges separating the glaciers and the snow-fields more or less completely. The play of colors, from the first touches of the morning sun on the summit, down the snow-fields and the ice and lava until the forests are aglow, is a never-ending delight, the rosy lava and the fine flushings of the snow being ineffably lovely. Thus one saunters on and on in the glorious radiance in utter peace and forgetfulness of time.

Yet, strange to say, there are days even here somewhat dull-looking, when the mountain seems uncommunicative, sending out no appreciable invitation, as if not at home. At such times its height seems much less, as if, crouching and weary, it were taking rest. But Shasta is always at home to those who love her, and is ever in a thrill of enthusiastic activity—burning fires within, grinding glaciers without, and fountains ever flowing. Every crystal dances responsive to the touches of the sun, and currents of sap in the growing cells of all the vegetation are ever in a vital whirl and rush, and though many feet and wings are folded, how many are astir! And the wandering winds, how busy they are, and what a breadth of sound and motion they make, glinting and bubbling about the crags of the summit, sifting through the woods, feeling their way from grove to grove, ruffling the loose hair on the shoulders of the bears, fanning and rocking young birds in their cradles, making a trumpet of every corolla, and carrying their fragrance around the world.

In unsettled weather, when storms are growing, the mountain looms immensely higher, and its miles of height become apparent to all, especially in the gloom of the gathering clouds, or when the storm is done and they are rolling away, torn on the edges and melting while in the sunshine. Slight rain-storms are likely to be encountered in a trip round the mountain, but one may easily find shelter beneath well-thatched trees that shed the rain like a roof. Then the shining of the wet leaves is delightful, and the steamy fragrance, and the burst of bird-song from a multitude of thrushes and finches and warblers that have nests in the chaparral.

The nights, too, are delightful, watching with Shasta beneath the great starry dome. A thousand thousand voices are heard, but so finely blended they seem a part of the night itself, and make a deeper silence. And how grandly do the great logs and branches of your campfire give forth the heat and light that during their long century-lives they have so slowly gathered from the sun, storing it away in beautiful dotted cells and beads of amber gum! The neighboring trees look into the charmed circle as if the noon of another day had come, familiar flowers and grasses that chance to be near seem far more beautiful and impressive than by day, and as the dead trees give forth their light all the other riches of their lives seem to be set free and with the rejoicing flames rise again to the sky. In setting out from Strawberry Valley, by bearing off to the northwestward a few miles you may see

> . . . beneath dim aisles, in odorous beds,
> The slight Linnæa hang its twin-born heads,
> And [bless] the monument of the man of flowers,
> Which breathes his sweet fame through the northern
> bowers.

This is one of the few places in California where the charming linnæa is found, though it is common to the northward through Oregon and Washington. Here, too, you may find the curious but unlovable darlingtonia, a carnivorous plant that devours bumblebees, grasshoppers, ants, moths, and other insects, with insatiable appetite. In approaching it, its suspicious-looking yellow-spotted hood and watchful attitude will be likely to make you go cautiously through the bog where it stands, as if you were approaching a dangerous snake. It also occurs in a bog near Sothern's Station on the stage-road, where I first saw it, and in other similar bogs throughout the mountains hereabouts.

The "Big Spring" of the Sacramento is about a mile and a half above Sisson's, issuing from the base of a drift-covered hill. It is lined with emerald algae and mosses, and shaded with alder, willow, and thorn bushes, which give it a fine setting. Its waters, apparently unaffected by flood or drouth, heat or cold, fall at once into white rapids with a rush and dash, as if glad to escape from the darkness to begin their wild course down the cañon to the plain.

Muir's Peak, a few miles to the north of the spring, rises about three thousand feet above the plain on which it stands, and is easily climbed. The view is very fine and well repays the slight walk to its summit, from which much of your way about the mountain may be studied and chosen. The view obtained of the Whitney Glacier should tempt you to visit it, since it is the largest of the Shasta glaciers and its lower portion abounds in beautiful and interesting cascades and crevasses. It is three or four miles long and terminates at an elevation of about nine thousand five hundred feet above sealevel, in moraine-sprinkled ice-cliffs sixty feet high. The long gray slopes leading up to the glacier seem remarkably smooth and unbroken. They are much interrupted, nevertheless, with abrupt, jagged precipitous gorges, which, though offering instructive sections of the lavas for examination, would better be shunned by most people. This may be done by keeping well down on the base until fronting the glacier before beginning the ascent.

The gorge through which the glacier is drained is rawlooking, deep and narrow, and indescribably jagged. The walls in many places overhang; in others they are beveled, loose, and shifting where the channel has been eroded by cinders, ashes, strata of firm lavas, and glacial drift, telling of many a change from frost to fire and their attendant floods of mud and water. Most of the drainage of the glacier vanishes at once in the porous rocks to reappear in springs in the distant valley, and it is only in time of flood that the channel carries much water; then there are several fine falls in the gorge, six hundred feet or more in height. Snow lies in it the year round at an elevation of eight thousand five hundred feet, and in sheltered spots a thousand feet lower. Tracing this wild changing channel-gorge, gully, or cañon, the sections will show Mount Shasta as a huge palimpsest, containing the records, layer upon layer, of strangely contrasted events in its fiery-icy history. But look well to your footing, for the way will test the skill of the most cautious mountaineers.

Regaining the low ground at the base of the mountain and holding on in your grand orbit, you pass through a belt of juniper woods, called "The Cedars," to Sheep Rock at the foot of the Shasta Pass. Here you strike the old emigrant road, which leads over the low divide to the eastern slopes of the mountain. In a north-northwesterly direction from the foot of the pass you may chance to find Pluto's Cave, already mentioned; but it is not easily found, since its several mouths are on a level with the general surface of the ground, and have been made simply by the falling-in of portions of the roof. Far the most beautiful and richly furnished of the mountain caves of California occur in a thick belt of metamorphic limestone that is pretty generally developed along the western flank of the Sierra from the McCloud River to the Kaweah, a distance of nearly four hundred miles. These volcanic caves are not wanting in interest, and it is well to light a pitch-pine torch and take a walk in these dark ways of the underworld whenever opportunity offers, if for no other reason to see with new appreciation on returning to the sunshine the beauties that lie so thick about us.

Sheep Rock is about twenty miles from Sisson's, and is one of the principal winter pasture-grounds of the wild sheep, from which it takes its name. It is a mass of lava presenting to the gray sage plain of Shasta Valley a bold craggy front two thousand feet high. Its summit lies at an elevation of five thousand five hundred feet above the sea, and has several square miles of comparatively level surface, where bunch-grass grows and the snow does not lie deep, thus allowing the hardy sheep to pick up a living through the winter months when deep snows have driven them down from the lofty ridges of Shasta.

From here it might be well to leave the immediate base of the mountain for a few days and visit the Lava Beds made famous by the Modoc War. They lie about forty miles to the northeastward, on the south shore of Rhett or Tule[1] Lake, at an elevation above sea-level of about forty-five hundred feet. They are a portion of a flow of dense black vesicular lava, dipping northeastward at a low angle, but little changed as yet by the weather, and about as destitute of soil as a glacial pavement. The surface, though smooth in a general way as seen from a distance, is dotted with hillocks and rough crater-like pits, and traversed by a network of yawning fissures, forming a combination of topographical conditions of very striking character. The way lies by Mount Bremer, over stretches of gray sage plains, interrupted by rough lava-slopes timbered with juniper and yellow pine, and with here and there a green meadow and a stream.

This is a famous game region, and you will be likely to meet small bands of antelope, mule deer, and wild sheep. Mount Bremer is the most noted stronghold of the sheep in the whole Shasta region. Large flocks dwell here from year to year, winter and sum-

[1]Pronounced Too'-lay.

mer, descending occasionally into the adjacent sage plains and lava-beds to feed, but ever ready to take refuge in the jagged crags of their mountain at every alarm. While traveling with a company of hunters I saw about fifty in one flock.

The Van Bremer brothers, after whom the mountain is named, told me that they once climbed the mountain with their rifles and hounds on a grand hunt; but, after keeping up the pursuit for a week, their boots and clothing gave way, and the hounds were lamed and worn out without having run down a single sheep, notwithstanding they ran night and day. On smooth spots, level or ascending, the hounds gained on the sheep, but on descending ground, and over rough masses of angular rocks they fell hopelessly behind. Only half a dozen sheep were shot as they passed the hunters stationed near their paths circling round the rugged summit. The full-grown bucks weigh nearly three hundred and fifty pounds.

The mule deer are nearly as heavy. Their long, massive ears give them a very striking appearance. One large buck that I measured stood three feet and seven inches high at the shoulders, and when the ears were extended horizontally the distance across from tip to tip was two feet and one inch.

From the Van Bremer ranch the way to the Lava Beds leads down the Bremer Meadows past many a smooth grassy knoll and jutting cliff, along the shore of Lower Klamath Lake, and thence across a few miles of sage plain to the brow of the wall-like bluff of lava four hundred and fifty feet above Tule Lake. Here you are looking southeastward, and the Modoc landscape, which at once takes possession of you, lies revealed in front. It is composed of three principal parts; on your left lies the bright expanse of Tule Lake, on your right an evergreen forest, and between the two are the black Lava Beds.

When I first stood there, one bright day before sundown, the lake was fairly blooming in purple light, and was so responsive to the sky in both calmness and color it seemed itself a sky. No mountain shore hides its loveliness. It lies wide open for many a mile, veiled in no mystery but the mystery of light. The forest also was flooded with sun-purple, not a spire moving, and Mount Shasta was seen towering above it rejoicing in the ineffable beauty of the alpenglow. But neither the glorified woods on the one hand, nor the lake on the other, could at first hold the eye. That dark mysterious lava plain between them compelled attention. Here you trace yawning fissures, there clusters of somber pits; now you mark where the lava is bent and corrugated in swelling ridges and domes, again where it breaks into a rough mass of loose blocks. Tufts of grass grow far apart here and there and small bushes of hardy sage, but they have a singed appearance and can do little to hide the blackness. Deserts are charming to those who know how to see them—all kinds of bogs, barrens, and heathy moors; but the Modoc Lava Beds have for me an uncanny look. As I gazed the purple deepened over all the landscape. Then fell the gloaming, making everything still more forbidding and mysterious. Then, darkness like death.

Next morning the crisp, sunshiny air made even the Modoc landscape less hopeless, and we ventured down the bluff to the edge of the Lava Beds. Just at the foot of the bluff we came to a square enclosed by a stone wall. This is a graveyard where lie buried thirty soldiers, most of whom met their fate out in the Lava Beds, as we learn by the boards marking the graves—a gloomy place to die in, and deadly-looking even without Modocs. The poor fellows that lie here deserve far more pity than they have ever received. Picking our way over the strange ridges and hollows of the beds, we soon came to a circular flat about twenty yards in diameter, on the shore of the lake, where the comparative smoothness of the lava and a few handfuls of soil have caused the grass tufts to grow taller. This is where General Canby was slain while seeking to make peace with the treacherous Modocs.

Two or three miles farther on is the main stronghold of the Modocs, held by them so long and defiantly against all the soldiers that could be brought to the attack. Indians usually choose to hide in tall grass and bush and behind trees, where they can crouch and glide like panthers, without casting up defenses that would betray their positions; but the Modoc castle is in the rock. When the Yosemite Indians made raids on the settlers of the lower Merced, they withdrew with their spoils into Yosemite Valley; and the Modocs boasted that in case of war they had a stone house into which no white man could come as long as they cared to defend it. Yosemite was not held for a single day against the pursuing troops; but the Modocs held their fort for months, until, weary of being hemmed in, they chose to withdraw.

It consists of numerous redoubts formed by the unequal subsidence of portions of the lava-flow, and a complicated network of redans abundantly supplied with salient and reëntering angles, being united each to the other and to the redoubts by a labyrinth of open and covered corridors, some of which expand at intervals into spacious caverns, forming as a whole the most complete natural Gibraltar I ever saw. Other castles scarcely less strong are connected with this by subterranean passages known only to the Indians, while the unnatural blackness of the rock out of which Nature has constructed these defenses, and the weird, inhuman physiognomy of the whole region are well calculated to inspire terror.

Deadly was the task of storming such a place. The breech-loading rifles of the Indians thrust through chinks between the rocks were ready to pick off every soldier who showed himself for a moment, while the Indians lay utterly invisible. They were familiar with byways both over and under ground, and could at any time sink suddenly out of sight like squirrels among the loose boulders. Our bewildered soldiers heard them shooting, now before, now behind them, as they glided from place to place through fissures and subterranean passes, all the while as invisible as Gyges wearing his magic ring. To judge from the few I have seen, Modocs are not very amiable-looking people at best. When, therefore, they were crawling stealthily in the gloomy caverns, unkempt and begrimed and with the glare of war in their eyes, they must have seemed very demons of the volcanic pit.

Captain Jack's cave is one of the many somber cells of the castle. It measures twenty-five or thirty feet in diameter at the entrance, and extends but a short distance in a horizontal direction. The floor is littered with the bones of the animals slaughtered for food during the war. Some eager archæologist may hereafter discover this cabin and startle his world by announcing another of the Stone Age caves. The sun shines freely into its mouth, and graceful bunches of grass and eriogonums and sage grow about it, doing what they can toward its redemption from degrading associations and making it beautiful.

Where the lava meets the lake there are some fine curving

bays, beautifully embroidered with rushes and polygonums, a favorite resort of waterfowl. On our return, keeping close along
shore, we caused a noisy plashing and beating of wings among
cranes and geese. The ducks, less wary, kept their places, merely
swimming in and out through openings in the rushes, rippling the
glassy water, and raising spangles in their wake. The countenance
of the lava-beds became less and less forbidding. Tufts of pale
grasses, relieved on the jet rocks, looked like ornaments on a man-
tel, thick-furred mats of emerald mosses appeared in damp spots
next the shore, and I noticed one tuft of small ferns. From year to
year in the kindly weather the beds are thus gathering beauty—
beauty for ashes.

Returning to Sheep Rock and following the old emigrant
road, one is soon back again beneath the snows and shadows of
Shasta, and the Ash Creek and McCloud glaciers come into view
on the east side of the mountain. They are broad, rugged, cre-
vassed cloudlike masses of down-grinding ice, pouring forth
streams of muddy water as measures of the work they are doing in
sculpturing the rocks beneath them; very unlike the long, majestic
glaciers of Alaska that riverlike go winding down the valleys
through the forests to the sea. These, with a few others as yet name-
less, are lingering remnants of once great glaciers that occupied the
cañons now taken by the rivers, and in a few centuries will, under
present conditions, vanish altogether.

The rivers of the granite south half of the Sierra are outspread
on the peaks in a shining network of small branches, that divide
again and again into small dribbling, purling, oozing threads drawing their sources from the snow and ice of the surface. They seldom
sink out of sight, save here and there in moraines or glaciers, or,

early in the season, beneath banks and bridges of snow, soon to issue again. But in the north half, laden with rent and porous lava, small tributary streams are rare, and the rivers, flowing for a time beneath the sky of rock, at length burst forth into the light in generous volume from seams and caverns, filtered, cool, and sparkling, as if their bondage in darkness, safe from the vicissitudes of the weather in their youth, were only a blessing.

Only a very small portion of the water derived from the melting ice and snow of Shasta flows down its flanks on the surface. Probably ninety-nine per cent of it is at once absorbed and drained away beneath the porous lava-folds of the mountain to gush forth, filtered and pure, in the form of immense springs, so large, some of them, that they give birth to rivers that start on their journey beneath the sun, full-grown and perfect without any childhood. Thus the Shasta River issues from a large lakelike spring in Shasta Valley, and about two thirds of the volume of the McCloud gushes forth in a grand spring on the east side of the mountain, a few miles back from its immediate base.

To find the big spring of the McCloud, or "Mud Glacier," which you will know by its size (it being the largest on the east side), you make your way through sunny, parklike woods of yellow pine, and a shaggy growth of chaparral, and come in a few hours to the river flowing in a gorge of moderate depth, cut abruptly down into the lava plain. Should the volume of the stream where you strike it seem small, then you will know that you are above the spring; if large, nearly equal to its volume at its confluence with the Pitt River, then you are below it; and in either case have only to follow the river up or down until you come to it.

Under certain conditions you may hear the roar of the water

rushing from the rock at a distance of half a mile, or even more; or you may not hear it until within a few rods. It comes in a grand, eager gush from a horizontal seam in the face of the wall of the river-gorge in the form of a partially interrupted sheet nearly seventy-five yards in width, and at a height above the river-bed of about forty feet, as nearly as I could make out without the means of exact measurement. For about fifty yards this flat current is in one unbroken sheet, and flows in a lacework of plashing, upleaping spray over boulders that are clad in green silky algæ and watermosses to meet the smaller part of the river, which takes its rise farther up. Joining the river at right angles to its course, it at once swells its volume to three times its size above the spring.

The vivid green of the boulders beneath the water is very striking, and colors the entire stream with the exception of the portions broken into foam. The color is chiefly due to a species of algæ which seems common in springs of this sort. That any kind of plant can hold on and grow beneath the wear of so boisterous a current seems truly wonderful, even after taking into consideration the freedom of the water from cutting drift, and the constancy of its volume and temperature throughout the year. The temperature is about 45°, and the height of the river above the sea is here about three thousand feet. Asplenium, epilobium, heuchera, hazel, dogwood, and alder make a luxurious fringe and setting; and the forests of Douglas spruce along the banks are the finest I have ever seen in the Sierra.

From the spring you may go with the river—a fine traveling companion—down to the sportsman's fishing station, where, if you are getting hungry, you may replenish your stores; or, bearing off around the mountain by Huckleberry Valley, complete your circuit without interruption, emerging at length from beneath the outspread arms of the sugar pine at Strawberry Valley, with all the new wealth and health gathered in your walk; not tired in the least, and only eager to repeat the round.

Tracing rivers to their fountains makes the most charming of travels. As the lifeblood of the landscapes, the best of the wilderness comes to their banks, and not one dull passage is found in all their eventful histories. Tracing the McCloud to its highest springs, and over the divide to the fountains of Fall River, near Fort Crook, thence down that river to its confluence with the Pitt, on from there to the volcanic region about Lassen's Butte, through the Big Meadows among the sources of the Feather River, and down through forests of sugar pine to the fertile plains of Chico—this is a glorious saunter and imposes no hardship. Food may be had at moderate intervals, and the whole circuit forms one ever-deepening, broadening stream of enjoyment.

Fall River is a very remarkable stream. It is only about ten miles long, and is composed of springs, rapids, and falls—springs beautifully shaded at one end of it, a showy fall one hundred and eighty feet high at the other, and a rush of crystal rapids between. The banks are fringed with rubus, rose, plum, cherry, spiræa, azalea, honeysuckle, hawthorn, ash, alder, elder, aster, goldenrod, beautiful grasses, sedges, rushes, mosses, and ferns with fronds as large as the leaves of palms—all in the midst of a richly forested landscape. Nowhere within the limits of California are the forests of yellow pine so extensive and exclusive as on the headwaters of the Pitt. They cover the mountains and all the lower slopes that border the wide, open valleys which abound there, pressing forward in imposing ranks, seemingly the hardiest and most firmly established of all the northern coniferæ.

The volcanic region about Lassen's Butte I have already in part described. Miles of its flanks are dotted with hot springs, many of them so sulphurous and boisterous and noisy in their boiling that they seem inclined to become geysers like those of the Yellowstone.

The ascent of Lassen's Butte is an easy walk, and the views from the summit are extremely telling. Innumerable lakes and craters surround the base; forests of the charming Williamson spruce fringe lake and crater alike; the sunbeaten plains to east and west make a striking show, and the wilderness of peaks and ridges stretch indefinitely away on either hand. The lofty, icy Shasta, towering high above all, seems but an hour's walk from you, though the distance in an air-line is about sixty miles.

The "Big Meadows" lie near the foot of Lassen's Butte, a beautiful spacious basin set in the heart of the richly forested mountains, scarcely surpassed in the grandeur of its surroundings by Tahoe. During the Glacial Period it was a *mer de glace*, then a lake, and now a level meadow shining with bountiful springs and streams. In the number and size of its big spring of fountains it excels even Shasta. One of the largest that I measured forms a lakelet nearly a hundred yards in diameter, and, in the generous flood it sends forth offers one of the most telling symbols of Nature's affluence to be found in the mountains.

The great wilds of our country, once held to be boundless and inexhaustible, are being rapidly invaded and overrun in every direction, and everything destructible in them is being destroyed. How far destruction may go it is not easy to guess. Every landscape, low and high, seems doomed to be trampled and harried. Even the sky is not safe from scathe—blurred and blackened whole summers together with the smoke of fires that devour the woods.

The Shasta region is still a fresh unspoiled wilderness, accessible and available for travelers of every kind and degree. Would it not then be a fine thing to set it apart like the Yellowstone and Yosemite as a National Park for the welfare and benefit of all mankind, preserving its fountains and forests and all its glad life in primeval beauty? Very little of the region can ever be more valuable for any other use—certainly not for gold nor for grain. No private right or interest need suffer, and thousands yet unborn would come from far and near and bless the country for its wise and benevolent forethought.

6

The City of the Saints[1]

THE mountains rise grandly round about this curious city, the Zion of the new Saints, so grandly that the city itself is hardly visible. The Wahsatch Range, snow-laden and adorned with glacier-sculptured peaks, stretches continuously along the eastern horizon, forming the boundary of the Great Salt Lake Basin; while across the valley of the Jordan southwestward from here, you behold the Oquirrh Range, about as snowy and lofty as the Wahsatch. To the northwest your eye skims the blue levels of the great lake, out of the midst of which rise island mountains, and beyond, at a distance of fifty miles, is seen the picturesque wall of the lakeside mountains blending with the lake and the sky.

The glacial developments of these superb ranges are sharply sculptured peaks and crests, with ample wombs between them where the ancient snows of the glacial period were collected and transformed into ice, and ranks of profound shadowy cañons, while moraines commensurate with the lofty fountains extend into the valleys, forming far the grandest series of glacial monuments I have yet seen this side of the Sierra.

In beginning this letter I meant to describe the city, but in the company of these noble old mountains, it is not easy to bend one's attention upon anything else. Salt Lake cannot be called a very

[1]Letter dated "Salt Lake City, Utah, May 15, 1877." [Editor.]

beautiful town, neither is there anything ugly or repulsive about it. From the slopes of the Wahsatch foothills, or old lake benches, toward Fort Douglas it is seen to occupy the sloping gravelly delta of City Creek, a fine, hearty stream that comes pouring from the snows of the mountains through a majestic glacial cañon; and it is just where this stream comes forth into the light on the edge of the valley of the Jordan that the Mormons have built their new Jerusalem.

At first sight there is nothing very marked in the external appearance of the town excepting its leafiness. Most of the houses are veiled with trees, as if set down in the midst of one grand orchard; and seen at a little distance they appear like a field of glacier boulders overgrown with aspens, such as one often meets in the upper valleys of the California Sierra, for only the angular roofs are clearly visible.

Perhaps nineteen twentieths of the houses are built of bluish-gray adobe bricks, and are only one or two stories high, forming fine cottage homes which promise simple comfort within. They are set well back from the street, leaving room for a flower garden, while almost every one has a thrifty orchard at the sides and around the back. The gardens are laid out with great simplicity, indicating love for flowers by people comparatively poor, rather than deliberate efforts of the rich for showy artistic effects. They are like the pet gardens of children, about as artless and humble, and harmonize with the low dwellings to which they belong. In almost every one you find daisies, and mint, and lilac bushes, and rows of plain English tulips. Lilacs and tulips are the most characteristic flowers, and nowhere have I seen them in greater perfection. As Oakland is preëminently a city of roses, so is this Mormon Saints' Rest a city of lilacs and tulips. The flowers, at least, are saintly, and they are surely loved. Scarce a home, however obscure, is without them, and the simple, unostentatious manner in which they are planted and gathered in pots and boxes about the windows shows how truly they are prized.

The surrounding commons, the marshy levels of the Jordan, and dry, gravelly lake benches on the slopes of the Wahsatch foot-hills are now gay with wild flowers, chief among which are a species of phlox, with an abundance of rich pink corollas, growing among sagebrush in showy tufts, and a beautiful papilionaceous plant, with silky leaves and large clusters of purple flowers, banner, wings, and keel exquisitely shaded, a mertensia, hydrophyllum, white boragewort, orthocarpus, several species of violets, and a tall scarlet gilia. It is delightful to see how eagerly all these are sought after by the children, both boys and girls. Every day that I have gone botanizing I have met groups of little Latter-Days with their precious bouquets, and at such times it was hard to believe the dark, bloody passages of Mormon history.

But to return to the city. As soon as City Creek approaches its upper limit its waters are drawn off right and left, and distributed in brisk rills, one on each side of every street, the regular slopes of the delta upon which the city is built being admirably adapted to this system of street irrigation. These streams are all pure and spar-kling in the upper streets, but, as they are used to some extent as sewers, they soon manifest the consequence of contact with civi-lization, though the speed of their flow prevents their becoming offensive, and little Saints not over particular may be seen drinking from them everywhere.

The streets are remarkably wide and the buildings low, making them appear yet wider than they really are. Trees are planted along the sidewalks—elms, poplars, maples, and a few catalpas and hawthorns; yet they are mostly small and irregular, and nowhere form avenues half so leafy and imposing as one would be led to expect. Even in the business streets there is but little regularity in the buildings—now a row of plain adobe structures, half store, half dwelling, then a high mercantile block of red brick or sandstone, and again a row of adobe cottages nestled back among apple trees. There is one immense store with its sign upon the roof, in letters big enough to be read miles away, "Z.C.M.I." (Zion's Coöperative Mercantile Institution), while many a small, codfishy corner grocery bears the legend "Holiness to the Lord, Z.C.M.I." But little evidence will you find in this Zion, with its fifteen thousand souls, of great wealth, though many a Saint is seeking it as keenly as any Yankee Gentile. But on the other hand, searching throughout all the city, you will not find any trace of squalor or extreme poverty.

Most of the women I have chanced to meet, especially those from the country, have a weary, repressed look, as if for the sake of their religion they were patiently carrying burdens heavier than they were well able to bear. But, strange as it must seem to Gentiles, the many wives of one man, instead of being repelled from one another by jealousy, appear to be drawn all the closer together, as if the real marriage existed between the wives only. Groups of half a dozen or so may frequently be seen on the streets in close conversation, looking as innocent and unspeculative as a lot of heifers, while the masculine Saints pass them by as if they belonged to a distinct species. In the Tabernacle last Sunday, one of the elders of the church, in discoursing upon the good things of life, the possessions of Latter-Day Saints, enumerated fruitful fields, horses, cows, wives, and implements, the wives being placed as above, between the cows and implements, without receiving any superior emphasis.

Polygamy, as far as I have observed, exerts a more degrading influence upon husbands than upon wives. The love of the latter finds expression in flowers and children, while the former seem to be rendered incapable of pure love of anything. The spirit of Mormonism is intensely exclusive and un-American. A more withdrawn, compact, sealed-up body of people could hardly be found on the face of the earth than is gathered here, notwithstanding railroads, telegraphs, and the penetrating lights that go sifting through society everywhere in this revolutionary, question-asking century. Most of the Mormons I have met seem to be in a state of perpetual apology, which can hardly be fully accounted for by Gentile attacks. At any rate it is unspeakably offensive to any free man.

"We Saints," they are continually saying, "are not as bad as we are called. We don't murder those who differ with us, but rather treat them with all charity. You may go through our town night or day and no harm shall befall you. Go into our houses and you will be well used. We are as glad as you are that Lee was punished," etc. While taking a saunter the other evening we were overtaken by a characteristic Mormon, "an 'umble man," who made us a very deferential salute and then walked on with us about half a mile. We discussed whatsoever of Mormon doctrines came to mind with American freedom, which he defended as best he could, speaking in an excited but deprecating tone. When hard pressed he would say: "I don't understand these deep things, but the elders do. I'm only an 'umble tradesman." In taking leave he thanked us for the pleasure of our querulous conversation, removed his hat, and bowed lowly in a sort of Uriah Heep manner, and then went to his humble home. How many humble wives it contained, we did not learn.

Fine specimens of manhood are by no means wanting, but the number of people one meets here who have some physical defect or who attract one's attention by some mental peculiarity that manifests itself through the eyes, is astonishingly great in so small a city. It would evidently be unfair to attribute these defects to Mormonism, though Mormonism has undoubtedly been the magnet that elected and drew these strange people together from all parts of the world.

But however "the peculiar doctrines" and "peculiar practices" of Mormonism have affected the bodies and the minds of the old Saints, the little Latter-Day boys and girls are as happy and natural as possible, running wild, with plenty of good hearty parental indulgence, playing, fighting, gathering flowers in delightful innocence; and when we consider that most of the parents have been drawn from the thickly settled portion of the Old World, where they have long suffered the repression of hunger and hard toil, these Mormon children, "Utah's best crop," seem remarkably bright and promising.

From children one passes naturally into the blooming wilderness, to the pure religion of sunshine and snow, where all the good and the evil of this strange people lifts and vanishes from the mind like mist from the mountains.

7

A Great Storm in Utah[1]

UTAH has just been blessed with one of the grandest storms I have ever beheld this side of the Sierra. The mountains are laden with fresh snow; wild streams are swelling and booming adown the cañons, and out in the valley of the Jordan a thousand rain-pools are gleaming in the sun.

With reference to the development of fertile storms bearing snow and rain, the greater portion of the calendar springtime of Utah has been winter. In all the upper cañons of the mountains the snow is now from five to ten feet deep or more, and most of it has fallen since March. Almost every other day during the last three weeks small local storms have been falling on the Wahsatch and Oquirrh Mountains, while the Jordan Valley remained dry and sun-filled. But on the afternoon of Thursday, the 17th ultimo, wind, rain, and snow filled the whole basin, driving wildly over valley and plain from range to range, bestowing their benefactions in most cordial and harmonious storm-measures. The oldest Saints say they have never witnessed a more violent storm of this kind since the first settlement of Zion, and while the gale from the northwest, with which the storm began, was rocking their adobe walls, uprooting trees and darkening the streets with billows of dust and sand, some of them seemed inclined to guess that the terrible

---

[1]Letter dated "Salt Lake City, Utah, May 19, 1877." [Editor.]

phenomenon was one of the signs of the times of which their preachers are so constantly reminding them, the beginning of the outpouring of the treasured wrath of the Lord upon the Gentiles for the killing of Joseph Smith. To me it seemed a cordial outpouring of Nature's love; but it is easy to differ with salt Latter-Days in everything—storms, wives, politics, and religion.

About an hour before the storm reached the city I was so fortunate as to be out with a friend on the banks of the Jordan enjoying the scenery. Clouds, with peculiarly restless and self-conscious gestures, were marshaling themselves along the mountain-tops, and sending out long, overlapping wings across the valley; and even where no cloud was visible, an obscuring film absorbed the sunlight, giving rise to a cold, bluish darkness. Nevertheless, distant objects along the boundaries of the landscape were revealed with wonderful distinctness in this weird, subdued, cloud-sifted light. The mountains, in particular, with the forests on their flanks, their mazy lacelike cañons, the wombs of the ancient glaciers, and their marvelous profusion of ornate sculpture, were most impressively manifest. One would fancy that a man might be clearly seen walking on the snow at a distance of twenty or thirty miles.

While we were reveling in this rare, ungarish grandeur, turning from range to range, studying the darkening sky and listening to the still small voices of the flowers at our feet, some of the denser clouds came down, crowning and wreathing the highest peaks and dropping long gray fringes whose smooth linear structure showed that snow was beginning to fall. Of these partial storms there were soon ten or twelve, arranged in two rows, while the main Jordan Valley between them lay as yet in profound calm. At 4:30 P.M. a dark brownish cloud appeared close down on the plain towards the lake, extending from the northern extremity of the Oquirrh Range in a northeasterly direction as far as the eye could reach. Its peculiar color and structure excited our attention without enabling us to decide certainly as to its character, but we were not left long in doubt, for in a few minutes it came sweeping over the valley in wild uproar, a torrent of wind thick with sand and dust, advancing with a most majestic front, rolling and overcombing like a gigantic sea-wave. Scarcely was it in plain sight ere it was upon us, racing across the Jordan, over the city, and up the slopes of the Wahsatch, eclipsing all the landscapes in its course—the bending trees, the dust streamers, and the wild onrush of everything movable giving it an appreciable visibility that rendered it grand and inspiring.

This gale portion of the storm lasted over an hour, then down came the blessed rain and the snow all through the night and the next day, the snow and rain alternating and blending in the valley. It is long since I have seen snow coming into a city. The crystal flakes falling in the foul streets was a pitiful sight.

Notwithstanding the vaunted refining influences of towns, purity of all kinds—pure hearts, pure streams, pure snow—must here be exposed to terrible trials. City Creek, coming from its high glacial fountains, enters the streets of this Mormon Zion pure as an angel, but how does it leave it? Even roses and lilies in gardens most loved are tainted with a thousand impurities as soon as they unfold. I heard Brigham Young in the Tabernacle the other day warning his people that if they did not mend their manners angels would not come into their houses, though perchance they might be sauntering by with little else to do than chat with them. Possibly there may be Salt Lake families sufficiently pure for angel society, but I was not pleased with the reception they gave the small snow angels that God sent among them the other night. Only the children hailed them with delight. The old Latter-Days seemed to shun them. I should like to see how Mr. Young, the Lake Prophet, would meet such messengers.

But to return to the storm. Toward the evening of the 18th it began to wither. The snowy skirts of the Wahsatch Mountains appeared beneath the lifting fringes of the clouds, and the sun shone out through colored windows, producing one of the most glorious after-storm effects I ever witnessed. Looking across the Jordan, the gray sagey slopes from the base of the Oquirrh Mountains were covered with a thick, plushy cloth of gold, soft and ethereal as a cloud, not merely tinted and gilded like a rock with autumn sunshine, but deeply muffled beyond recognition. Surely nothing in heaven, nor any mansion of the Lord in all his worlds, could be more gloriously carpeted. Other portions of the plain were flushed with red and purple, and all the mountains and the clouds above them were painted in corresponding loveliness. Earth and sky, round and round the entire landscape, was one ravishing revelation of color, infinitely varied and interblended.

I have seen many a glorious sunset beneath lifting storm-clouds on the mountains, but nothing comparable with this. I felt as if new-arrived in some other far-off world. The mountains, the plains, the sky, all seemed new. Other experiences seemed but to have prepared me for this, as souls are prepared for heaven. To describe the colors on a single mountain would, if it were possible at all, require many a volume—purples, and yellows, and delicious pearly grays divinely toned and interblended, and so richly put on one seemed to be looking down through the ground as through a sky. The disbanding clouds lingered lovingly about the mountains, filling the cañons like tinted wool, rising and drooping around the topmost peaks, fondling their rugged bases, or, sailing alongside, trailed their lustrous fringes through the pines as if taking a last view of their accomplished work. Then came darkness, and the glorious day was done.

This afternoon the Utah mountains and valleys seem to belong to our own very world again. They are covered with common sunshine. Down here on the banks of the Jordan, larks and redwings are swinging on the rushes; the balmy air is instinct with immortal life; the wild flowers, the grass, and the farmers' grain are fresh as if, like the snow, they had come out of heaven, and the last of the angel clouds are fleeing from the mountains.

8

Bathing in Salt Lake[1]

WHEN the north wind blows, bathing in Salt Lake is a glorious baptism, for then it is all wildly awake with waves, blooming like a prairie in snowy crystal foam. Plunging confidently into the midst of the grand uproar you are hugged and welcomed, and swim without effort, rocking and heaving up and down, in delightful rhythm, while the winds sing in chorus and the cool, fragrant brine searches every fiber of your body; and at length you are tossed ashore with a glad Godspeed, braced and salted and clean as a saint.

The nearest point on the shore-line is distant about ten miles from Salt Lake City, and is almost inaccessible on account of the boggy character of the ground, but, by taking the Western Utah Railroad, at a distance of twenty miles you reach what is called Lake Point, where the shore is gravelly and wholesome and abounds in fine retreating bays that seem to have been made on purpose for bathing. Here the northern peaks of the Oquirrh Range plant their feet in the clear blue brine, with fine curving insteps, leaving no space for muddy levels. The crystal brightness of the water, the wild flowers, and the lovely mountain scenery make this a favorite summer resort for pleasure and health seekers. Numerous excursion trains are run from the city, and parties, some

[1]Letter dated "Lake Point, Utah, May 20, 1877." [Editor.]

of them numbering upwards of a thousand, come to bathe, and dance, and roam the flowery hillsides together.

But at the time of my first visit in May, I fortunately found myself alone. The hotel and bathhouse, which form the chief improvements of the place, were sleeping in winter silence, notwithstanding the year was in full bloom. It was one of those genial sundays when flowers and flies come thronging to the light, and birds sing their best. The mountain-ranges, stretching majestically north and south, were piled with pearly cumuli, the sky overhead was pure azure, and the wind-swept lake was all aroll and aroar with whitecaps.

I sauntered along the shore until I came to a sequestered cove, where buttercups and wild peas were blooming close down to the limit reached by the waves. Here, I thought, is just the place for a bath; but the breakers seemed terribly boisterous and forbidding as they came rolling up the beach, or dashed white against the rocks that bounded the cove on the east. The outer ranks, ever broken, ever builded, formed a magnificent rampart, sculptured and corniced like the hanging wall of a bergschrund, and appeared hopelessly insurmountable, however easily one might ride the swelling waves beyond. I feasted awhile on their beauty, watching their coming in from afar like faithful messengers, to tell their stories one by one; then I turned reluctantly away, to botanize and wait a calm. But the calm did not come that day, nor did I wait long. In an hour or two I was back again to the same little cove. The waves still sang the old storm song, and rose in high crystal walls, seemingly hard enough to be cut in sections, like ice.

Without any definite determination I found myself undressed, as if some one else had taken me in hand; and while one of the largest waves was ringing out its message and spending itself on the beach, I ran out with open arms to the next, ducked beneath its breaking top, and got myself into right lusty relationship with the brave old lake. Away I sped in free, glad motion, as if, like a fish, I had been afloat all my life, now low out of sight in the smooth, glassy valleys, now bounding aloft on firm combing crests, while the crystal foam beat against my breast with keen, crisp clashing, as if composed of pure salt. I bowed to every wave, and each lifted me right royally to its shoulders, almost setting me erect on my feet, while they all went speeding by like living creatures, blooming and rejoicing in the brightness of the day, and chanting the history of their grand mountain home.

A good deal of nonsense has been written concerning the difficulty of swimming in this heavy water. "One's head would go down, and heels come up, and the acrid brine would burn like fire." I was conscious only of a joyous exhilaration, my limbs seemingly heeding their own business, without any discomfort or confusion; so much so, that without previous knowledge my experience on this occasion would not have led me to detect anything peculiar. In calm weather, however, the sustaining power of the water might probably be more marked. This was by far the most exciting and effective wave excursion I ever made this side of the Rocky Mountains; and when at its close I was heaved ashore among the sunny grasses and flowers, I found myself a new creature indeed, and went bounding along the beach with blood all aglow, reinforced by the best salts of the mountains, and ready for any race.

Since the completion of the transcontinental and Utah rail-

Bathing in Salt Lake

ways, this magnificent lake in the heart of the continent has become as accessible as any watering-place on either coast; and I am sure that thousands of travelers, sick and well, would throng its shores every summer were its merits but half known. Lake Point is only an hour or two from the city, and has hotel accommodations and a steamboat for excursions; and then, besides the bracing waters, the climate is delightful. The mountains rise into the cool sky furrowed with cañons almost yosemitic in grandeur, and filled with a glorious profusion of flowers and trees. Lovers of science, lovers of wildness, lovers of pure rest will find here more than they may hope for.

As for the Mormons one meets, however their doctrines be regarded, they will be found as rich in human kindness as any people in all our broad land, while the dark memories that cloud their earlier history will vanish from the mind as completely as when we bathe in the fountain azure of the Sierra.

9

Mormon Lilies[1]

LILIES are rare in Utah; so also are their companions the ferns and orchids, chiefly on account of the fiery saltness of the soil and climate. You may walk the deserts of the Great Basin in the bloom time of the year, all the way across from the snowy Sierra to the snowy Wahsatch, and your eyes will be filled with many a gay malva, and poppy, and abronia, and cactus, but you may not see a single true lily, and only a very few liliaceous plants of any kind. Not even in the cool, fresh glens of the mountains will you find these favorite flowers, though some of these desert ranges almost rival the Sierra in height. Nevertheless, in the building and planting of this grand Territory the lilies were not forgotten. Far back in the dim geologic ages, when the sediments of the old seas were being gathered and outspread in smooth sheets like leaves of a book, and when these sediments became dry land, and were baked and crumbled into the sky as mountain-ranges; when the lava-floods of the Fire Period were being lavishly poured forth from innumerable rifts and craters; when the ice of the Glacial Period was laid like a mantle over every mountain and valley—throughout all these immensely protracted periods, in the throng of these majestic operations, Nature kept her flower children in mind. She considered the lilies, and, while planting the plains with sage and

[1]Letter dated "Salt Lake, July, 1877." [Editor.]

the hills with cedar, she has covered at least one mountain with golden erythroniums and fritillarias as its crowning glory, as if willing to show what she could do in the lily line even here.

Looking southward from the south end of Salt Lake, the two northmost peaks of the Oquirrh Range are seen swelling calmly into the cool sky without any marked character, excepting only their snow crowns, and a few small weedy-looking patches of spruce and fir, the simplicity of their slopes preventing their real loftiness from being appreciated. Gray, sagey plains circle around their bases, and up to a height of a thousand feet or more their sides are tinged with purple, which I afterwards found is produced by a close growth of dwarf oak just coming into leaf. Higher you may detect faint tintings of green on a gray ground, from young grasses and sedges; then come the dark pine woods filling glacial hollows, and over all the smooth crown of snow.

While standing at their feet, the other day, shortly after my memorable excursion among the salt waves of the lake, I said: "Now I shall have another baptism. I will bathe in the high sky, among cool wind-waves from the snow." From the more southerly of the two peaks a long ridge comes down, bent like a bow, one end in the hot plains, the other in the snow of the summit. After carefully scanning the jagged towers and battlements with which it is roughened, I determined to make it my way, though it presented but a feeble advertisement of its floral wealth. This apparent barrenness, however, made no great objection just then, for I was scarce hoping for flowers, old or new, or even for fine scenery. I wanted in particular to learn what the Oquirrh rocks were made of, what trees composed the curious patches of forest; and, perhaps more than all, I was animated by a mountaineer's eagerness to get my feet into the snow once more, and my head into the clear sky, after lying dormant all winter at the level of the sea.

But in every walk with Nature one receives far more than he seeks. I had not gone more than a mile from Lake Point ere I found the way profusely decked with flowers, mostly compositæ and purple leguminosæ, a hundred corollas or more to the square yard, with a corresponding abundance of winged blossoms above them, moths and butterflies, the leguminosæ of the insect kingdom. This floweriness is maintained with delightful variety all the way up through rocks and bushes to the snow—violets, lilies, gilias, œnotheras, wallflowers, ivesias, saxifrages, smilax, and miles of blooming bushes, chiefly azalea, honeysuckle, brier rose, buckthorn, and eriogonum, all meeting and blending in divine accord.

Two liliaceous plants in particular, *Erythronium grandiflorum* and *Fritillaria pudica*, are marvelously beautiful and abundant. Never before, in all my walks, have I met so glorious a throng of these fine showy liliaceous plants. The whole mountain-side was aglow with them, from a height of fifty-five hundred feet to the very edge of the snow. Although remarkably fragile, both in form and in substance, they are endowed with plenty of deep-seated vitality, enabling them to grow in all kinds of places—down in leafy glens, in the lee of wind-beaten ledges, and beneath the brushy tangles of azalea, and oak, and prickly roses—everywhere forming the crowning glory of the flowers. If the neighboring mountains are as rich in lilies, then this may well be called the Lily Range.

After climbing about a thousand feet above the plain I came to a picturesque mass of rock, cropping up through the underbrush on one of the steepest slopes of the mountain. After examining some tufts of grass and saxifrage that were growing in its fissured surface, I was going to pass it by on the upper side, where the bushes were more open, but a company composed of the two lilies I have mentioned were blooming on the lower side, and though they were as yet out of sight, I suddenly changed my mind and went down to meet them, as if attracted by the ringing of their bells. They were growing in a small, nestlike opening between the rock and the bushes, and both the erythronium and the fritillaria were in full flower. These were the first of the species I had seen, and I need not try to tell the joy they made. They are both lowly plants,— lowly as violets,—the tallest seldom exceeding six inches in height, so that the most searching winds that sweep the mountains scarce reach low enough to shake their bells.

The fritillaria has five or six linear, obtuse leaves, put on irregularly near the bottom of the stem, which is usually terminated by one large bell-shaped flower; but its more beautiful companion, the erythronium, has two radical leaves only, which are large and oval, and shine like glass. They extend horizontally in opposite directions, and form a beautiful glossy ground, over which the one large down-looking flower is swung from a simple stem, the petals being strongly recurved, like those of *Lilium superbum*. Occasionally a specimen is met which has from two to five flowers hung in a loose panicle. People oftentimes travel far to see curious plants like the carnivorous darlingtonia, the fly-catcher, the walking fern, etc. I hardly know how the little bells I have been describing would be regarded by seekers of this class, but every true flower-lover who comes to consider these Utah lilies will surely be well rewarded, however long the way.

Pushing on up the rugged slopes, I found many delightful

seclusions—moist nooks at the foot of cliffs, and lilies in every one of them, not growing close together like daisies, but well apart, with plenty of room for their bells to swing free and ring. I found hundreds of them in full bloom within two feet of the snow. In winter only the bulbs are alive, sleeping deep beneath the ground, like field mice in their nests; then the snow-flowers fall above them, lilies over lilies, until the spring winds blow, and these winter lilies wither in turn; then the hiding erythroniums and fritillarias rise again, responsive to the first touches of the sun.

I noticed the tracks of deer in many places among the lily gardens, and at the height of about seven thousand feet I came upon the fresh trail of a flock of wild sheep, showing that these fine mountaineers still flourish here above the range of Mormon rifles. In the planting of her wild gardens, Nature takes the feet and teeth of her flocks into account, and makes use of them to trim and cultivate, and keep them in order, as the bark and buds of the tree are tended by woodpeckers and linnets.

The evergreen woods consist, as far as I observed, of two species, a spruce and a fir, standing close together, erect and arrowy in a thrifty, compact growth; but they are quite small, say from six to twelve or fourteen inches in diameter, and about forty feet in height. Among their giant relatives of the Sierra the very largest would seem mere saplings. A considerable portion of the south side of the mountain is planted with a species of aspen, called "quaking asp" by the wood-choppers. It seems to be quite abundant on many of the eastern mountains of the basin, and forms a marked feature of their upper forests.

Wading up the curves of the summit was rather toilsome, for the snow, which was softened by the blazing sun, was from ten to twenty feet deep, but the view was one of the most impressively sublime I ever beheld. Snowy, ice-sculptured ranges bounded the horizon all around, while the great lake, eighty miles long and fifty miles wide, lay fully revealed beneath a lily sky. The shore-lines, marked by a ribbon of white sand, were seen sweeping around many a bay and promontory in elegant curves, and picturesque islands rising to mountain heights, and some of them capped with pearly cumuli. And the wide prairie of water glowing in the gold and purple of evening presented all the colors that tint the lips of shells and the petals of lilies—the most beautiful lake this side of the Rocky Mountains. Utah Lake, lying thirty-five miles to the south, was in full sight also, and the river Jordan, which links the two together, may be traced in silvery gleams throughout its whole course.

Descending the mountain, I followed the windings of the main central glen on the north, gathering specimens of the cones and sprays of the evergreens, and most of the other new plants I had met; but the lilies formed the crowning glory of my bouquet— the grandest I had carried in many a day. I reached the hotel on the lake about dusk with all my fresh riches, and my first mountain ramble in Utah was accomplished. On my way back to the city, the next day, I met a grave old Mormon with whom I had previously held some Latter-Day discussions. I shook my big handful of lilies in his face and shouted, "Here are the true saints, ancient and Latter-Day, enduring forever!" After he had recovered from his astonishment he said, "They are nice."

The other liliaceous plants I have met in Utah are two species of zigadenas, *Fritillaria atropurpurea*, *Calochortus Nuttallii*, and three or four handsome alliums. One of these lilies, the calochortus, several species of which are well known in California as the "Mariposa tulips," has received great consideration at the hands of the Mormons, for to it hundreds of them owe their lives. During the famine years between 1853 and 1858, great destitution prevailed, especially in the southern settlements, on account of drouth and grasshoppers, and throughout one hunger winter in particular, thousands of the people subsisted chiefly on the bulbs of these tulips, called "sego" by the Indians, who taught them its use.

Liliaceous women and girls are rare among the Mormons. They have seen too much hard, repressive toil to admit of the development of lily beauty either in form or color. In general they are thickset, with large feet and hands, and with sun-browned faces, often curiously freckled like the petals of *Fritillaria atropurpurea*. They are fruit rather than flower—good brown bread. But down in the San Pitch Valley at Gunnison, I discovered a genuine lily, happily named Lily Young. She is a granddaughter of Brigham Young, slender and graceful, with lily-white cheeks tinted with clear rose. She was brought up in the old Salt Lake Zion House, but by some strange chance has been transplanted to this wilderness, where she blooms alone, the "Lily of San Pitch." Pitch is an old Indian, who, I suppose, pitched into the settlers and thus acquired fame enough to give name to the valley. Here I feel uneasy about the name of this lily, for the compositors have a perverse trick of making me say all kinds of absurd things wholly unwarranted by plain copy, and I fear that the "Lily of San Pitch" will appear in print as the widow of Sam Patch. But, however this may be, among my memories of this strange land, that Oquirrh mountain, with its golden lilies, will ever rise in clear relief, and associated with them will always be the Mormon lily of San Pitch.

10

The San Gabriel Valley[1]

THE sun valley of San Gabriel is one of the brightest spots to be found in all our bright land, and most of its brightness is wildness—wild south sunshine in a basin rimmed about with mountains and hills. Cultivation is not wholly wanting, for here are the choicest of all the Los Angeles orange groves, but its glorious abundance of ripe sun and soil is only beginning to be coined into fruit. The drowsy bits of cultivation accomplished by the old missionaries and the more recent efforts of restless Americans are scarce as yet visible, and when comprehended in general views form nothing more than mere freckles on the smooth brown bosom of the Valley.

I entered the sunny south half a month ago, coming down along the cool sea, and landing at Santa Monica. An hour's ride over stretches of bare, brown plain, and through cornfields and orange groves, brought me to the handsome, conceited little town of Los Angeles, where one finds Spanish adobes and Yankee shingles meeting and overlapping in very curious antagonism. I believe there are some fifteen thousand people here, and some of their buildings are rather fine, but the gardens and the sky interested me more. A palm is seen here and there poising its royal crown in the rich light, and the banana, with its magnificent ribbon leaves, pro-

---

[1] Letter dated "September 1, 1877." [Editor.]

ducing a marked tropical effect—not semi-tropical, as they are so fond of saying here, while speaking of their fruits. Nothing I have noticed strikes me as semi, save the brusque little bits of civilization with which the wilderness is checkered. These are semi-barbarous or less; everything else in the region has a most exuberant pronounced wholeness. The city held me but a short time, for the San Gabriel Mountains were in sight, advertising themselves grandly along the northern sky, and I was eager to make my way into their midst.

At Pasadena I had the rare good fortune to meet my old friend Doctor Congar, with whom I had studied chemistry and mathematics fifteen years ago. He exalted San Gabriel above all other inhabitable valleys, old and new, on the face of the globe. "I have rambled," said he, "ever since we left college, tasting innumerable climates, and trying the advantages offered by nearly every new State and Territory. Here I have made my home, and here I shall stay while I live. The geographical position is exactly right, soil and climate perfect, and everything that heart can wish comes to our efforts—flowers, fruits, milk and honey, and plenty of money. And there," he continued, pointing just beyond his own precious possessions, "is a block of land that is for sale; buy it and be my neighbor; plant five acres with orange trees, and by the time your last mountain is climbed their fruit will be your fortune." He then led me down the valley, through the few famous old groves in full bearing, and on the estate of Mr. Wilson showed me a ten-acre grove eighteen years old, the last year's crop from which was sold for twenty thousand dollars. "There," said he, with triumphant enthusiasm, "what do you think of that? Two thousand dollars per acre per annum for land worth only one hundred dollars."

The San Gabriel Valley

The number of orange trees planted to the acre is usually from forty-nine to sixty-nine; they then stand from twenty-five to thirty feet apart each way, and, thus planted, thrive and continue fruitful to a comparatively great age. J. DeBarth Shorb, an enthusiastic believer in Los Angeles and oranges, says, "We have trees on our property fully forty years old, and eighteen inches in diameter, that are still vigorous and yielding immense crops of fruit, although they are only twenty feet apart." Seedlings are said to begin to bear remunerative crops in their tenth year, but by superior cultivation this long unproductive period may be somewhat lessened, while trees from three to five years old may be purchased from the nurserymen, so that the newcomer who sets out an orchard may begin to gather fruit by the fifth or sixth year. When first set out, and for some years afterward, the trees are irrigated by making rings of earth around them, which are connected with small ditches, through which the water is distributed to each tree. Or, where the ground is nearly level, the whole surface is flooded from time to time as required. From 309 trees, twelve years old from the seed, DeBarth Shorb says that in the season of 1874 he obtained an average of $20.50 per tree, or $1435 per acre, over and above cost of transportation to San Francisco, commission on sales, etc. He considers $1000 per acre a fair average at present prices, after the trees have reached the age of twelve years. The average price throughout the county for the last five years has been about $20 or $25 per thousand; and, inasmuch as the area adapted to orange culture is limited, it is hoped that this price may not greatly fall for many years.

The lemon and lime are also cultivated here to some extent, and considerable attention is now being given to the Florida banana, and the olive, almond, and English walnut. But the orange interest heavily overshadows every other, while vines have of late years been so unremunerative they are seldom mentioned.

This is preëminently a fruit land, but the fame of its productions has in some way far outrun the results that have as yet been attained. Experiments have been tried, and good beginnings made, but the number of really valuable, well-established groves is scarce as one to fifty, compared with the newly planted. Many causes, however, have combined of late to give the business a wonderful impetus, and new orchards are being made every day, while the few old groves, aglow with golden fruit, are the burning and shining lights that direct and energize the sanguine newcomers.

After witnessing the bad effect of homelessness, developed to so destructive an extent in California, it would reassure every lover of his race to see the hearty home-building going on here and the blessed contentment that naturally follows it. Travel-worn pioneers, who have been tossed about like boulders in flood-time, are thronging hither as to a kind of terrestrial heaven, resolved to rest. They build, and plant, and settle, and so come under natural influences. When a man plants a tree he plants himself. Every root is an anchor, over which he rests with grateful interest, and becomes sufficiently calm to feel the joy of living. He necessarily makes the acquaintance of the sun and the sky. Favorite trees fill his mind, and, while tending them like children, and accepting the benefits they bring, he becomes himself a benefactor. He sees down through the brown common ground teeming with colored fruits, as if it were transparent, and learns to bring them to the surface. What he wills he can raise by true enchantment. With slips and rootlets, his magic wands, they appear at his bidding.

The San Gabriel Valley

These, and the seeds he plants, are his prayers, and, by them brought into right relations with God, he works grander miracles every day than ever were written.

The Pasadena Colony, located on the southwest corner of the well-known San Pasqual Rancho, is scarce three years old, but it is growing rapidly, like a pet tree, and already forms one of the best contributions to culture yet accomplished in the county. It now numbers about sixty families, mostly drawn from the better class of vagabond pioneers, who, during their rolling-stone days have managed to gather sufficient gold moss to purchase from ten to forty acres of land. They are perfectly hilarious in their newly found life, work like ants in a sunny noonday, and, looking far into the future, hopefully count their orange chicks ten years or more before they are hatched; supporting themselves in the mean time on the produce of a few acres of alfalfa, together with garden vegetables and the quick-growing fruits, such as figs, grapes, apples, etc., the whole reinforced by the remaining dollars of their land purchase money. There is nothing more remarkable in the character of the colony than the literary and scientific taste displayed. The conversation of most I have met here is seasoned with a smack of mental ozone, Attic salt, which struck me as being rare among the tillers of California soil. People of taste and money in search of a home would do well to prospect the resources of this aristocratic little colony.

If we look now at these southern valleys in general, it will appear at once that with all their advantages they lie beyond the reach of poor settlers, not only on account of the high price of irrigable land—one hundred dollars per acre and upwards—but because of the scarcity of labor. A settler with three or four thousand dollars would be penniless after paying for twenty acres of orange land and building ever so plain a house, while many years would go by ere his trees yielded an income adequate to the maintenance of his family.

Nor is there anything sufficiently reviving in the fine climate to form a reliable inducement for very sick people. Most of this class, from all I can learn, come here only to die, and surely it is better to die comfortably at home, avoiding the thousand discomforts of travel, at a time when they are so hard to bear. It is indeed pitiful to see so many invalids, already on the verge of the grave, making a painful way to quack climates, hoping to change age to youth, and the darkening twilight of their day to morning. No such health-fountain has been found, and this climate, fine as it is, seems, like most others, to be adapted for well people only. From all I could find out regarding its influence upon patients suffering from pulmonary difficulties, it is seldom beneficial to any great extent in advanced cases. The cold sea-winds are less fatal to this class of sufferers than the corresponding winds further north, but, notwithstanding they are tempered on their passage inland over warm, dry ground, they are still more or less injurious.

The summer climate of the fir and pine woods of the Sierra Nevada would, I think, be found infinitely more reviving; but because these woods have not been advertised like patent medicines, few seem to think of the spicy, vivifying influences that pervade their fountain freshness and beauty.

11

The San Gabriel Mountains[1]

AFTER saying so much for human culture in my last, perhaps I may now be allowed a word for wildness—the wildness of this southland, pure and untamable as the sea.

In the mountains of San Gabriel, overlooking the lowland vines and fruit groves, Mother Nature is most ruggedly, thornily savage. Not even in the Sierra have I ever made the acquaintance of mountains more rigidly inaccessible. The slopes are exceptionally steep and insecure to the foot of the explorer, however great his strength or skill may be, but thorny chaparral constitutes their chief defense. With the exception of little park and garden spots not visible in comprehensive views, the entire surface is covered with it, from the highest peaks to the plain. It swoops into every hollow and swells over every ridge, gracefully complying with the varied topography, in shaggy, ungovernable exuberance, fairly dwarfing the utmost efforts of human culture out of sight and mind.

But in the very heart of this thorny wilderness, down in the dells, you may find gardens filled with the fairest flowers, that any child would love, and unapproachable linns lined with lilies and ferns, where the ousel builds its mossy hut and sings in chorus with the white falling water. Bears, also, and panthers, wolves, wildcats,

[1]Letter written during the first week of September, 1877. [Editor.]

wood rats, squirrels, foxes, snakes, and innumerable birds, all find grateful homes here, adding wildness to wildness in glorious profusion and variety.

Where the coast ranges and the Sierra Nevada come together we find a very complicated system of short ranges, the geology and topography of which is yet hidden, and many years of laborious study must be given for anything like a complete interpretation of them. The San Gabriel is one or more of these ranges, forty or fifty miles long, and half as broad, extending from the Cajon Pass on the east, to the Santa Monica and Santa Susanna ranges on the west. San Antonio, the dominating peak, rises towards the eastern extremity of the range to a height of about six thousand feet, forming a sure landmark throughout the valley and all the way down to the coast, without, however, possessing much striking individuality. The whole range, seen from the plain, with the hot sun beating upon its southern slopes, wears a terribly forbidding aspect. There is nothing of the grandeur of snow, or glaciers, or deep forests, to excite curiosity or adventure; no trace of gardens or waterfalls. From base to summit all seems gray, barren, silent—dead, bleached bones of mountains, overgrown with scrubby bushes, like gray moss. But all mountains are full of hidden beauty, and the next day after my arrival at Pasadena I supplied myself with bread and eagerly set out to give myself to their keeping.

On the first day of my excursion I went only as far as the mouth of Eaton Cañon, because the heat was oppressive, and a pair of new shoes were chafing my feet to such an extent that walking began to be painful. While looking for a camping-ground among the boulder beds of the cañon, I came upon a strange, dark man of doubtful parentage. He kindly invited me to camp with

The San Gabriel Mountains

him, and led me to his little hut. All my conjectures as to his nationality failed, and no wonder, since his father was Irish and mother Spanish, a mixture not often met even in California. He happened to be out of candles, so we sat in the dark while he gave me a sketch of his life, which was exceedingly picturesque. Then he showed me his plans for the future. He was going to settle among these cañon boulders, and make money, and marry a Spanish woman. People mine for irrigating water along the foothills as for gold. He is now driving a prospecting tunnel into a spur of the mountains back of his cabin. "My prospect is good," he said, "and if I strike a strong flow, I shall soon be worth five or ten thousand dollars. That flat out there," he continued, referring to a small, irregular patch of gravelly detritus that had been sorted out and deposited by Eaton Creek during some flood season, "is large enough for a nice orange grove, and, after watering my own trees, I can sell water down the valley; and then the hillside back of the cabin will do for vines, and I can keep bees, for the white sage and black sage up the mountains is full of honey. You see, I've got a good thing." All this prospective affluence in the sunken, boulder-choked flood-bed of Eaton Creek! Most home-seekers would as soon think of settling on the summit of San Antonio.

Half an hour's easy rambling up the cañon brought me to the foot of "The Fall," famous throughout the valley settlements as the finest yet discovered in the range. It is a charming little thing, with a voice sweet as a songbird's, leaping some thirty-five or forty feet into a round, mirror pool. The cliff back of it and on both sides is completely covered with thick, furry mosses, and the white fall shines against the green like a silver instrument in a velvet case. Here come the Gabriel lads and lassies from the commonplace orange groves, to make love and gather ferns and dabble away their hot holidays in the cool pool. They are fortunate in finding so fresh a retreat so near their homes. It is the Yosemite of San Gabriel. The walls, though not of the true Yosemite type either in form or sculpture, rise to a height of nearly two thousand feet. Ferns are abundant on all the rocks within reach of the spray, and picturesque maples and sycamores spread a grateful shade over a rich profusion of wild flowers that grow among the boulders, from the edge of the pool a mile or more down the dell-like bottom of the valley, the whole forming a charming little poem of wildness—the vestibule of these shaggy mountain temples.

The foot of the fall is about a thousand feet above the level of the sea, and here climbing begins. I made my way out of the valley on the west side, followed the ridge that forms the western rim of the Eaton Basin to the summit of one of the principal peaks, thence crossed the middle of the basin, forcing a way over its many subordinate ridges, and out over the eastern rim, and from first to last during three days spent in this excursion, I had to contend with the richest, most self-possessed and uncompromising chaparral I have ever enjoyed since first my mountaineering began.

For a hundred feet or so the ascent was practicable only by means of bosses of the club moss that clings to the rock. Above this the ridge is weathered away to a slender knife-edge for a distance of two or three hundred yards, and thence to the summit it is a bristly mane of chaparral. Here and there small openings occur, commanding grand views of the valley and beyond to the ocean. These are favorite outlooks and resting-places for the wild animals, in particular for bears, wolves, and wildcats. In the densest places I came upon woodrat villages whose huts were from four to eight feet high, built in the same style of architecture as those of the muskrats.

The day was nearly done. I reached the summit and I had time to make only a hasty survey of the topography of the wild basin now outspread maplike beneath, and to drink in the rare loveliness of the sunlight before hastening down in search of water. Pushing through another mile of chaparral, I emerged into one of the most beautiful parklike groves of live oak I ever saw. The ground beneath was planted only with aspidiums and brier roses. At the foot of the grove I came to the dry channel of one of the tributary streams, but, following it down a short distance, I descried a few specimens of the scarlet mimulus; and I was assured that water was near. I found about a bucketful in a granite bowl, but it was full of leaves and beetles, making a sort of brown coffee that could be rendered available only by filtering it through sand and charcoal. This I resolved to do in case the night came on before I found better. Following the channel a mile farther down to its confluence with another, larger tributary, I found a lot of boulder pools, clear as crystal, and brimming full, linked together by little glistening currents just strong enough to sing. Flowers in full bloom adorned the banks, lilies ten feet high, and luxuriant ferns arching over one another in lavish abundance, while a noble old live oak spread its rugged boughs over all, forming one of the most perfect and most secluded of Nature's gardens. Here I camped, making my bed on smooth cobblestones.

Next morning, pushing up the channel of a tributary that takes its rise on Mount San Antonio, I passed many lovely gardens watered by oozing currentlets, every one of which had lilies in them in the full pomp of bloom, and a rich growth of ferns, chiefly woodwardias and aspidiums and maidenhairs; but toward the base of the mountain the channel was dry, and the chaparral closed over from bank to bank, so that I was compelled to creep more than a mile on hands and knees.

In one spot I found an opening in the thorny sky where I could stand erect, and on the further side of the opening discovered a small pool. "Now, *here,*" I said, "I must be careful in creeping, for the birds of the neighborhood come here to drink, and the rattlesnakes come here to catch them." I then began to cast my eye along the channel, perhaps instinctively feeling a snaky atmosphere, and finally discovered one rattler between my feet. But there was a bashful look in his eye, and a withdrawing, deprecating kink in his neck that showed plainly as words could tell that he would not strike, and only wished to be let alone. I therefore passed on, lifting my foot a little higher than usual, and left him to enjoy his life in this his own home.

My next camp was near the heart of the basin, at the head of a grand system of cascades from ten to two hundred feet high, one following the other in close succession and making a total descent of nearly seventeen hundred feet. The rocks above me leaned over in a threatening way and were full of seams, making the camp a very unsafe one during an earthquake.

Next day the chaparral, in ascending the eastern rim of the basin, was, if possible, denser and more stubbornly bayoneted than ever. I followed bear trails, where in some places I found tufts of their hair that had been pulled out in squeezing a way through; but there was much of a very interesting character that far overpaid all my pains. Most of the plants are identical with those of the Sierra, but there are quite a number of Mexican species. One coniferous tree was all I found. This is a spruce of a species new to me, *Douglasii macrocarpa*.[1]

My last camp was down at the narrow, notched bottom of a dry channel, the only open way for the life in the neighborhood. I therefore lay between two fires, built to fence out snakes and wolves.

From the summit of the eastern rim I had a glorious view of the valley out to the ocean, which would require a whole book for its description. My bread gave out a day before reaching the settlements, but I felt all the fresher and clearer for the fast.

[1]The spruce, or hemlock, then known as *Abies Douglasii* var. *macrocarpa* is now called *Pseudotsuga macrocarpa*.]

12

Nevada Farms[1]

To the farmer who comes to this thirsty land from beneath rainy skies, Nevada seems one vast desert, all sage and sand, hopelessly irredeemable now and forever. And this, under present conditions, is severely true. For notwithstanding it has gardens, grainfields, and hayfields generously productive, these compared with the arid stretches of valley and plain, as beheld in general views from the mountain-tops, are mere specks lying inconspicuously here and there, in out-of-the-way places, often thirty or forty miles apart.

In leafy regions, blessed with copious rains, we learn to measure the productive capacity of the soil by its natural vegetation. But this rule is almost wholly inapplicable here, for, notwithstanding its savage nakedness, scarce at all veiled by a sparse growth of sage and linosyris,[2] the desert soil of the Great Basin is as rich in the elements that in rainy regions rise and ripen into food as that of any other State in the Union. The rocks of its numerous mountain-ranges have been thoroughly crushed and ground by glaciers, thrashed and vitalized by the sun, and sifted and outspread in lake-basins by powerful torrents that attended the breaking-up of the glacial period, as if in every way Nature had been making haste to prepare the land for the husbandman. Soil, climate, to-

[1]Written at Ward, Nevada, in September, 1878. [Editor.]
[2]See footnote on p. 26.

Nevada Farms

pographical conditions, all that the most exacting could demand, are present, but one thing, water, is wanting. The present rainfall would be wholly inadequate for agriculture, even if it were advantageously distributed over the lowlands, while in fact the greater portion is poured out on the heights in sudden and violent thundershowers called "cloud-bursts," the waters of which are fruitlessly swallowed up in sandy gulches and deltas a few minutes after their first boisterous appearance. The principal mountain-chains, trending nearly north and south, parallel with the Sierra and the Wahsatch, receive a good deal of snow during winter, but no great masses are stored up as fountains for large perennial streams capable of irrigating considerable areas. Most of it is melted before the end of May and absorbed by moraines and gravelly taluses, which send forth small rills that slip quietly down the upper cañons through narrow strips of flowery verdure, most of them sinking and vanishing before they reach the base of their fountain ranges. Perhaps not one in ten of the whole number flow out into the open plains, not a single drop reaches the sea, and only a few are large enough to irrigate more than one farm of moderate size.

It is upon these small outflowing rills that most of the Nevada ranches are located, lying countersunk beneath the general level, just where the mountains meet the plains, at an average elevation of five thousand feet above sea-level. All the cereals and garden vegetables thrive here, and yield bountiful crops. Fruit, however, has been, as yet, grown successfully in only a few specially favored spots.

Another distinct class of ranches are found sparsely distributed along the lowest portions of the plains, where the ground is kept moist by springs, or by narrow threads of moving water called rivers, fed by some one or more of the most vigorous of the mountain rills that have succeeded in making their escape from the mountains. These are mostly devoted to the growth of wild hay, though in some the natural meadow grasses and sedges have been supplemented by timothy and alfalfa; and where the soil is not too strongly impregnated with salts, some grain is raised. Reese River Valley, Big Smoky Valley, and White River Valley offer fair illustrations of this class. As compared with the foothill ranches, they are larger and less inconspicuous, as they lie in the wide, unshadowed levels of the plains—wavy-edged flecks of green in a wilderness of gray.

Still another class equally well defined, both as to distribution and as to products, is restricted to that portion of western Nevada and the eastern border of California which lies within the redeeming influences of California waters. Three of the Sierra rivers descend from their icy fountains into the desert like angels of mercy to bless Nevada. These are the Walker, Carson, and Truckee; and in the valleys through which they flow are found by far the most extensive hay and grain fields within the bounds of the State. Irrigating streams are led off right and left through innumerable channels, and the sleeping ground, starting at once into action, pours forth its wealth without stint.

But notwithstanding the many porous fields thus fertilized, considerable portions of the waters of all these rivers continue to reach their old deathbeds in the desert, indicating that in these salt valleys there still is room for coming farmers. In middle and eastern Nevada, however, every rill that I have seen in a ride of three thousand miles, at all available for irrigation, has been claimed and put to use.

Nevada Farms

It appears, therefore, that under present conditions the limit of agricultural development in the dry basin between the Sierra and the Wahsatch has been already approached, a result caused not alone by natural restrictions as to the area capable of development, but by the extraordinary stimulus furnished by the mines to agricultural effort. The gathering of gold and silver, hay and barley, have gone on together. Most of the mid-valley bogs and meadows, and foothill rills capable of irrigating from ten to fifty acres, were claimed more than twenty years ago.

A majority of these pioneer settlers are plodding Dutchmen, living content in the back lanes and valleys of Nature; but the high price of all kinds of farm products tempted many of even the keen Yankee prospectors, made wise in California, to bind themselves down to this sure kind of mining. The wildest of wild hay, made chiefly of carices and rushes, was sold at from two to three hundred dollars per ton on ranches. The same kind of hay is still worth from fifteen to forty dollars per ton, according to the distance from mines and comparative security from competition. Barley and oats are from forty to one hundred dollars a ton, while all sorts of garden products find ready sale at high prices.

With rich mine markets and salubrious climate, the Nevada farmer can make more money by loose, ragged methods than the same class of farmers in any other State I have yet seen, while the almost savage isolation in which they live seems grateful to them. Even in those cases where the advent of neighbors brings no disputes concerning water-rights and ranges, they seem to prefer solitude, most of them having been elected from adventurers from California—the pioneers of pioneers. The passing stranger, however, is always welcomed and supplied with the best the home affords, and around the fireside, while he smokes his pipe, very little encouragement is required to bring forth the story of the farmer's life—hunting, mining, fighting, in the early Indian times, etc. Only the few who are married hope to return to California to educate their children, and the ease with which money is made renders the fulfillment of these hopes comparatively sure.

After dwelling thus long on the farms of this dry wonderland, my readers may be led to fancy them of more importance as compared with the unbroken fields of Nature than they really are. Making your way along any of the wide gray valleys that stretch from north to south, seldom will your eye be interrupted by a single mark of cultivation. The smooth lakelike ground sweeps on indefinitely, growing more and more dim in the glowing sunshine, while a mountain-range from eight to ten thousand feet high bounds the view on either hand. No singing water, no green sod, no moist nook to rest in—mountain and valley alike naked and shadowless in the sun-glare; and though, perhaps, traveling a well-worn road to a gold or silver mine, and supplied with repeated instructions, you can scarce hope to find any human habitation from day to day, so vast and impressive is the hot, dusty, alkaline wildness.

But after riding some thirty or forty miles, and while the sun may be sinking behind the mountains, you come suddenly upon signs of cultivation. Clumps of willows indicate water, and water indicates a farm. Approaching more nearly, you discover what may be a patch of barley spread out unevenly along the bottom of a flood-bed, broken perhaps, and rendered less distinct by boulder-piles and the fringing willows of a stream. Speedily you can confidently say that the grain-patch is surely such; its ragged bounds become clear; a sand-roofed cabin comes to view littered with sun-cracked implements and with an outer girdle of potato, cabbage, and alfalfa patches.

The immense expanse of mountain-girt valleys, on the edges of which these hidden ranches lie, make even the largest fields seem comic in size. The smallest, however, are by no means insignificant in a pecuniary view. On the east side of the Toyabe Range I discovered a jolly Irishman who informed me that his income from fifty acres, reinforced by a sheep-range on the adjacent hills, was from seven to nine thousand dollars per annum. His irrigating brook is about four feet wide and eight inches deep, flowing about two miles per hour.

On Duckwater Creek, Nye County, Mr. Irwin has reclaimed a tule swamp several hundred acres in extent, which is now chiefly devoted to alfalfa. On twenty-five acres he claims to have raised this year thirty-seven tons of barley. Indeed, I have not yet noticed a meager crop of any kind in the State. Fruit alone is conspicuously absent.

On the California side of the Sierra grain will not ripen at a much greater elevation than four thousand feet above sea-level. The valleys of Nevada lie at a height of from four to six thousand feet, and both wheat and barley ripen, wherever water may be had, up to seven thousand feet. The harvest, of course, is later as the elevation increases. In the valleys of the Carson and Walker Rivers, four thousand feet above the sea, the grain harvest is about a month later than in California. In Reese River Valley, six thousand feet, it begins near the end of August. Winter grain ripens somewhat earlier, while occasionally one meets a patch of barley in some cool, high-lying cañon that will not mature before the middle of September.

Unlike California, Nevada will probably be always richer in gold and silver than in grain. Utah farmers hope to change the climate of the east side of the basin by prayer, and point to the recent rise in the waters of the Great Salt Lake as a beginning of moister times. But Nevada's only hope, in the way of any considerable increase in agriculture, is from artesian wells. The cleft and porous character of the mountain rocks, tilted at every angle, and the presence of springs bursting forth in the valleys far from the mountain sources, indicate accumulations of water from the melting snows that have escaped evaporation, which, no doubt, may in many places now barren be brought to the surface in flowing wells. The experiment has been tried on a small scale with encouraging success. But what is now wanted seems to be the boring of a few specimen wells of a large size out in the main valleys. The encouragement that successful experiments of this kind would give to emigration seeking farms forms an object well worthy the attention of the Government. But all that California farmers in the grand central valley require is the preservation of the forests and the wise distribution of the glorious abundance of water from the snow stored on the west flank of the Sierra.

Whether any considerable area of these sage plains will ever thus be made to blossom in grass and wheat, experience will show. But in the mean time Nevada is beautiful in her wildness, and if tillers of the soil can thus be brought to see that possibly Nature may have other uses even for *rich* soil besides the feeding of human beings, then will these foodless "deserts" have taught a fine lesson.

13

Nevada Forests[1]

WHEN the traveler from California has crossed the Sierra and gone a little way down the eastern flank, the woods come to an end about as suddenly and completely as if, going westward, he had reached the ocean. From the very noblest forests in the world he emerges into free sunshine and dead alkaline lake-levels. Mountains are seen beyond, rising in bewildering abundance, range beyond range. But however closely we have been accustomed to associate forests and mountains, these always present a singularly barren aspect, appearing gray and forbidding and shadeless, like heaps of ashes dumped from the blazing sky.

But wheresoever we may venture to go in all this good world, nature is ever found richer and more beautiful than she seems, and nowhere may you meet with more varied and delightful surprises than in the byways and recesses of this sublime wilderness—lovely asters and abronias on the dusty plains, rose-gardens around the mountain wells, and resiny woods, where all seemed so desolate, adorning the hot foothills as well as the cool summits, fed by cordial and benevolent storms of rain and hail and snow; all of these scant and rare as compared with the immeasurable exuberance of California, but still amply sufficient throughout the barest deserts for a clear manifestation of God's love.

[1]Written at Eureka, Nevada, in October, 1878. [Editor.]

Steep Trails

Though Nevada is situated in what is called the "Great Basin," no less than sixty-five groups and chains of mountains rise within the bounds of the State to a height of about from eight thousand to thirteen thousand feet above the level of the sea, and as far as I have observed, every one of these is planted, to some extent, with coniferous trees, though it is only upon the highest that we find anything that may fairly be called a forest. The lower ranges and the foothills and slopes of the higher are roughened with small scrubby junipers and nut pines, while the dominating peaks, together with the ridges that swing in grand curves between them, are covered with a closer and more erect growth of pine, spruce, and fir, resembling the forests of the Eastern States both as to size and general botanical characteristics. Here is found what is called the heavy timber, but the tallest and most fully developed sections of the forests, growing down in sheltered hollows on moist moraines, would be regarded in California only as groves of saplings, and so, relatively, they are, for by careful calculation we find that more than a thousand of these trees would be required to furnish as much timber as may be obtained from a single specimen of our Sierra giants.

The height of the timber-line in eastern Nevada, near the middle of the Great Basin, is about eleven thousand feet above sea-level; consequently the forests, in a dwarfed, storm-beaten condition, pass over the summits of nearly every range in the State, broken here and there only by mechanical conditions of the surface rocks. Only three mountains in the State have as yet come under my observation whose summits rise distinctly above the tree-line. These are Wheeler's Peak, twelve thousand three hundred feet high, Mount Moriah, about twelve thousand feet, and Granite

Nevada Forests

Mountain, about the same height, all of which are situated near the boundary-line between Nevada and Utah Territory.

In a rambling mountaineering journey of eighteen hundred miles across the state, I have met nine species of coniferous trees,—four pines, two spruces, two junipers, and one fir,—about one third the number found in California. By far the most abundant and interesting of these is the *Pinus Fremontiana*,[1] or nut pine. In the number of individual trees and extent of range this curious little conifer surpasses all the others combined. Nearly every mountain in the State is planted with it from near the base to a height of from eight thousand to nine thousand feet above the sea. Some are covered from base to summit by this one species, with only a sparse growth of juniper on the lower slopes to break the continuity of these curious woods, which, though dark-looking at a little distance, are yet almost shadeless, and without any hint of the dark glens and hollows so characteristic of other pine woods. Tens of thousands of acres occur in one continuous belt. Indeed, viewed comprehensively, the entire State seems to be pretty evenly divided into mountain-ranges covered with nut pines and plains covered with sage—now a swath of pines stretching from north to south, now a swath of sage; the one black, the other gray; one severely level, the other sweeping on complacently over ridge and valley and lofty crowning dome.

The real character of a forest of this sort would never be guessed by the inexperienced observer. Traveling across the sage levels in the dazzling sunlight, you gaze with shaded eyes at the mountains rising along their edges, perhaps twenty miles away, but

[1] Now called *Pinus monophylla*, or one-leaf piñon. [Editor.]

no invitation that is at all likely to be understood is discernible. Every mountain, however high it swells into the sky, seems utterly barren. Approaching nearer, a low brushy growth is seen, strangely black in aspect, as though it had been burned. This is a nut pine forest, the bountiful orchard of the red man. When you ascend into its midst you find the ground beneath the trees, and in the openings also, nearly naked, and mostly rough on the surface—a succession of crumbling ledges of lava, limestones, slate, and quartzite, coarsely strewn with soil weathered from them. Here and there occurs a bunch of sage or linosyris, or a purple aster, or a tuft of dry bunch-grass.

The harshest mountain-sides, hot and waterless, seem best adapted to the nut pine's development. No slope is too steep, none too dry; every situation seems to be gratefully chosen, if only it be sufficiently rocky and firm to afford secure anchorage for the tough, grasping roots. It is a sturdy, thickset little tree, usually about fifteen feet high when full grown, and about as broad as high, holding its knotty branches well out in every direction in stiff zigzags, but turning them gracefully upward at the ends in rounded bosses. Though making so dark a mass in the distance, the foliage is a pale grayish green, in stiff, awl-shaped fascicles. When examined closely these round needles seem inclined to be two-leaved, but they are mostly held firmly together, as if to guard against evaporation. The bark on the older sections is nearly black, so that the boles and branches are clearly traced against the prevailing gray of the mountains on which they delight to dwell.

The value of this species to Nevada is not easily overestimated. It furnishes fuel, charcoal, and timber for the mines, and, together with the enduring juniper, so generally associated with it, supplies the ranches with abundance of firewood and rough fencing. Many a square mile has already been denuded in supplying these demands, but, so great is the area covered by it, no appreciable loss has as yet been sustained. It is pretty generally known that this tree yields edible nuts, but their importance and excellence as human food is infinitely greater than is supposed. In fruitful seasons like this one, the pine-nut crop of Nevada is, perhaps, greater than the entire wheat crop of California, concerning which so much is said and felt throughout the food-markets of the world.

The Indians alone appreciate this portion of Nature's bounty and celebrate the harvest home with dancing and feasting. The cones, which are a bright grass-green in color and about two inches long by one and a half in diameter, are beaten off with poles just before the scales open, gathered in heaps of several bushels, and lightly scorched by burning a thin covering of brushwood over them. The resin, with which the cones are bedraggled, is thus burned off, the nuts slightly roasted, and the scales made to open. Then they are allowed to dry in the sun, after which the nuts are easily thrashed out and are ready to be stored away. They are about half an inch long by a quarter of an inch in diameter, pointed at the upper end, rounded at the base, light-brown in general color, and handsomely dotted with purple, like birds' eggs. The shells are thin, and may be crushed between the thumb and finger. The kernels are white and waxy-looking, becoming brown by roasting, sweet and delicious to every palate, and are eaten by birds, squirrels, dogs, horses, and man. When the crop is abundant the Indians bring in large quantities for sale; they are eaten around every fireside in the State, and oftentimes fed to horses instead of barley.

Looking over the whole continent, none of Nature's bounties

seems to me so great as this in the way of food, none so little appreciated. Fortunately for the Indians and wild animals that gather around Nature's board, this crop is not easily harvested in a monopolizing way. If it could be gathered like wheat the whole would be carried away and dissipated in towns, leaving the brave inhabitants of these wilds to starve.

Long before the harvest-time, which is in September and October, the Indians examine the trees with keen discernment, and inasmuch as the cones require two years to mature from the first appearance of the little red rosettes of the fertile flowers, the scarcity or abundance of the crop may be predicted more than a year in advance. Squirrels, and worms, and Clarke crows, make haste to begin the harvest. When the crop is ripe the Indians make ready their long beating-poles; baskets, bags, rags, mats, are gotten together. The squaws out among the settlers at service, washing and drudging, assemble at the family huts; the men leave their ranch work; all, old and young, are mounted on ponies, and set off in great glee to the nut lands, forming cavalcades curiously picturesque. Flaming scarfs and calico skirts stream loosely over the knotty ponies, usually two squaws astride of each, with the small baby midgets bandaged in baskets slung on their backs, or balanced upon the saddle-bow, while the nut-baskets and water-jars project from either side, and the long beating-poles, like old-fashioned lances, angle out in every direction.

Arrived at some central point already fixed upon, where water and grass is found, the squaws with baskets, the men with poles, ascend the ridges to the laden trees, followed by the children; beating begins with loud noise and chatter; the burs fly right and left, lodging against stones and sagebrush; the squaws and children gather them with fine natural gladness; smoke-columns speedily mark the joyful scene of their labors as the roasting-fires are kindled; and, at night, assembled in circles, garrulous as jays, the first grand nut feast begins. Sufficient quantities are thus obtained in a few weeks to last all winter.

The Indians also gather several species of berries and dry them to vary their stores, and a few deer and grouse are killed on the mountains, besides immense numbers of rabbits and hares; but the pine-nuts are their main dependence—their staff of life, their bread.

Insects also, scarce noticed by man, come in for their share of this fine bounty. Eggs are deposited, and the baby grubs, happy fellows, find themselves in a sweet world of plenty, feeding their way through the heart of the cone from one nut-chamber to another, secure from rain and wind and heat, until their wings are grown and they are ready to launch out into the free ocean of air and light.

14

Nevada's Timber Belt[1]

THE pine woods on the tops of the Nevada mountains are already shining and blooming in winter snow, making a most blessedly refreshing appearance to the weary traveler down on the gray plains. During the fiery days of summer the whole of this vast region seems so perfectly possessed by the sun that the very memories of pine trees and snow are in danger of being burned away, leaving one but little more than dust and metal. But since these first winter blessings have come, the wealth and beauty of the landscapes have come fairly into view, and one is rendered capable of looking and seeing.

The grand nut-harvest is over, as far as the Indians are concerned, though perhaps less than one bushel in a thousand of the whole crop has been gathered. But the squirrels and birds are still busily engaged, and by the time that Nature's ends are accomplished, every nut will doubtless have been put to use.

All of the nine Nevada conifers mentioned in my last letter are also found in California, excepting only the Rocky Mountain spruce, which I have not observed westward of the Snake Range. So greatly, however, have they been made to vary by differences of soil and climate, that most of them appear as distinct species. Without seeming in any way dwarfed or repressed in habit, they

[1]Written at Pioche, Nevada, in October, 1878. [Editor.]

nowhere develop to anything like California dimensions. A height of fifty feet and diameter of twelve or fourteen inches would probably be found to be above the average size of those cut for lumber. On the margin of the Carson and Humboldt Sink the larger sage bushes are called "heavy timber"; and to the settlers here any tree seems large enough for saw-logs.

Mills have been built in the most accessible cañons of the higher ranges, and sufficient lumber of an inferior kind is made to supply most of the local demand. The principal lumber trees of Nevada are the white pine (*Pinus flexilis*), foxtail pine, and Douglas spruce, or "red pine," as it is called here. Of these the first named is most generally distributed, being found on all the higher ranges throughout the State. In botanical characters it is nearly allied to the Weymouth, or white, pine of the Eastern States, and to the sugar and mountain pines of the Sierra. In open situations it branches near the ground and tosses out long down-curving limbs all around, often gaining in this way a very strikingly picturesque habit. It is seldom found lower than nine thousand feet above the level of the sea, but from this height it pushes upward over the roughest ledges to the extreme limit of tree growth—about eleven thousand feet.

On the Hot Creek, White Pine, and Golden Gate ranges we find a still hardier and more picturesque species, called the foxtail pine, from its long dense leaf-tassels. About a foot or eighteen inches of the ends of the branches are densely packed with stiff outstanding needles, which radiate all around like an electric fox- or squirrel-tail. The needles are about an inch and a half long, slightly curved, elastic, and glossily polished, so that the sunshine sifting through them makes them burn with a fine silvery luster, while their number and elastic temper tell delightfully in the singing winds.

This tree is preëminently picturesque, far surpassing not only its companion species of the mountains in this respect, but also the most noted of the lowland oaks and elms. Some stand firmly erect, feathered with radiant tail tassels down to the ground, forming slender, tapering towers of shining verdure; others with two or three specialized branches pushed out at right angles to the trunk and densely clad with the tasseled sprays, take the form of beautiful ornamental crosses. Again, in the same woods you find trees that are made up of several boles united near the ground, and spreading in easy curves at the sides in a plane parallel to the axis of the mountain, with the elegant tassels hung in charming order between them, the whole making a perfect harp, ranged across the main wind-lines just where they may be most effective in the grand storm harmonies. And then there is an infinite variety of arching forms, standing free or in groups, leaning away from or toward each other in curious architectural structures,—innumerable tassels drooping under the arches and radiating above them, the outside glowing in the light, masses of deep shade beneath, giving rise to effects marvelously beautiful,—while on the roughest ledges of crumbling limestone are lowly old giants, five or six feet in diameter, that have braved the storms of more than a thousand years. But, whether old or young, sheltered or exposed to the wildest gales, this tree is ever found to be irrepressibly and extravagantly picturesque, offering a richer and more varied series of forms to the artist than any other species I have yet seen.

One of the most interesting mountain excursions I have made in the State was up through a thick spicy forest of these trees to the top of the highest summit of the Troy Range, about ninety miles to the south of Hamilton. The day was full of perfect Indian-summer sunshine, calm and bracing. Jays and Clarke crows made a pleasant stir in the foothill pines and junipers; grasshoppers danced in the hazy light, and rattled on the wing in pure glee, reviving suddenly from the torpor of a frosty October night to exuberant summer joy. The squirrels were working industriously among the falling nuts; ripe willows and aspens made gorgeous masses of color on the russet hillsides and along the edges of the small streams that threaded the higher ravines; and on the smooth sloping uplands, beneath the foxtail pines and firs, the ground was covered with brown grasses enriched with sunflowers, columbines, and larkspurs and patches of linosyris, mostly frost-nipped and gone to seed, yet making fine bits of yellow and purple in the general brown.

At a height of about ninety-five hundred feet we passed through a magnificent grove of aspens, about a hundred acres in extent, through which the mellow sunshine sifted in ravishing splendor, showing every leaf to be as beautiful in color as the wing of a butterfly, and making them tell gloriously against the evergreens. These extensive groves of aspen are a marked feature of the Nevada woods. Some of the lower mountains are covered with them, giving rise to remarkably beautiful effects in general views— waving, trembling masses of pale, translucent green in spring and summer, yellow and orange in autumn, while in winter, after every leaf has fallen, the white bark of the boles and branches seen in mass seems like a cloud of mist that has settled close down on the mountain, conforming to all its hollows and ridges like a mantle, yet roughened on the surface with innumerable ascending spires.

Just above the aspens we entered a fine, close growth of foxtail pine, the tallest and most evenly planted I had yet seen. It extended along a waving ridge tending north and south and down both sides with but little interruption for a distance of about five miles. The trees were mostly straight in the bole, and their shade covered the ground in the densest places, leaving only small openings to the sun. A few of the tallest specimens measured over eighty feet, with a diameter of eighteen inches; but many of the younger trees, growing in tufts, were nearly fifty feet high, with a diameter of only five or six inches, while their slender shafts were hidden from top to bottom by a close, fringy growth of tasseled branchlets. A few white pines and balsam firs occur here and there, mostly around the edges of sunny openings, where they enrich the air with their rosiny fragrance, and bring out the peculiar beauties of the predominating foxtails by contrast.

Birds find grateful homes here—grouse, chickadees, and linnets, of which we saw large flocks that had a delightfully enlivening effect. But the woodpeckers are remarkably rare. Thus far I have noticed only one species, the golden-winged; and but few of the streams are large enough or long enough to attract the blessed ousel, so common in the Sierra.

On Wheeler's Peak, the dominating summit of the Snake Mountains, I found all the conifers I had seen on the other ranges of the State, excepting the foxtail pine, which I have not observed further east than the White Pine range, but in its stead the beautiful Rocky Mountain spruce. First, as in the other ranges, we find the juniper and nut pine; then, higher, the white pine and balsam fir; then the Douglas spruce and this new Rocky Mountain spruce, which is common eastward from here, though this range is, as far as I have observed, its western limit. It is one of the largest and most important of Nevada conifers, attaining a height of from sixty to eighty feet and a diameter of nearly two feet, while now and then an exceptional specimen may be found in shady dells a hundred feet high or more.

The foliage is bright yellowish and bluish green, according to exposure and age, growing all around the branchlets, though inclined to turn upward from the under sides, like that of the plushy firs of California, making remarkably handsome fernlike plumes. While yet only mere saplings five or six inches thick at the ground, they measure fifty or sixty feet in height and are beautifully clothed with broad, level, fronded plumes down to the base, preserving a strict arrowy outline, though a few of the larger branches shoot out in free exuberance, relieving the spire from any unpicturesque stiffness of aspect, while the conical summit is crowded with thousands of rich brown cones to complete its beauty.

We made the ascent of the peak just after the first storm had whitened its summit and brightened the atmosphere. The footslopes are like those of the Troy Range, only more evenly clad with grasses. After tracing a long, rugged ridge of exceedingly hard quartzite, said to be veined here and there with gold, we came to the North Dome, a noble summit rising about a thousand feet above the timber-line, its slopes heavily tree-clad all around, but most perfectly on the north. Here the Rocky Mountain spruce forms the bulk of the forest. The cones were ripe; most of them had shed their winged seeds, and the shell-like scales were conspicuously spread, making rich masses of brown from the tops of the fertile trees down halfway to the ground, cone touching cone in lavish clusters. A single branch that might be carried in the hand would be found to bear a hundred or more.

Some portions of the wood were almost impenetrable, but in

general we found no difficulty in mazing comfortably on over fallen logs and under the spreading boughs, while here and there we came to an opening sufficiently spacious for standpoints, where the trees around their margins might be seen from top to bottom. The winter sunshine streamed through the clustered spires, glinting and breaking into a fine dust of spangles on the spiky leaves and beads of amber gum, and bringing out the reds and grays and yellows of the lichened boles which had been freshened by the late storm; while the tip of every spire looking up through the shadows was dipped in deepest blue.

The ground was strewn with burs and needles and fallen trees; and, down in the dells, on the north side of the dome, where strips of aspen are imbedded in the spruces, every breeze sent the ripe leaves flying, some lodging in the spruce boughs, making them bloom again, while the fresh snow beneath looked like a fine painting.

Around the dome and well up toward the summit of the main peak, the snow-shed was well marked with tracks of mule deer and the pretty stitching and embroidery of field mice, squirrels, and grouse; and on the way back to camp I came across a strange track, somewhat like that of a small bear, but more spreading at the toes. It proved to be that of a wolverine. In my conversations with hunters, both Indians and white men assure me that there are no bears in Nevada, notwithstanding the abundance of pine-nuts, of which they are so fond, and the accessibility of these basin ranges from their favorite haunts in the Sierra Nevada and Wahsatch Mountains. The mule deer, antelope, wild sheep, wolverine, and two species of wolves are all of the larger animals that I have seen or heard of in the State.

15

Glacial Phenomena in Nevada[1]

THE monuments of the Ice Age in the Great Basin have been greatly obscured and broken, many of the more ancient of them having perished altogether, leaving scarce a mark, however faint, of their existence—a condition of things due not alone to the long-continued action of post-glacial agents, but also in great part to the perishable character of the rocks of which they were made. The bottoms of the main valleys, once grooved and planished like the glacier pavements of the Sierra, lie buried beneath sediments and detritus derived from the adjacent mountains, and now form the arid sage plains; characteristic U-shaped cañons have become V-shaped by the deepening of their bottoms and straightening of their sides, and decaying glacier headlands have been undermined and thrown down in loose taluses, while most of the moraines and striæ and scratches have been blurred or weathered away. Nevertheless, enough remains of the more recent and the more enduring phenomena to cast a good light well back upon the conditions of the ancient ice-sheet that covered this interesting region, and upon the system of distinct glaciers that loaded the tops of the mountains and filled the cañons long after the ice-sheet had been broken up.

The first glacial traces that I noticed in the basin are on the Wassuck, Augusta, and Toyabe ranges, consisting of ridges and

[1]Written at Eureka, Nevada, in November, 1878. [Editor.]

cañons, whose trends, contours, and general sculpture are in great part specifically glacial, though deeply blurred by subsequent denudation. These discoveries were made during the summer of 1876–77. And again, on the 17th of last August, while making the ascent of Mount Jefferson, the dominating mountain of the Toquima Range, I discovered an exceedingly interesting group of moraines, cañons with V-shaped cross sections, wide *névé* amphitheatres, moutonnéed rocks, glacier meadows, and one glacier lake, all as fresh and telling as if the glaciers to which they belonged had scarcely vanished.

The best preserved and most regular of the moraines are two laterals about two hundred feet in height and two miles long, extending from the foot of a magnificent cañon valley on the north side of the mountain and trending first in a northerly direction, then curving around to the west, while a well-characterized terminal moraine, formed by the glacier towards the close of its existence, unites them near their lower extremities at a height of eighty-five hundred feet. Another pair of older lateral moraines, belonging to a glacier of which the one just mentioned was a tributary, extend in a general northwesterly direction nearly to the level of Big Smoky Valley, about fifty-five hundred feet above sea-level.

Four other cañons, extending down the eastern slopes of this grand old mountain into Monito Valley, are hardly less rich in glacial records, while the effects of the mountain-shadows in controlling and directing the movements of the residual glaciers to which all these phenomena belonged are everywhere delightfully apparent in the trends of the cañons and ridges, and in the massive sculpture of the *névé* wombs at their heads. This is a very marked and imposing mountain, attracting the eye from a great distance. It presents a smooth and gently curved outline against the sky, as observed from the plains, and is whitened with patches of enduring snow. The summit is made up of irregular volcanic tables, the most extensive of which is about two and a half miles long, and like the smaller ones is broken abruptly down on the edges by the action of the ice. Its height is approximately eleven thousand three hundred feet above the sea.

A few days after making these interesting discoveries, I found other well-preserved glacial traces on Arc Dome, the culminating summit of the Toyabe Range. On its northeastern slopes there are two small glacier lakes, and the basins of two others which have recently been filled with down-washed detritus. One small residual glacier lingered until quite recently beneath the coolest shadows of the dome, the moraines and *névé*-fountains of which are still as fresh and unwasted as many of those lying at the same elevation on the Sierra—ten thousand feet—while older and more wasted specimens may be traced on all the adjacent mountains. The sculpture, too, of all the ridges and summits of this section of the range is recognized at once as glacial, some of the larger characters being still easily readable from the plains at a distance of fifteen or twenty miles.

The Hot Creek Mountains, lying to the east of the Toquima and Monito ranges, reach the culminating point on a deeply serrate ridge at a height of ten thousand feet above the sea. This ridge is found to be made up of a series of imposing towers and pinnacles which have been eroded from the solid mass of the mountain by a group of small residual glaciers that lingered in their shadows long after the larger ice rivers had vanished. On its western declivities are found a group of well-characterized moraines, cañons, and *roches moutonnées*, all of which are unmistakably fresh and telling. The moraines in particular could hardly fail to attract the eye of any observer. Some of the short laterals of the glaciers that drew their fountain snows from the jagged recesses of the summit are from one to two hundred feet in height, and scarce at all wasted as yet, notwithstanding the countless storms that have fallen upon them, while cool rills flow between them, watering charming gardens of arctic plants—saxifrages, larkspurs, dwarf birch, ribes, and parnassia, etc.—beautiful memories of the Ice Age, representing a once greatly extended flora.

In the course of explorations made to the eastward of here, between the 38th and 40th parallels, I observed glacial phenomena equally fresh and demonstrative on all the higher mountains of the White Pine, Golden Gate, and Snake ranges, varying from those already described only as determined by differences of elevation, relations to the snow-bearing winds, and the physical characteristics of the rock-formations.

On the Jeff Davis group of the Snake Range, the dominating summit of which is nearly thirteen thousand feet in elevation, and the highest ground in the basin, every marked feature is a glacier monument—peaks, valleys, ridges, meadows, and lakes. And because here the snow-fountains lay at a greater height, while the rock, an exceedingly hard quartzite, offered superior resistance to post-glacial agents, the ice-characters are on a larger scale, and are more sharply defined than any we have noticed elsewhere, and it is probably here that the last lingering glacier of the basin was located. The summits and connecting ridges are mere blades and points, ground sharp by the glaciers that descended on both sides to the main valleys. From one standpoint I counted nine of these glacial channels with their moraines sweeping grandly out to the plains to deep sheer-walled *névé*-fountains at their heads, making a most vivid picture of the last days of the Ice Period.

I have thus far directed attention only to the most recent and appreciable of the phenomena; but it must be borne in mind that less recent and less obvious traces of glacial action abound on *all* the ranges throughout the entire basin, where the fine striæ and grooves have been obliterated, and most of the moraines have been washed away, or so modified as to be no longer recognizable, and even the lakes and meadows, so characteristic of glacial regions, have almost entirely vanished. For there are other monuments, far more enduring than these, remaining tens of thousands of years after the more perishable records are lost. Such are the cañons, ridges, and peaks themselves, the glacial peculiarities of whose trends and contours cannot be hid from the eye of the skilled observer until changes have been wrought upon them far more destructive than those to which these basin ranges have yet been subjected.

It appears, therefore, that the last of the basin glaciers have but recently vanished, and that the almost innumerable ranges trending north and south between the Sierra and the Wahsatch Mountains were loaded with glaciers that descended to the adjacent valleys during the last glacial period, and that it is to this mighty host of ice-streams that all the more characteristic of the present features of these mountain-ranges are due.

But grand as is this vision delineated in these old records, this is not all; for there is not wanting evidence of a still grander glaciation extending over all the valleys now forming the sage plains as well as the mountains. The basins of the main valleys alternating with the mountain-ranges, and which contained lakes during at least the closing portion of the Ice Period, were eroded wholly, or in part, from a general elevated tableland, by immense glaciers that flowed north and south to the ocean. The mountains as well as the valleys present abundant evidence of this grand origin.

The flanks of all the interior ranges are seen to have been heavily abraded and ground away by the ice acting in a direction parallel with their axes. This action is most strikingly shown upon projecting portions where the pressure has been greatest. These are shorn off in smooth planes and bossy outswelling curves, like the outstanding portions of cañon-walls. Moreover, the extremities of the ranges taper out like those of dividing ridges which have been ground away by dividing and confluent glaciers. Furthermore, the horizontal sections of separate mountains, standing isolated in the great valleys, are lens-shaped like those of mere rocks that rise in the channels of ordinary cañon glaciers, and which have been overflowed or past-flowed, while in many of the smaller valleys *roches moutonnées* occur in great abundance.

Again, the mineralogical and physical characters of the two ranges bounding the sides of many of the valleys indicate that the valleys were formed simply by the removal of the material between the ranges. And again, the rim of the general basin, where it is elevated, as for example on the southwestern portion, instead of being a ridge sculptured on the sides like a mountain-range, is found to be composed of many short ranges, parallel to one another, and to the interior ranges, and so modeled as to resemble a row of convex lenses set on edge and half buried beneath a general surface, without manifesting any dependence upon synclinal or anticlinal axes—a series of forms and relations that could have resulted only from the outflow of vast basin glaciers on their courses to the ocean.

I cannot, however, present all the evidence here bearing upon these interesting questions, much less discuss it in all its relations. I will, therefore, close this letter with a few of the more important generalizations that have grown up out of the facts that I have observed. First, at the beginning of the glacial period the region now known as the Great Basin was an elevated tableland, not furrowed as at present with mountains and valleys, but comparatively bald and featureless.

Second, this tableland, bounded on the east and west by lofty mountain-ranges, but comparatively open on the north and south, was loaded with ice, which was discharged to the ocean northward and southward, and in its flow brought most, if not all, the present interior ranges and valleys into relief by erosion.

Third, as the glacial winter drew near its close the ice vanished from the lower portions of the basin, which then became lakes, into which separate glaciers descended from the mountains. Then these mountain glaciers vanished in turn, after sculpturing the ranges into their present condition.

Fourth, the few immense lakes extending over the lowlands, in the midst of which many of the interior ranges stood as islands, became shallow as the ice vanished from the mountains, and separated into many distinct lakes, whose waters no longer reached the ocean. Most of these have disappeared by the filling of their basins with detritus from the mountains, and now form sage plains and "alkali flats."

The transition from one to the other of these various conditions was gradual and orderly: first, a nearly simple tableland; then a grand *mer de glace* shedding its crawling silver currents to the sea, and becoming gradually more wrinkled as unequal erosion roughened its bed, and brought the highest peaks and ridges above the surface; then a land of lakes, an almost continuous sheet of water stretching from the Sierra to the Wahsatch, adorned with innumerable island mountains; then a slow desiccation and decay to present conditions of sage and sand.

16

Nevada's Dead Towns[1]

NEVADA is one of the very youngest and wildest of the States; nevertheless it is already strewn with ruins that seem as gray and silent and time-worn as if the civilization to which they belonged had perished centuries ago. Yet, strange to say, all these ruins are results of mining efforts made within the last few years. Wander where you may throughout the length and breadth of this mountain-barred wilderness, you everywhere come upon these dead mining towns, with their tall chimney-stacks, standing forlorn amid broken walls and furnaces, and machinery half buried in sand, the very names of many of them already forgotten amid the excitements of later discoveries, and now known only through tradition—tradition ten years old.

While exploring the mountain-ranges of the State during a considerable portion of three summers, I think that I have seen at least five of these deserted towns and villages for every one in ordinary life. Some of them were probably only camps built by bands of prospectors, and inhabited for a few months or years, while some specially interesting cañon was being explored, and then carelessly abandoned for more promising fields. But many were real towns, regularly laid out and incorporated, containing well-built hotels,

---

[1]Date and place of writing not given. Published in the *San Francisco Evening Bulletin*, January 15, 1879. [Editor.]

churches, school-houses, post-offices, and jails, as well as the mills on which they all depended; and whose well-graded streets were filled with lawyers, doctors, brokers, hangmen, real-estate agents, etc., the whole population numbering several thousand.

A few years ago the population of Hamilton is said to have been nearly eight thousand; that of Treasure Hill, six thousand; of Shermantown, seven thousand; of Swansea, three thousand. All of these were incorporated towns with mayors, councils, fire departments, and daily newspapers. Hamilton has now about one hundred inhabitants, most of whom are merely waiting in dreary inaction for something to turn up. Treasure Hill has about half as many, Shermantown one family, and Swansea none, while on the other hand the graveyards are far too full.

In one cañon of the Toyabe Range, near Austin, I found no less than five dead towns without a single inhabitant. The streets and blocks of "real estate" graded on the hillsides are rapidly falling back into the wilderness. Sage-brushes are growing up around the forges of the blacksmith shops, and lizards bask on the crumbling walls.

While traveling southward from Austin down Big Smoky Valley, I noticed a remarkably tall and imposing column, rising like a lone pine out of the sage-brush on the edge of a dry gulch. This proved to be a smokestack of solid masonry. It seemed strangely out of place in the desert, as if it had been transported entire from the heart of some noisy manufacturing town and left here by mistake. I learned afterwards that it belonged to a set of furnaces that were built by a New York company to smelt ore that never was found. The tools of the workmen are still lying in place beside the furnaces, as if dropped in some sudden Indian or earthquake panic and never afterwards handled. These imposing ruins, together with the desolate town, lying a quarter of a mile to the northward, present a most vivid picture of wasted effort. Coyotes now wander unmolested through the brushy streets, and of all the busy throng that so lavishly spent their time and money here only one man remains—a lone bachelor with one suspender.

Mining discoveries and progress, retrogression and decay, seem to have been crowded more closely against each other here than on any other portion of the globe. Some one of the band of adventurous prospectors who came from the exhausted placers of California would discover some rich ore—how much or little mattered not at first. These specimens fell among excited seekers after wealth like sparks in gunpowder, and in a few days the wilderness was disturbed with the noisy clang of miners and builders. A little town would then spring up, and before anything like a careful survey of any particular lode would be made, a company would be formed, and expensive mills built. Then, after all the machinery was ready for the ore, perhaps little, or none at all, was to be found. Meanwhile another discovery was reported, and the young town was abandoned as completely as a camp made for a single night; and so on, until some really valuable lode was found, such as those of Eureka, Austin, Virginia, etc., which formed the substantial groundwork for a thousand other excitements.

Passing through the dead town of Schellbourne last month, I asked one of the few lingering inhabitants why the town was built. "For the mines," he replied. "And where are the mines?" "On the mountains back here." "And why were they abandoned?" I asked. "Are they exhausted?" "Oh, no," he replied, "they are not exhausted; on the contrary, they have never been worked at all, for unfortunately, just as we were about ready to open them, the Cherry Creek mines were discovered across the valley in the Egan Range, and everybody rushed off there, taking what they could with them—houses, machinery, and all. But we are hoping that somebody with money and speculation will come and revive us yet."

The dead mining excitements of Nevada were far more intense and destructive in their action than those of California, because the prizes at stake were greater, while more skill was required to gain them. The long trains of gold-seekers making their way to California had ample time and means to recover from their first attacks of mining fever while crawling laboriously across the plains, and on their arrival on any portion of the Sierra gold belt, they at once began to make money. No matter in what gulch or cañon they worked, some measure of success was sure, however unskillful they might be. And though while making ten dollars a day they might be agitated by hopes of making twenty, or of striking their picks against hundred- or thousand-dollar nuggets, men of ordinary nerve could still work on with comparative steadiness, and remain rational.

But in the case of the Nevada miner, he too often spent himself in years of weary search without gaining a dollar, traveling hundreds of miles from mountain to mountain, burdened with wasting hopes of discovering some hidden vein worth millions, enduring hardships of the most destructive kind, driving innumerable tunnels into the hillsides, while his assayed specimens again and again proved worthless. Perhaps one in a hundred of these brave prospectors would "strike it rich," while ninety-nine died

alone in the mountains or sank out of sight in the corners of sa-
loons, in a haze of whiskey and tobacco smoke.

The healthful ministry of wealth is blessed; and surely it is a
fine thing that so many are eager to find the gold and silver that lie
hid in the veins of the mountains. But in the search the seekers too
often become insane, and strike about blindly in the dark like raving madmen. Seven hundred and fifty tons of ore from the original
Eberhardt mine on Treasure Hill yielded a million and a half dollars, the whole of this immense sum having been obtained within
two hundred and fifty feet of the surface, the greater portion within
one hundred and forty feet. Other ore-masses were scarcely less
marvelously rich, giving rise to one of the most violent excitements
that ever occurred in the history of mining. All kinds of people—
shoemakers, tailors, farmers, etc., as well as miners—left their
own right work and fell in a perfect storm of energy upon the White
Pine Hills, covering the ground like grasshoppers, and seeming
determined by the very violence of their efforts to turn every stone
to silver. But with few exceptions, these mining storms pass away
about as suddenly as they rise, leaving only ruins to tell of the
tremendous energy expended, as heaps of giant boulders in the
valley tell of the spent power of the mountain floods.

In marked contrast with this destructive unrest is the orderly
deliberation into which miners settle in developing a truly valuable
mine. At Eureka we were kindly led through the treasure chambers
of the Richmond and Eureka Consolidated, our guides leisurely
leading the way from level to level, calling attention to the precious
ore-masses which the workmen were slowly breaking to pieces with
their picks, like navvies wearing away the day in a railroad cutting;

while down at the smelting works the bars of bullion were handled with less eager haste than the farmer shows in gathering his sheaves.

The wealth Nevada has already given to the world is indeed wonderful, but the only grand marvel is the energy expended in its development. The amount of prospecting done in the face of so many dangers and sacrifices, the innumerable tunnels and shafts bored into the mountains, the mills that have been built—these would seem to require a race of giants. But, in full view of the substantial results achieved, the pure waste manifest in the ruins one meets never fails to produce a saddening effect.

The dim old ruins of Europe, so eagerly sought after by travelers, have something pleasing about them, whatever their historical associations; for they at least lend some beauty to the landscape. Their picturesque towers and arches seem to be kindly adopted by nature, and planted with wild flowers and wreathed with ivy; while their rugged angles are soothed and freshened and embossed with green mosses, fresh life and decay mingling in pleasing measures, and the whole vanishing softly like a ripe, tranquil day fading into night. So, also, among the older ruins of the East there is a fitness felt. They have served their time, and like the weather-beaten mountains are wasting harmoniously. The same is in some degree true of the dead mining towns of California.

But those lying to the eastward of the Sierra throughout the ranges of the Great Basin waste in the dry wilderness like the bones of cattle that have died of thirst. Many of them do not represent any good accomplishment, and have no right to be. They are monuments of fraud and ignorance—sins against science. The drifts and tunnels in the rocks may perhaps be regarded as the prayers of the prospector, offered for the wealth he so earnestly craves; but, like prayers of any kind not in harmony with nature, they are unanswered. But, after all, effort, however misapplied, is better than stagnation. Better toil blindly, beating every stone in turn for grains of gold, whether they contain any or not, than lie down in apathetic decay.

The fever period is fortunately passing away. The prospector is no longer the raving, wandering ghoul of ten years ago, rushing in random lawlessness among the hills, hungry and footsore; but cool and skillful, well supplied with every necessary, and clad in his right mind. Capitalists, too, and the public in general, have become wiser, and do not take fire so readily from mining sparks; while at the same time a vast amount of real work is being done, and the ratio between growth and decay is constantly becoming better.

17

Puget Sound

WASHINGTON TERRITORY, recently admitted[1] into the Union as a
State, lies between latitude 46° and 49° and longitude 117° and
125°, forming the northwest shoulder of the United States. The
majestic range of the Cascade Mountains naturally divides the
State into two distinct parts, called Eastern and Western Washington, differing greatly from each other in almost every way, the western section being less than half as large as the eastern, and, with its
copious rains and deep fertile soil, being clothed with forests of
evergreens, while the eastern section is dry and mostly treeless,
though fertile in many parts, and producing immense quantities
of wheat and hay. Few States are more fertile and productive in one
way or another than Washington, or more strikingly varied in natural features or resources.

Within her borders every kind of soil and climate may be
found—the densest woods and dryest plains, the smoothest levels
and roughest mountains. She is rich in square miles (some seventy
thousand of them), in coal, timber, and iron, and in sheltered
inland waters that render these resources advantageously accessible. She also is already rich in busy workers, who work hard,
though not always wisely, hacking, burning, blasting their way

---

[1]November 11, 1889; Muir's description probably was written toward the end of
the same year. [Editor.]

deeper into the wilderness, beneath the sky, and beneath the ground. The wedges of development are being driven hard, and none of the obstacles or defenses of nature can long withstand the onset of this immeasurable industry.

Puget Sound, so justly famous the world over for the surpassing size and excellence and abundance of its timber, is a long, many-fingered arm of the sea reaching southward from the head of the Strait of Juan de Fuca into the heart of the grand forests of the western portion of Washington, between the Cascade Range and the mountains of the coast. It is less than a hundred miles in length, but so numerous are the branches into which it divides, and so many its bays, harbors, and islands, that its entire shore-line is said to measure more than eighteen hundred miles. Throughout its whole vast extent ships move in safety, and find shelter from every wind that blows, the entire mountain-girt sea forming one grand unrivaled harbor and center for commerce.

The forest trees press forward to the water around all the windings of the shores in most imposing array, as if they were courting their fate, coming down from the mountains far and near to offer themselves to the axe, thus making the place a perfect paradise for the lumberman. To the lover of nature the scene is enchanting. Water and sky, mountain and forest, clad in sunshine and clouds, are composed in landscapes sublime in magnitude, yet exquisitely fine and fresh, and full of glad, rejoicing life. The shining waters stretch away into the leafy wilderness, now like the reaches of some majestic river and again expanding into broad roomy spaces like mountain lakes, their farther edges fading gradually and blending with the pale blue of the sky. The wooded shores with an outer fringe of flowering bushes sweep onward in beautiful curves around bays, and capes, and jutting promontories innumerable; while the islands, with soft, waving outlines, lavishly adorned with spruces and cedars, thicken and enrich the beauty of the waters; and the white spirit mountains looking down from the sky keep watch and ward over all, faithful and changeless as the stars.

All the way from the Strait of Juan de Fuca up to Olympia, a hopeful town situated at the head of one of the farthest-reaching of the fingers of the Sound, we are so completely inland and surrounded by mountains that it is hard to realize that we are sailing on a branch of the salt sea. We are constantly reminded of Lake Tahoe. There is the same clearness of the water in calm weather without any trace of the ocean swell, the same picturesque winding and sculpture of the shore-line and flowery, leafy luxuriance; only here the trees are taller and stand much closer together, and the backgrounds are higher and far more extensive. Here, too, we find greater variety amid the marvelous wealth of islands and inlets, and also in the changing views dependent on the weather. As we double cape after cape and round the uncounted islands, new combinations come to view in endless variety, sufficient to fill and satisfy the lover of wild beauty through a whole life.

Oftentimes in the stillest weather, when all the winds sleep and no sign of storms is felt or seen, silky clouds form and settle over all the land, leaving in sight only a circle of water with indefinite bounds like views in mid-ocean; then, the clouds lifting, some islet will be presented standing alone, with the tops of its trees dipping out of sight in pearly gray fringes; or, lifting higher, and perhaps letting in a ray of sunshine through some rift overhead, the whole island will be set free and brought forward in vivid relief amid the gloom, a girdle of silver light of dazzling brightness on the water about its shores, then darkening again and vanishing back into the general gloom. Thus island after island may be seen, singly or in groups, coming and going from darkness to light like a scene of enchantment, until at length the entire cloud ceiling is rolled away, and the colossal cone of Mount Rainier is seen in spotless white looking down over the forests from a distance of sixty miles, but so lofty and so massive and clearly outlined as to impress itself upon us as being just back of a strip of woods only a mile or two in breadth.

For the tourist sailing to Puget Sound from San Francisco there is but little that is at all striking in the scenery within reach by the way until the mouth of the Strait of Juan de Fuca is reached. The voyage is about four days in length and the steamers keep within sight of the coast, but the hills fronting the sea up to Oregon are mostly bare and uninviting, the magnificent redwood forests stretching along this portion of the California coast seeming to keep well back, away from the heavy winds, so that very little is seen of them; while there are no deep inlets or lofty mountains visible to break the regular monotony. Along the coast of Oregon the woods of spruce and fir come down to the shore, kept fresh and vigorous by copious rains, and become denser and taller to the northward until, rounding Cape Flattery, we enter the Strait of Fuca, where, sheltered from the ocean gales, the forests begin to hint the grandeur they attain in Puget Sound. Here the scenery in general becomes exceedingly interesting; for now we have arrived at the grand mountain-walled channel that forms the entrance to that marvelous network of inland waters that extends along the margin of the continent to the northward for a thousand miles.

This magnificent inlet was named for Juan de Fuca, who discovered it in 1592 while seeking a mythical strait, supposed to exist somewhere in the north, connecting the Atlantic and Pacific. It is about seventy miles long, ten or twelve miles wide, and extends to the eastward in a nearly straight line between the south end of Vancouver Island and the Olympic Range of mountains on the mainland.

Cape Flattery, the western termination of the Olympic Range, is terribly rugged and jagged, and in stormy weather is utterly inaccessible from the sea. Then the ponderous rollers of the deep Pacific thunder amid its caverns and cliffs with the foam and uproar of a thousand Yosemite waterfalls. The bones of many a noble ship lie there, and many a sailor. It would seem unlikely that any living thing should seek rest in such a place, or find it. Nevertheless, frail and delicate flowers bloom there, flowers of both the land and the sea; heavy, ungainly seals disport in the swelling waves, and find grateful retreats back in the inmost bores of its storm-lashed caverns; while in many a chink and hollow of the highest crags, not visible from beneath, a great variety of water-fowl make homes and rear their young.

But not always are the inhabitants safe, even in such wave-defended castles as these, for the Indians of the neighboring shores venture forth in the calmest summer weather in their frail canoes to spear the seals in the narrow gorges amid the grinding, gurgling din of the restless waters. At such times also the hunters make out to scale many of the apparently inaccessible cliffs for the eggs and young of the gulls and other water-birds, occasionally losing their lives in these perilous adventures, which give rise to many an exciting story told around the camp-fires at night when the storms roar loudest.

Puget Sound

Passing through the strait, we have the Olympic Mountains close at hand on the right, Vancouver Island on the left, and the snowy peak of Mount Baker straight ahead in the distance. During calm weather, or when the clouds are lifting and rolling off the mountains after a storm, all these views are truly magnificent. Mount Baker is one of that wonderful series of old volcanoes that once flamed along the summits of the Sierras and Cascades from Lassen to Mount St. Elias. Its fires are sleeping now, and it is loaded with glaciers, streams of ice having taken the place of streams of glowing lava. Vancouver Island presents a charming variety of hill and dale, open sunny spaces and sweeps of dark forest rising in swell beyond swell to the high land in the distance.

But the Olympic Mountains most of all command attention, seen tellingly near and clear in all their glory, rising from the water's edge into the sky to a height of six or eight thousand feet. They bound the strait on the south side throughout its whole extent, forming a massive sustained wall, flowery and bushy at the base, a zigzag of snowy peaks along the top, which have ragged-edged fields of ice and snow beneath them, enclosed in wide amphitheaters opening to the waters of the strait through spacious forest-filled valleys enlivened with fine, dashing streams. These valleys mark the courses of the Olympic glaciers at the period of their greatest extension, when they poured their tribute into that portion of the great northern ice-sheet that overswept the south end of Vancouver Island and filled the strait with flowing ice as it is now filled with ocean water.

The steamers of the Sound usually stop at Esquimalt on their way up, thus affording tourists an opportunity to visit the interesting town of Victoria, the capital of British Columbia. The Victoria harbor is too narrow and difficult of access for the larger class of ships; therefore a landing has to be made at Esquimalt. The distance, however, is only about three miles, and the way is delightful, winding on through a charming forest of Douglas spruce, with here and there groves of oak and madrone, and a rich undergrowth of hazel, dogwood, willow, alder, spiræa, rubus, huckleberry, and wild rose. Pretty cottages occur at intervals along the road, covered with honeysuckle, and many an upswelling rock, freshly glaciated and furred with yellow mosses and lichen, telling interesting stories of the icy past.

Victoria is a quiet, handsome, breezy town, beautifully located on finely modulated ground at the mouth of the Canal de Haro, with charming views in front, of islands and mountains and far-reaching waters, ever changing in the shifting lights and shades of the clouds and sunshine. In the background there are a mile or two of field and forest and sunny oak openings; then comes the forest primeval, dense and shaggy and well-nigh impenetrable.

Notwithstanding the importance claimed for Victoria as a commercial center and the capital of British Columbia, it has a rather young, loose-jointed appearance. The government buildings and some of the business blocks on the main streets are well built and imposing in bulk and architecture. These are far less interesting and characteristic, however, than the mansions set in the midst of spacious pleasure-grounds and the lovely home cottages embowered in honeysuckle and climbing roses. One soon discovers that this is no Yankee town. The English faces and the way that English is spoken alone would tell that; while in business quarters there is a staid dignity and moderation that is very noticeable, and a want of American push and hurrah. Love of land and of privacy in homes is made manifest in the residences, many of which are built in the middle of fields and orchards or large city blocks, and in the loving care with which these home-grounds are planted. They are very beautiful. The fineness of the climate, with its copious measure of warm moisture distilling in dew and fog, and gentle, bathing, laving rain, give them a freshness and flower-iness that is worth going far to see.

Victoria is noted for its fine drives, and every one who can should either walk or drive around the outskirts of the town, not only for the fine views out over the water but to see the cascades of bloom pouring over the gables of the cottages, and the fresh wild woods with their flowery, fragrant underbrush. Wild roses abound almost everywhere. One species, blooming freely along the wood-land paths, is from two to three inches in diameter, and more fra-grant than any other wild rose I ever saw excepting the sweetbriar. This rose and three species of spiræa fairly fill the air with fragrance after a shower. And how brightly then do the red berries of the dogwood shine out from the warm yellow-green of leaves and mosses!

But still more interesting and significant are the glacial phe-nomena displayed hereabouts. All this exuberant tree, bush, and herbaceous vegetation, cultivated or wild, is growing upon mo-raine beds outspread by waters that issued from the ancient glaciers at the time of their recession, and scarcely at all moved or in any way modified by post-glacial agencies. The town streets and the roads are graded in moraine material, among scratched and grooved rock-bosses that are as unweathered and telling as any to be found in the glacier-channels of Alaska. The harbor also is clearly of glacial origin. The rock islets that rise here and there, forming so marked a feature of the harbor, are unchanged *roches moutonnées*, and the shores are grooved, scratched, and rounded, and in every way as glacial in all their characteristics as those of a newborn glacial lake.

Most visitors to Victoria go to the stores of the Hudson's Bay Company, presumably on account of the romantic associations, or to purchase a bit of fur or some other wild-Indianish trinket as a memento. At certain seasons of the year, when the hairy harvests are gathered in, immense bales of skins may be seen in these unsavory warehouses, the spoils of many thousand hunts over mountain and plain, by lonely river and shore. The skins of bears, wolves, beavers, otters, fishers, martens, lynxes, panthers, wolverine, reindeer, moose, elk, wild goats, sheep, foxes, squirrels, and many other of our "poor earth-born companions and fellow-mortals" may here be found.

Vancouver is the southmost and the largest of the countless islands forming the great archipelago that stretches a thousand miles to the northward. Its shores have been known a long time, but little is known of the lofty mountainous interior on account of the difficulties in the way of explorations—lake, bogs, and shaggy tangled forests. It is mostly a pure, savage wilderness, without roads or clearings, and silent so far as man is concerned. Even the Indians keep close to the shore, getting a living by fishing, dwelling together in villages, and traveling almost wholly by canoes. White settlements are few and far between. Good agricultural lands occur here and there on the edge of the wilderness, but they are hard to clear, and have received but little attention thus far. Gold, the grand attraction that lights the way into all kinds of wildernesses and makes rough places smooth, has been found, but only in small quantities, too small to make much motion. Almost all the industry of the island is employed upon lumber and coal, in which, so far as known, its chief wealth lies.

Leaving Victoria for Port Townsend, after we are fairly out on the free open water, Mount Baker is seen rising solitary over a dark breadth of forest, making a glorious show in its pure white raiment. It is said to be about eleven thousand feet high, is loaded with glaciers, some of which come well down into the woods, and never, so far as I have heard, has been climbed, though in all probability it is not inaccessible. The task of reaching its base through the dense woods will be likely to prove of greater difficulty than the climb to the summit.

In a direction a little to the left of Mount Baker and much nearer, may be seen the island of San Juan, famous in the young history of the country for the quarrels concerning its rightful ownership between the Hudson's Bay Company and Washington Territory, quarrels which nearly brought on war with Great Britain. Neither party showed any lack of either pluck or gunpowder. General Scott was sent out by President Buchanan to negotiate, which resulted in a joint occupancy of the island. Small quarrels, however, continued to arise until the year 1874, when the peppery question was submitted to the Emperor of Germany for arbitration. Then the whole island was given to the United States.

San Juan is one of a thickset cluster of islands that fills the waters between Vancouver and the mainland, a little to the north of Victoria. In some of the intricate channels between these islands the tides run at times like impetuous rushing rivers, rendering navigation rather uncertain and dangerous for the small sailing-vessels that ply between Victoria and the settlements on the coast of British

Columbia and the larger islands. The water is generally deep enough everywhere, too deep in most places for anchorage, and, the winds shifting hither and thither or dying away altogether, the ships, getting no direction from their helms, are carried back and forth or are caught in some eddy where two currents meet and whirled round and round to the dismay of the sailors, like a chip in a river whirlpool.

All the way over to Port Townsend the Olympic Mountains well maintain their massive, imposing grandeur, and present their elaborately carved summits in clear relief, many of which are out of sight in coming up the strait on account of our being too near the base of the range. Turn to them as often as we may, our admiration only grows the warmer the longer we dwell upon them. The highest peaks are Mount Constance and Mount Olympus, said to be about eight thousand feet high.

In two or three hours after leaving Victoria, we arrive at the handsome little town of Port Townsend, situated at the mouth of Puget Sound, on the west side. The residential portion of the town is set on the level top of the bluff that bounds Port Townsend Bay, while another nearly level space of moderate extent, reaching from the base of the bluff to the shore-line, is occupied by the business portion, thus making a town of two separate and distinct stories, which are connected by long, ladder-like flights of stairs. In the streets of the lower story, while there is no lack of animation, there is but little business noise as compared with the amount of business transacted. This in great part is due to the scarcity of horses and wagons. Farms and roads back in the woods are few and far between. Nearly all the tributary settlements are on the coast, and communication is almost wholly by boats, canoes, and schooners. Hence country stages and farmers' wagons and buggies, with the whir and din that belong to them, are wanting.

This being the port of entry, all vessels have to stop here, and they make a lively show about the wharves and in the bay. The winds stir the flags of every civilized nation, while the Indians in their long-beaked canoes glide about from ship to ship, satisfying their curiosity or trading with the crews. Keen traders these Indians are, and few indeed of the sailors or merchants from any country ever get the better of them in bargains. Curious groups of people may often be seen in the streets and stores, made up of English, French, Spanish, Portuguese, Scandinavians, Germans, Greeks, Moors, Japanese, and Chinese, of every rank and station and style of dress and behavior; settlers from many a nook and bay and island up and down the coast; hunters from the wilderness; tourists on their way home by the Sound and the Columbia River or to Alaska or California.

The upper story of Port Townsend is charmingly located, wide bright waters on one side, flowing evergreen woods on the other. The streets are well laid out and well tended, and the houses, with their luxuriant gardens about them, have an air of taste and refinement seldom found in towns set on the edge of a wild forest. The people seem to have come here to make true homes, attracted by the beauty and fresh breezy healthfulness of the place as well as by business advantages, trusting to natural growth and advancement instead of restless "booming" methods. They perhaps have caught some of the spirit of calm moderation and enjoyment from their English neighbors across the water. Of late, however, this sober tranquillity has begun to give way, some whiffs from the whirlwind of real-estate speculation up the Sound having at length touched the town and ruffled the surface of its calmness.

A few miles up the bay is Fort Townsend, which makes a pretty picture with the green woods rising back of it and the calm water in front. Across the mouth of the Sound lies the long, narrow Whidbey Island, named by Vancouver for one of his lieutenants. It is about thirty miles in length, and is remarkable in this region of crowded forests and mountains as being comparatively open and low. The soil is good and easily worked, and a considerable portion of the island has been under cultivation for many years. Fertile fields, open, parklike groves of oak, and thick masses of evergreens succeed one another in charming combinations to make this "the garden spot of the Territory."

Leaving Port Townsend for Seattle and Tacoma, we enter the Sound and sail down into the heart of the green, aspiring forests, and find, look where we may, beauty ever changing, in lavish profusion. Puget Sound, "the Mediterranean of America" as it is sometimes called, is in many respects one of the most remarkable bodies of water in the world. Vancouver, who came here nearly a hundred years ago and made a careful survey of it, named the larger northern portion of it "Admiralty Inlet" and one of the long, narrow branches "Hood's Canal," applying the name "Puget Sound" only to the comparatively small southern portion. The latter name, however, is now applied generally to the entire inlet, and is commonly shortened by the people hereabouts to "the Sound." The natural wealth and commercial advantages of the Sound region were quickly recognized, and the cause of the activity prevailing here is not far to seek. Vancouver, long before civilization touched these shores, spoke of it in terms of unstinted praise. He was sent out by the British government with the principal object in view of "acquiring accurate knowledge as to the nature and extent of any water communication which may tend in any considerable degree to facilitate an intercourse for the purposes of commerce between the northwest coast and the country on the opposite side of the continent," vague traditions having long been current concerning a strait supposed to unite the two oceans. Vancouver reported that he found the coast from San Francisco to Oregon and beyond to present a nearly straight solid barrier to the sea, without openings, and we may well guess the joy of the old navigator on the discovery of these waters after so long and barren a search to the southward.

His descriptions of the scenery—Mounts Baker, Rainier, St. Helen's, etc.—were as enthusiastic as those of the most eager landscape-lover of the present day, when scenery is in fashion. He says in one place: "To describe the beauties of this region will, on some future occasion, be a very grateful task for the pen of a skillful panegyrist. The serenity of the climate, the immeasurable pleasing landscapes, and the abundant fertility that unassisted nature puts forth, require only to be enriched by the industry of man with villages, mansions, cottages, and other buildings, to render it the most lovely country that can be imagined. The labor of the inhabitants would be amply rewarded in the bounties which nature seems ready to bestow on cultivation." "A picture so pleasing could not fail to call to our remembrance certain delightful and beloved situations in old England." So warm, indeed, were the praises he sung that his statements were received in England with a good deal of hesitation. But they were amply corroborated by Wilkes and others who followed many years later. "Nothing," says Wilkes, "can exceed the beauty of these waters and their safety. Not a shoal exists in the Straits of Juan de Fuca, Admiralty Inlet, Puget Sound or Hood's Canal, that can in any way interrupt their navigation by a 74-gun ship. I venture nothing in saying there is no country in the world that possesses waters like these." And again, quoting from the United States Coast Survey, "For depth of water, boldness of approaches, freedom from hidden dangers, and the immeasurable sea of gigantic timber coming down to the very shores, these waters are unsurpassed, unapproachable."

The Sound region has a fine, fresh, clean climate, well washed both winter and summer with copious rains and swept with winds and clouds that come from the mountains and the sea. Every hidden nook in the depths of the woods is searched and refreshed, leaving no stagnant air; beaver meadows and lake-basins and low and willowy bogs, all are kept wholesome and sweet the year round. Cloud and sunshine alternate in bracing, cheering succession, and health and abundance follow the storms. The outer sea-margin is sublimely dashed and drenched with ocean brine, the spicy scud sweeping at times far inland over the bending woods, the giant trees waving and chanting in hearty accord as if surely enjoying it all.

Heavy, long-continued rains occur in the winter months. Then every leaf, bathed and brightened, rejoices. Filtering drops and currents through all the shaggy undergrowth of the woods go with tribute to the small streams, and these again to the larger. The rivers swell, but there are no devastating floods; for the thick felt of roots and mosses holds the abounding waters in check, stored in a thousand thousand fountains. Neither are there any violent hurricanes here. At least, I never have heard of any, nor have I come upon their tracks. Most of the streams are clear and cool always, for their waters are filtered through deep beds of mosses, and flow beneath shadows all the way to the sea. Only the streams from the glaciers are turbid and muddy. On the slopes of the mountains where they rush from their crystal caves, they carry not only small particles of rock-mud, worn off the sides and bottoms of the channels of the glaciers, but grains of sand and pebbles and large boulders tons in weight, rolling them forward on their way rumbling and bumping to their appointed places at the foot of steep slopes, to be built into rough bars and beds, while the smaller material is carried farther and outspread in flats, perhaps for coming wheatfields and gardens, the finest of it going out to sea, floating on the tides for weeks and months ere it finds rest on the bottom.

Snow seldom falls to any great depth on the lowlands, though it comes in glorious abundance on the mountains. And only on the mountains does the temperature fall much below the freezing-point. In the warmest summer weather a temperature of eighty-five degrees or even more occasionally is reached, but not for long at a time, as such heat is speedily followed by a breeze from the sea. The most charming days here are days of perfect calm, when all the winds are holding their breath and not a leaf stirs. Then the surface of the Sound shines like a silver mirror over all its vast extent, reflecting its lovely islands and shores; and long sheets of spangles flash and dance in the wake of every swimming seabird and boat. The sun, looking down on the tranquil landscape, seems conscious of the presence of every living thing on which he is pouring his blessings, while they in turn, with perhaps the exception of man, seem conscious of the presence of the sun as a benevolent father and stand hushed and waiting.

18

The Forests of Washington

WHEN we force our way into the depths of the forests, following any of the rivers back to their fountains, we find that the bulk of the woods is made up of the Douglas spruce (*Pseudotsuga Douglasii*), named in honor of David Douglas, an enthusiastic botanical explorer of early Hudson's Bay times. It is not only a very large tree but a very beautiful one, with lively bright-green drooping foliage, handsome pendent cones, and a shaft exquisitely straight and regular. For so large a tree it is astonishing how many find nourishment and space to grow on any given area. The magnificent shafts push their spires into the sky close together with as regular a growth as that of a well-tilled field of grain. And no ground has been better tilled for the growth of trees than that on which these forests are growing. For it has been thoroughly ploughed and rolled by the mighty glaciers from the mountains, and sifted and mellowed and outspread in beds hundreds of feet in depth by the broad streams that issued from their fronts at the time of their recession, after they had long covered all the land.

The largest tree of this species that I have myself measured was nearly twelve feet in diameter at a height of five feet from the ground, and, as near as I could make out under the circumstances, about three hundred feet in length. It stood near the head of the Sound not far from Olympia. I have seen a few others, both near the coast and thirty or forty miles back in the interior, that were from eight to ten feet in diameter, measured above their bulging insteps; and many from six to seven feet. I have heard of some that were said to be three hundred and twenty-five feet in height and fifteen feet in diameter, but none that I measured were so large, though it is not at all unlikely that such colossal giants do exist where conditions of soil and exposure are surpassingly favorable. The average size of all the trees of this species found up to an elevation on the mountain-slopes of, say, two thousand feet above sea-level, taking into account only what may be called mature trees two hundred and fifty to five hundred years of age, is perhaps, at a vague guess, not more than a height of one hundred and seventy-five or two hundred feet and a diameter of three feet; though, of course, throughout the richest sections the size is much greater.

In proportion to its weight when dry, the timber from this tree is perhaps stronger than that of any other conifer in the country. It is tough and durable and admirably adapted in every way for ship-building, piles, and heavy timber in general. But its hardness and liability to warp render it much inferior to white or sugar pine for fine work. In the lumber markets of California it is known as "Oregon pine" and is used almost exclusively for spars, bridge-timbers, heavy planking, and the framework of houses.

The same species extends northward in abundance through British Columbia and southward through the coast and middle regions of Oregon and California. It is also a common tree in the cañons and hollows of the Wahsatch Mountains in Utah, where it is called "red pine" and on portions of the Rocky Mountains and some of the short ranges of the Great Basin. Along the coast of California it keeps company with the redwood wherever it can find a favorable opening. On the western slope of the Sierra, with the yellow pine and incense cedar, it forms a pretty well-defined belt at a height of from three thousand to six thousand feet above the sea, and extends into the San Gabriel and San Bernardino Mountains in southern California. But, though widely distributed, it is only in these cool, moist northlands that it reaches its finest development, tall, straight, elastic, and free from limbs to an immense height, growing down to tide-water, where ships of the largest size may lie close alongside and load at the least possible cost.

Growing with the Douglas we find the white spruce, or "Sitka pine," as it is sometimes called. This also is a very beautiful and majestic tree, frequently attaining a height of two hundred feet or more and a diameter of five or six feet. It is very abundant in southeastern Alaska, forming the greater part of the best forests there. Here it is found mostly around the sides of beaver-dam and other meadows and on the borders of the streams, especially where the ground is low. One tree that I saw felled at the head of the Hop-Ranch meadows on the upper Snoqualmie River, though far from being the largest I have seen, measured a hundred and eighty feet in length and four and a half in diameter, and was two hundred and fifty-seven years of age.

In habit and general appearance it resembles the Douglas spruce, but it is somewhat less slender and the needles grow close together all around the branchlets and are so stiff and sharp-pointed on the younger branches that they cannot well be handled without gloves. The timber is tough, close-grained, white, and looks more like pine than any other of the spruces. It splits freely, makes excellent shingles, and in general use in house-building takes the place of pine. I have seen logs of this species a hundred feet long and two feet in diameter at the upper end. It was named in honor of the old Scotch botanist Archibald Menzies, who came to this coast with Vancouver in 1792.[1]

The beautiful hemlock spruce with its warm yellow-green foliage is also common in some portions of these woods. It is tall and slender and exceedingly graceful in habit before old age comes on, but the timber is inferior and is seldom used for any other than the roughest work, such as wharf-building.

The Western arbor-vitæ[2] (*Thuja gigantea*) grows to a size truly gigantic on low rich ground. Specimens ten feet in diameter and a hundred and forty feet high are not at all rare. Some that I have heard of are said to be fifteen and even eighteen feet thick. Clad in rich, glossy plumes, with gray lichens covering their smooth, tapering boles, perfect trees of this species are truly noble objects and well worthy the place they hold in these glorious forests. It is of this tree that the Indians make their fine canoes.

Of the other conifers that are so happy as to have place here, there are three firs, three or four pines, two cypresses, a yew, and another spruce, the *Abies Pattoniana*.[3] This last is perhaps the most beautiful of all the spruces, but, being comparatively small and growing only far back on the mountains, it receives but little attention from most people. Nor is there room in a work like this for anything like a complete description of it, or of the others I have just mentioned. Of the three firs, one (*Picea grandis*),[4] grows near the coast and is one of the largest trees in the forest, sometimes

[1] [This tree, now known to botanists as *Picea sitchensis*, was named *Abies Menziesii* by Lindley in 1833.]
[2] Also known as "canoe cedar," and described in Jepson's *Silva of California* under the more recent specific name *Thuja plicata*. [Editor.]
[3] Now classified as *Tsuga mertensiana* Sarg. [Editor.]
[4] Now *Abies grandis* Lindley. [Editor.]

attaining a height of two hundred and fifty feet. The timber, however, is inferior in quality and not much sought after while so much that is better is within reach. One of the others (*P. amabilis*, var. *nobilis*) forms magnificent forests by itself at a height of about three thousand to four thousand feet above the sea. The rich plushy, plumelike branches grow in regular whorls around the trunk, and on the topmost whorls, standing erect, are the large, beautiful cones. This is far the most beautiful of all the firs. In the Sierra Nevada it forms a considerable portion of the main forest belt on the western slope, and it is there that it reaches its greatest size and greatest beauty. The third species (*P. subalpina*) forms, together with *Abies Pattoniana*, the upper edge of the timber-line on the portion of the Cascades opposite the Sound. A thousand feet below the extreme limit of tree-growth it occurs in beautiful groups amid parklike openings where flowers grow in extravagant profusion.

The pines are nowhere abundant in the State. The largest, the yellow pine (*Pinus ponderosa*), occurs here and there on margins of dry gravelly prairies, and only in such situations have I yet seen it in this State. The others (*P. monticola* and *P. contorta*) are mostly restricted to the upper slopes of the mountains, and though the former of these two attains a good size and makes excellent lumber, it is mostly beyond reach at present and is not abundant. One of the cypresses (*Cupressus Lawsoniana*)[1] grows near the coast and is a fine large tree, clothed like the arbor-vitæ in a glorious wealth of flat, feathery branches. The other is found here and there well up toward the edge of the timber-line. This is the fine Alaska cedar (*C. Nootkatensis*), the lumber from which is noted for its

[1]*Chamœcyparis lawsoniana* Parl. (Port Orford cedar) in Jepson's *Silva*. [Editor.]

durability, fineness of grain, and beautiful yellow color, and for its fragrance, which resembles that of sandal-wood. The Alaska Indians make their canoe-paddles of it and weave matting and coarse cloth from the fibrous brown bark.

Among the different kinds of hardwood trees are the oak, maple, madroña, birch, alder, and wild apple, while large cottonwoods are common along the rivers and shores of the numerous lakes.

The most striking of these to the traveler is the Menzies arbutus, or madroña, as it is popularly called in California. Its curious red and yellow bark, large thick glossy leaves, and panicles of waxy-looking greenish-white urn-shaped flowers render it very conspicuous. On the boles of the younger trees and on all the branches, the bark is so smooth and seamless that it does not appear as bark at all, but rather the naked wood. The whole tree, with the exception of the larger part of the trunk, looks as though it had been thoroughly peeled. It is found sparsely scattered along the shores of the Sound and back in the forests also on open margins, where the soil is not too wet, and extends up the coast on Vancouver Island beyond Nanaimo. But in no part of the State does it reach anything like the size and beauty of proportions that it attains in California, few trees here being more than ten or twelve inches in diameter and thirty feet high. It is, however, a very remarkable-looking object, standing there like some lost or runaway native of the tropics, naked and painted, beside that dark mossy ocean of northland conifers. Not even a palm tree would seem more out of place here.

The oaks, so far as my observation has reached, seem to be most abundant and to grow largest on the islands of the San Juan and Whidbey Archipelago. One of the three species of maples that I have seen is only a bush that makes tangles on the banks of the rivers. Of the other two one is a small tree, crooked and moss-grown, holding out its leaves to catch the light that filters down through the close-set spires of the great spruces. It grows almost everywhere throughout the entire extent of the forest until the higher slopes of the mountains are reached, and produces a very picturesque and delightful effect; relieving the bareness of the great shafts of the evergreens, without being close enough in its growth to hide them wholly, or to cover the bright mossy carpet that is spread beneath all the dense parts of the woods.

The other species is also very picturesque and at the same time very large, the largest tree of its kind that I have ever seen anywhere. Not even in the great maple woods of Canada have I seen trees either as large or with so much striking, picturesque character. It is widely distributed throughout western Washington, but is never found scattered among the conifers in the dense woods. It keeps together mostly in magnificent groves by itself on the damp levels along the banks of streams or lakes where the ground is subject to overflow. In such situations it attains a height of seventy-five to a hundred feet and a diameter of four to eight feet. The trunk sends out large limbs toward its neighbors, laden with long drooping mosses beneath and rows of ferns on their upper surfaces, thus making a grand series of richly ornamented interlacing arches, with the leaves laid thick overhead, rendering the underwood spaces delightfully cool and open. Never have I seen a finer forest ceiling or a more picturesque one, while the floor, covered with tall ferns and rubus and thrown into hillocks by the bulging roots, matches it well. The largest of these maple groves that I have yet found is on the right bank of the Snoqualmie River, about a mile above the falls. The whole country hereabouts is picturesque, and interesting in many ways, and well worthy a visit by tourists passing through the Sound region, since it is now accessible by rail from Seattle.

Looking now at the forests in a comprehensive way, we find in passing through them again and again from the shores of the Sound to their upper limits, that some portions are much older than others, the trees much larger, and the ground beneath them strewn with immense trunks in every stage of decay, representing several generations of growth, everything about them giving the impression that these are indeed the "forests primeval," while in the younger portions, where the elevation of the ground is the same as to the sea-level and the species of trees are the same as well as the quality of the soil, apart from the moisture which it holds, the trees seem to be and are mostly of the same age, perhaps from one hundred to two or three hundred years, with no gray-bearded, venerable patriarchs—forming tall, majestic woods without any grandfathers.

When we examine the ground we find that it is as free from those mounds of brown crumbling wood and mossy ancient fragments as are the growing trees from very old ones. Then, perchance, we come upon a section farther up the slopes towards the mountains that has no trees more than fifty years old, or even fifteen or twenty years old. These last show plainly enough that they have been devastated by fire, as the black, melancholy monuments rising here and there above the young growth bear witness. Then, with this fiery, suggestive testimony, on examining those sections whose trees are a hundred years old or two hundred, we find the same fire-records, though heavily veiled with mosses and lichens, showing that a century or two ago the forests that stood there had been swept away in some tremendous fire at a time when rare conditions of drouth made their burning possible. Then, the bare ground sprinkled with the winged seeds from the edges of the burned district, a new forest sprang up, nearly every tree starting at the same time, or within a few years, thus producing the uniformity of size we find in such places; while, on the other hand, in those sections of ancient aspect containing very old trees both standing and fallen, we find no traces of fire, nor from the extreme dampness of the ground can we see any possibility of fire ever running there.

Fire, then, is the great governing agent in forest-distribution and to a great extent also in the conditions of forest-growth. Where fertile lands are very wet one half the year and very dry the other, there can be no forests at all. Where the ground is damp, with drouth occurring only at intervals of centuries, fine forests may be found, other conditions being favorable. But it is only where fires never run that truly ancient forests of pitchy coniferous trees may exist. When the Washington forests are seen from the deck of a ship out in the middle of the Sound, or even from the top of some high, commanding mountain, the woods seem everywhere perfectly solid. And so in fact they are in general found to be. The largest openings are those of the lakes and prairies, the smaller of beaver-meadows, bogs, and the rivers; none of them large enough to make a distinct mark in comprehensive views.

Of the lakes there are said to be some thirty in King's County alone; the largest, Lake Washington, being twenty-six miles long and four miles wide. Another, which enjoys the duckish name of

The Forests of Washington

Lake Squak, is about ten miles long. Both are pure and beautiful, lying imbedded in the green wilderness. The rivers are numerous and are but little affected by the weather, flowing with deep, steady currents the year round. They are short, however, none of them drawing their sources from beyond the Cascade Range. Some are navigable for small steamers on their lower courses, but the openings they make in the woods are very narrow, the tall trees on their banks leaning over in some places, making fine shady tunnels.

The largest of the prairies that I have seen lies to the south of Tacoma on the line of the Portland and Tacoma Railroad. The ground is dry and gravelly, a deposit of water-washed cobbles and pebbles derived from moraines—conditions which readily explain the absence of trees here and on other prairies adjacent to Yelm. Berries grow in lavish abundance, enough for man and beast with thousands of tons to spare. The woods are full of them, especially about the borders of the waters and meadows where the sunshine may enter. Nowhere in the north does Nature set a more bountiful table. There are huckleberries of many species, red, blue, and black, some of them growing close to the ground, others on bushes eight to ten feet high; also salal berries, growing on a low, weak-stemmed bush, a species of gaultheria, seldom more than a foot or two high. This has pale pea-green glossy leaves two or three inches long and half an inch wide and beautiful pink flowers, urn-shaped, that make a fine, rich show. The berries are black when ripe, are extremely abundant, and, with the huckleberries, form an important part of the food of the Indians, who beat them into paste, dry them, and store them away for winter use, to be eaten with their oily fish. The salmon-berry also is very plentiful, growing in dense prickly tangles. The flowers are as large as wild roses and of the same color, and the berries measure nearly an inch in diameter. Besides these there are gooseberries, currants, raspberries, blackberries, and, in some favored spots, strawberries. The mass of the underbrush of the woods is made up in great part of these berry-bearing bushes, together with white-flowered spiræa twenty feet high, hazel, dogwood, wild rose, honeysuckle, symphoricarpus, etc. But in the depths of the woods, where little sunshine can reach the ground, there is but little underbrush of any kind, only a very light growth of huckleberry and rubus and young maples in most places. The difficulties encountered by the explorer in penetrating the wilderness are presented mostly by the streams and bogs, with their tangled margins, and the fallen timber and thick carpet of moss covering all the ground.

Notwithstanding the tremendous energy displayed in lumbering and the grand scale on which it is being carried on, and the number of settlers pushing into every opening in search of farmlands, the woods of Washington are still almost entirely virgin and wild, without trace of human touch, savage or civilized. Indians, no doubt, have ascended most of the rivers on their way to the mountains to hunt the wild sheep and goat to obtain wool for their clothing, but with food in abundance on the coast they had little to tempt them into the wilderness, and the monuments they have left in it are scarcely more conspicuous than those of squirrels and bears; far less so than those of the beavers, which in damming the streams have made clearings and meadows which will continue to mark the landscape for centuries. Nor is there much in these woods to tempt the farmer or cattle-raiser. A few settlers established homes on the prairies or open borders of the woods and in the valleys of the Chehalis and Cowlitz before the gold days of California. Most of the early immigrants from the Eastern States, however, settled in the fertile and open Willamette Valley of Oregon. Even now, when the search for land is so keen, with the exception of the bottom lands around the Sound and on the lower reaches of the rivers, there are comparatively few spots of cultivation in western Washington. On every meadow or opening of any kind some one will be found keeping cattle, planting hop-vines, or raising hay, vegetables, and patches of grain. All the large spaces available, even back near the summits of the Cascade Mountains, were occupied long ago. The newcomers, building their cabins where the beavers once built theirs, keep a few cows and industriously seek to enlarge their small meadow patches by chopping, girdling, and burning the edge of the encircling forest, gnawing like beavers, and scratching for a living among the blackened stumps and logs, regarding the trees as their greatest enemies—a sort of larger pernicious weed immensely difficult to get rid of.

But all these are as yet mere spots, making no visible scar in the distance and leaving the grand stretches of the forest as wild as they were before the discovery of the continent. For many years the axe has been busy around the shores of the Sound and chips have been falling in perpetual storm like flakes of snow. The best of the timber has been cut for a distance of eight or ten miles from the water and to a much greater distance along the streams deep enough to float the logs. Railroads, too, have been built to fetch in the logs from the best bodies of timber otherwise inaccessible except at great cost. None of the ground, however, has been completely denuded. Most of the young trees have been left, together with the hemlocks and other trees undesirable in kind or in some way defective, so that the neighboring trees appear to have closed over the gaps made by the removal of the larger and better ones, maintaining the general continuity of the forest and leaving no sign on the sylvan sea, at least as seen from a distance.

In felling the trees they cut them off usually at a height of six to twelve feet above the ground, so as to avoid cutting through the swollen base, where the diameter is so much greater. In order to reach this height the chopper cuts a notch about two inches wide and three or four deep and drives a board into it, on which he stands while at work. In case the first notch, cut as high as he can reach, is not high enough, he stands on the board that has been driven into the first notch and cuts another. Thus the axeman may often be seen at work standing eight or ten feet above the ground. If the tree is so large that with his long-handled axe the chopper is unable to reach to the farther side of it, then a second chopper is set to work, each cutting halfway across. And when the tree is about to fall, warned by the faint crackling of the strained fibers, they jump to the ground, and stand back out of danger from flying limbs, while the noble giant that had stood erect in glorious strength and beauty century after century, bows low at last and with gasp and groan and booming throb falls to earth.

Then with long saws the trees are cut into logs of the required length, peeled, loaded upon wagons capable of carrying a weight of eight or ten tons, hauled by a long string of oxen to the nearest available stream or railroad, and floated or carried to the Sound. There the logs are gathered into booms and towed by steamers to the mills, where workmen with steel spikes in their boots leap lightly with easy poise from one to another and by means of long pike-poles push them apart and, selecting such as are at the time required, push them to the foot of a chute and drive dogs into the ends, when they are speedily hauled in by the mill machinery alongside the saw-carriage and placed and fixed in position. Then with sounds of greedy hissing and growling they are rushed back and forth like enormous shuttles, and in an incredibly short time they are lumber and are aboard the ships lying at the mill wharves.

Many of the long, slender boles so abundant in these woods are saved for spars, and so excellent is their quality that they are in demand in almost every shipyard of the world. Thus these trees, felled and stripped of their leaves and branches, are raised again, transplanted and set firmly erect, given roots of iron and a new foliage of flapping canvas, and sent to sea. On they speed in glad, free motion, cheerily waving over the blue, heaving water, responsive to the same winds that rocked them when they stood at home in the woods. After standing in one place all their lives they now, like sight-seeing tourists, go round the world, meeting many a relative from the old home forest, some like themselves, wandering free, clad in broad canvas foliage, others planted head downward in mud, holding wharf platforms aloft to receive the wares of all nations.

The mills of Puget Sound and those of the redwood region of California are said to be the largest and most effective lumber-makers in the world. Tacoma alone claims to have eleven sawmills, and Seattle about as many; while at many other points on the Sound, where the conditions are particularly favorable, there are immense lumbering establishments, as at Ports Blakely, Madison, Discovery, Gamble, Ludlow, etc., with a capacity all together of over three million feet a day. Nevertheless, the observer coming up the Sound sees not nor hears anything of this fierce storm of steel that is devouring the forests, save perhaps the shriek of some whistle or the columns of smoke that mark the position of the mills. All else seems as serene and unscathed as the silent watching mountains.

19

People and Towns of Puget Sound

As one strolls in the woods about the logging-camps, most of the lumbermen are found to be interesting people to meet, kind and obliging and sincere, full of knowledge concerning the bark and sapwood and heartwood of the trees they cut, and how to fell them without unnecessary breakage, on ground where they may be most advantageously sawed into logs and loaded for removal. The work is hard, and all of the older men have a tired, somewhat haggard appearance. Their faces are doubtful in color, neither sickly nor quite healthy-looking, and seamed with deep wrinkles like the bark of the spruces, but with no trace of anxiety. Their clothing is full of rosin and never wears out. A little of everything in the woods is stuck fast to these loggers, and their trousers grow constantly thicker with age. In all their movements and gestures they are heavy and deliberate like the trees above them, and they walk with a swaying, rocking gait altogether free from quick, jerky fussiness, for chopping and log-rolling have quenched all that. They are also slow of speech, as if partly out of breath, and when one tries to draw them out on some subject away from logs, all the fresh, leafy, outreaching branches of the mind seem to have been withered and killed with fatigue, leaving their lives little more than dry lumber. Many a tree have these old axemen felled, but, round-shouldered and stooping, they too are beginning to lean over. Many of their companions are already beneath the moss, and among those that we see at work some are now dead at the top (bald), leafless, so to speak, and tottering to their fall.

A very different man, seen now and then at long intervals but usually invisible, is the free roamer of the wilderness—hunter, prospector, explorer, seeking he knows not what. Lithe and sinewy, he walks erect, making his way with the skill of wild animals, all his senses in action, watchful and alert, looking keenly at everything in sight, his imagination well nourished in the wealth of the wilderness, coming into contact with free nature in a thousand forms, drinking at the fountains of things, responsive to wild influences, as trees to the winds. Well he knows the wild animals his neighbors, what fishes are in the streams, what birds in the forests, and where food may be found. Hungry at times and weary, he has corresponding enjoyment in eating and resting, and all the wilderness is home. Some of these rare, happy rovers die alone among the leaves. Others half settle down and change in part into farmers; each, making choice of some fertile spot where the landscape attracts him, builds a small cabin, where, with few wants to supply from garden or field, he hunts and farms in turn, going perhaps once a year to the settlements, until night begins to draw near, and, like forest shadows, thickens into darkness and his day is done. In these Washington wilds, living alone, all sorts of men may perchance be found—poets, philosophers, and even full-blown transcendentalists, though you may go far to find them.

Indians are seldom to be met with away from the Sound, excepting about the few outlying hop-ranches, to which they resort in great numbers during the picking-season. Nor in your walks in the woods will you be likely to see many of the wild animals, however far you may go, with the exception of the Douglas squirrel and the mountain goat. The squirrel is everywhere, and the goat you can hardly fail to find if you climb any of the high mountains. The deer, once very abundant, may still be found on the islands and along the shores of the Sound, but the large gray wolves render their existence next to impossible at any considerable distance back in the woods of the mainland, as they can easily run them down unless they are near enough to the coast to make their escape by plunging into the water and swimming to the islands off shore. The elk and perhaps also the moose still exist in the most remote and inaccessible solitudes of the forest, but their numbers have been greatly reduced of late, and even the most experienced hunters have difficulty in finding them. Of bears there are two species, the black and the large brown, the former by far the more common of the two. On the shaggy bottom-lands where berries are plentiful, and along the rivers while salmon are going up to spawn, the black bear may be found, fat and at home. Many are killed every year, both for their flesh and skins. The large brown species likes higher and opener ground. He is a dangerous animal, a near relative of the famous grizzly, and wise hunters are very fond of letting him alone.

The towns of Puget Sound are of a very lively, progressive, and aspiring kind, fortunately with abundance of substance about them to warrant their ambition and make them grow. Like young sapling sequoias, they are sending out their roots far and near for nourishment, counting confidently on longevity and grandeur of stature. Seattle and Tacoma are at present far in the lead of all others in the race for supremacy, and these two are keen, active rivals, to all appearances well matched. Tacoma occupies near the head of the Sound a site of great natural beauty. It is the terminus of the Northern Pacific Railroad, and calls itself the "City of Destiny." Seattle is also charmingly located about twenty miles down the Sound from Tacoma, on Elliott Bay. It is the terminus of the Seattle, Lake-Shore, and Eastern Railroad, now in process of construction, and calls itself the "Queen City of the Sound" and the "Metropolis of Washington." What the populations of these towns number I am not able to say with anything like exactness. They are probably about the same size and they each claim to have about twenty thousand people; but their figures are so rapidly changing, and so often mixed up with counts that refer to the future that exact measurements of either of these places are about as hard to obtain as measurements of the clouds of a growing storm. Their edges run back for miles into the woods among the trees and stumps and brush which hide a good many of the houses and the stakes which mark the lots; so that, without being as yet very large towns, they seem to fade away into the distance.

But, though young and loose-jointed, they are fast taking on the forms and manners of old cities, putting on airs, as some would say, like boys in haste to be men. They are already towns "with all modern improvements, first-class in every particular," as is said of hotels. They have electric motors and lights, paved broadways and boulevards, substantial business blocks, schools, churches, factories, and foundries. The lusty, titanic clang of boiler-making may be heard there, and plenty of the languid music of pianos mingling with the babel noises of commerce carried on in a hundred tongues. The main streets are crowded with bright, wide-awake lawyers, ministers, merchants, agents for everything under the sun; ox-drivers and loggers in stiff, gummy overalls; back-slanting dudes, well-tailored and shiny; and fashions and bonnets of every feather and color bloom gayly in the noisy throng and advertise London and Paris. Vigorous life and strife are to be seen everywhere. The spirit of progress is in the air. Still it is hard to realize how much good work is being done here of a kind that makes for civilization—the enthusiastic, exulting energy displayed in the building of new towns, railroads, and mills, in the opening of mines of coal and iron, and the development of natural resources in general. To many, especially in the Atlantic States, Washington is hardly known at all. It is regarded as being yet a far wild west—a dim, nebulous expanse of woods—by those who do not know that railroads and steamers have brought the country out of the wilderness and abolished the old distances. It is now near to all the world and is in possession of a share of the best of all that civilization has to offer, while on some of the lines of advancement it is at the front.

Notwithstanding the sharp rivalry between different sections and towns, the leading men mostly pull together for the general good and glory,—building, buying, borrowing, to push the country to its place; keeping arithmetic busy in counting population present and to come, ships, towns, factories, tons of coal and iron, feet of lumber, miles of railroad,—Americans, Scandinavians, Irish, Scotch, and Germans being joined together in the white heat of work like religious crowds in time of revival who have forgotten sectarianism. It is a fine thing to see people in hot earnest about anything; therefore, however extravagant and high the brag ascending from Puget Sound, in most cases it is likely to appear pardonable and more.

Seattle was named after an old Indian chief who lived in this part of the Sound. He was very proud of the honor and lived long enough to lead his grandchildren about the streets. The greater part of the lower business portion of the town, including a long stretch of wharves and warehouses built on piles, was destroyed by fire a few months ago,[1] with immense loss. The people, however, are in no wise discouraged, and ere long the loss will be gain, inasmuch as a better class of buildings, chiefly of brick, are being erected in place of the inflammable wooden ones, which, with comparatively few exceptions, were built of pitchy spruce.

With their own scenery so glorious ever on show, one would at first thought suppose that these happy Puget Sound people would never go sightseeing from home like less favored mortals. But they do all the same. Some go boating on the Sound or on the lakes and rivers, or with their families make excursions at small cost on the steamers. Others will take the train to the Franklin and Newcastle or Carbon River coal-mines for the sake of the thirty- or forty-mile rides through the woods, and a look into the black depths of the underworld. Others again take the steamers for Victoria, Fraser River, or Vancouver, the new ambitious town at the terminus of the Canadian Railroad, thus getting views of the outer world in a near foreign country. One of the regular summer resorts of this region where people go for fishing, hunting, and the healing of diseases is the Green River Hot Springs, in the Cascade Mountains, sixty-one miles east of Tacoma, on the line of the Northern Pacific Railroad. Green River is a small rocky stream with picturesque banks, and derives its name from the beautiful pale-green hue of its waters.

Among the most interesting of all the summer rest and pleasure places is the famous "Hop Ranch" on the upper Snoqualmie

[1]1889.

River, thirty or forty miles eastward from Seattle. Here the dense forest opens, allowing fine free views of the adjacent mountains from a long stretch of ground which is half meadow, half prairie, level and fertile, and beautifully diversified with outstanding groves of spruces and alders and rich flowery fringes of spiræa and wild roses, the river meandering deep and tranquil through the midst of it. On the portions most easily cleared some three hundred acres of hop-vines have been planted and are now in full bearing, yielding, it is said, at the rate of about a ton of hops to the acre. They are a beautiful crop, these vines of the north, pillars of verdure in regular rows, seven feet apart and eight or ten feet in height; the long, vigorous shoots sweeping round in fine, wild freedom, and the light, leafy cones hanging in loose, handsome clusters.

Perhaps enough of hops might be raised in Washington for the wants of all the world, but it would be impossible to find pickers to handle the crop. Most of the picking is done by Indians, and to this fine, clean, profitable work they come in great numbers in their canoes, old and young, of many different tribes, bringing wives and children and household goods, in some cases from a distance of five or six hundred miles, even from far Alaska. Then they too grow rich and spend their money on red cloth and trinkets. About a thousand Indians are required as pickers at the Snoqualmie ranch alone, and a lively and merry picture they make in the field, arrayed in bright, showy calicoes, lowering the rustling vine-pillars with incessant song-singing and fun. Still more striking are their queer camps on the edges of the fields or over on the river-bank, with the firelight shining on their wild, jolly faces. But woe to the ranch should fire-water get there!

But the chief attractions here are not found in the hops, but in trout-fishing and bear-hunting, and in the two fine falls on the river. Formerly the trip from Seattle was a hard one, over corduroy roads; now it is reached in a few hours by rail along the shores of Lake Washington and Lake Squak, through a fine sample section of the forest and past the brow of the main Snoqualmie Fall. From the hotel at the ranch village the road to the fall leads down the right bank of the river through the magnificent maple woods I have mentioned elsewhere, and fine views of the fall may be had on that side, both from above and below. It is situated on the main river, where it plunges over a sheer precipice, about two hundred and forty feet high, in leaving the level meadows of the ancient lake-basin. In a general way it resembles the well-known Nevada Fall in Yosemite, having the same twisted appearance at the top and the free plunge in numberless comet-shaped masses into a deep pool seventy-five or eighty yards in diameter. The pool is of considerable depth, as is shown by the radiating well-beaten foam and mist, which is of a beautiful rose color at times, of exquisite fineness of tone, and by the heavy waves that lash the rocks in front of it.

Though to a Californian the height of this fall would not seem great, the volume of water is heavy, and all the surroundings are delightful. The maple forest, of itself worth a long journey, the beauty of the river-reaches above and below, and the views down the valley afar over the mighty forests, with all its lovely trimmings of ferns and flowers, make this one of the most interesting falls I have ever seen. The upper fall is about seventy-five feet high, with bouncing rapids at head and foot, set in a romantic dell thatched with dripping mosses and ferns and embowered in dense evergreens and blooming bushes, the distance to it from the upper end of the meadows being about eight miles. The road leads through majestic woods with ferns ten feet high beneath some of the thickets, and across a gravelly plain deforested by fire many years ago. Orange lilies are plentiful, and handsome shining mats of the kinnikinic, sprinkled with bright scarlet berries.

From a place called "Hunt's," at the end of the wagon-road, a trail leads through lush, dripping woods (never dry) to Thuja and Mertens, Menzies, and Douglas spruces. The ground is covered with the best moss-work of the moist lands of the north, made up mostly of the various species of hypnum, with some liverworts, marchantia, jungermannia, etc., in broad sheets and bosses, where never a dust-particle floated, and where all the flowers, fresh with mist and spray, are wetter than water-lilies. The pool at the foot of the fall is a place surpassingly lovely to look at, with the enthusiastic rush and song of the falls, the majestic trees overhead leaning over the brink like listeners eager to catch every word of the white refreshing waters, the delicate maidenhairs and aspleniums with fronds outspread gathering the rainbow sprays, and the myriads of hooded mosses, every cup fresh and shining.

20

An Ascent of Mount Rainier

AMBITIOUS climbers, seeking adventures and opportunities to test their strength and skill, occasionally attempt to penetrate the wilderness on the west side of the Sound, and push on to the summit of Mount Olympus. But the grandest excursion of all to be made hereabouts is to Mount Rainier, to climb to the top of its icy crown. The mountain is very high,[1] fourteen thousand four hundred feet, and laden with glaciers that are terribly roughened and interrupted by crevasses and ice-cliffs. Only good climbers should attempt to gain the summit, led by a guide of proved nerve and endurance. A good trail has been cut through the woods to the base of the mountain on the north; but the summit of the mountain never has been reached from this side, though many brave attempts have been made upon it.

Last summer I gained the summit from the south side, in a day and a half from the timber-line, without encountering any desperate obstacles that could not in some way be passed in good weather. I was accompanied by Keith, the artist, Professor Ingraham, and five ambitious young climbers from Seattle. We were led

---

[1] A careful re-determination of the height of Rainier, made by Professor A. G. McAdie in 1905, gave an altitude of 13,394 feet. The Standard Dictionary wrongly describes it as "the highest peak (13,363 feet) within the United States." The United States Baedeker and railroad literature overstate its altitude by more than a hundred feet. [Editor.]

An Ascent of Mount Rainier

by the veteran mountaineer and guide Van Trump, of Yelm, who many years before guided General Stevens in his memorable ascent, and later Mr. Bailey, of Oakland. With a cumbersome abundance of campstools and blankets we set out from Seattle, traveling by rail as far as Yelm Prairie, on the Tacoma and Oregon road. Here we made our first camp and arranged with Mr. Longmire, a farmer in the neighborhood, for pack and saddle animals. The noble King Mountain was in full view from here, glorifying the bright, sunny day with his presence, rising in godlike majesty over the woods, with the magnificent prairie as a foreground. The distance to the mountain from Yelm in a straight line is perhaps fifty miles; but by the mule and yellow-jacket trail we had to follow it is a hundred miles. For, notwithstanding a portion of this trail runs in the air, where the wasps work hardest, it is far from being an airline as commonly understood.

By night of the third day we reached the Soda Springs on the right bank of the Nisqually, which goes roaring by, gray with mud, gravel, and boulders from the caves of the glaciers of Rainier, now close at hand. The distance from the Soda Springs to the Camp of the Clouds is about ten miles. The first part of the way lies up the Nisqually Cañon, the bottom of which is flat in some places and the walls very high and precipitous, like those of the Yosemite Valley. The upper part of the cañon is still occupied by one of the Nisqually glaciers, from which this branch of the river draws its source, issuing from a cave in the gray, rock-strewn snout. About a mile below the glacier we had to ford the river, which caused some anxiety, for the current is very rapid and carried forward large boulders as well as lighter material, while its savage roar is bewildering.

At this point we left the cañon, climbing out of it by a steep zigzag up the old lateral moraine of the glacier, which was deposited when the present glacier flowed past at this height, and is about eight hundred feet high. It is now covered with a superb growth of *Picea amabilis;*[1] so also is the corresponding portion of the right lateral. From the top of the moraine, still ascending, we passed for a mile or two through a forest of mixed growth, mainly silver fir, Patton spruce, and mountain pine, and then came to the charming park region, at an elevation of about five thousand feet above sealevel. Here the vast continuous woods at length begin to give way under the dominion of climate, though still at this height retaining their beauty and giving no sign of stress of storm, sweeping upward in belts of varying width, composed mainly of one species of fir, sharp and spiry in form, leaving smooth, spacious parks, with here and there separate groups of trees standing out in the midst of the openings like islands in a lake. Every one of these parks, great and small, is a garden filled knee-deep with fresh, lovely flowers of every hue, the most luxuriant and the most extravagantly beautiful of all the alpine gardens I ever beheld in all my mountain-top wanderings.

We arrived at the Cloud Camp at noon, but no clouds were in sight, save a few gauzy ornamental wreaths adrift in the sunshine. Out of the forest at last there stood the mountain, wholly unveiled, awful in bulk and majesty, filling all the view like a separate, newborn world, yet withal so fine and so beautiful it might well fire the dullest observer to desperate enthusiasm. Long we gazed in silent admiration, buried in tall daisies and anemones by the side of a snowbank. Higher we could not go with the animals

---

[1] Doubtless the red silver fir, now classified as *Abies amabilis*. [Editor.]

and find food for them and wood for our own camp-fires, for just beyond this lies the region of ice, with only here and there an open spot on the ridges in the midst of the ice, with dwarf alpine plants, such as saxifrages and drabas, which reach far up between the glaciers, and low mats of the beautiful bryanthus, while back of us were the gardens and abundance of everything that heart could wish. Here we lay all the afternoon, considering the lilies and the lines of the mountains with reference to a way to the summit.

At noon next day we left camp and began our long climb. We were in light marching order, save one who pluckily determined to carry his camera to the summit. At night, after a long easy climb over wide and smooth fields of ice, we reached a narrow ridge, at an elevation of about ten thousand feet above the sea, on the divide between the glaciers of the Nisqually and the Cowlitz. Here we lay as best we could, waiting for another day, without fire of course, as we were now many miles beyond the timber-line and without much to cover us. After eating a little hardtack, each of us leveled a spot to lie on among lava-blocks and cinders. The night was cold, and the wind coming down upon us in stormy surges drove gritty ashes and fragments of pumice about our ears while chilling to the bone. Very short and shallow was our sleep that night; but day dawned at last, early rising was easy, and there was nothing about breakfast to cause any delay. About four o'clock we were off, and climbing began in earnest. We followed up the ridge on which we had spent the night, now along its crest, now on either side, or on the ice leaning against it, until we came to where it becomes massive and precipitous. Then we were compelled to crawl along a seam or narrow shelf, on its face, which we traced to its termination in the base of the great ice-cap. From this point all the climbing was over ice, which was here desperately steep but fortunately was at the same time carved into innumerable spikes and pillars which afforded good footholds, and we crawled cautiously on, warm with ambition and exercise.

At length, after gaining the upper extreme of our guiding ridge, we found a good place to rest and prepare ourselves to scale the dangerous upper curves of the dome. The surface almost everywhere was bare, hard, snowless ice, extremely slippery; and, though smooth in general, it was interrupted by a network of yawning crevasses, outspread like lines of defense against any attempt to win the summit. Here every one of the party took off his shoes and drove stout steel caulks about half an inch long into them, having brought tools along for the purpose, and not having made use of them until now so that the points might not get dulled on the rocks ere the smooth, dangerous ice was reached. Besides being well shod each carried an alpenstock, and for special difficulties we had a hundred feet of rope and an axe.

Thus prepared, we stepped forth afresh, slowly groping our way through tangled lines of crevasses, crossing on snow bridges here and there after cautiously testing them, jumping at narrow places, or crawling around the ends of the largest, bracing well at every point with our alpenstocks and setting our spiked shoes squarely down on the dangerous slopes. It was nerve-trying work, most of it, but we made good speed nevertheless, and by noon all stood together on the utmost summit, save one who, his strength failing for a time, came up later.

We remained on the summit nearly two hours, looking about us at the vast maplike views, comprehending hundreds of miles of the Cascade Range, with their black interminable forests and white

An Ascent of Mount Rainier

volcanic cones in glorious array reaching far into Oregon; the Sound region also, and the great plains of eastern Washington, hazy and vague in the distance. Clouds began to gather. Soon of all the land only the summits of the mountains, St. Helen's, Adams, and Hood, were left in sight, forming islands in the sky. We found two well-formed and well-preserved craters on the summit, lying close together like two plates on a table with their rims touching. The highest point of the mountain is located between the craters, where their edges come in contact. Sulphurous fumes and steam issue from several vents, giving out a sickening smell that can be detected at a considerable distance. The unwasted condition of these craters, and, indeed, to a great extent, of the entire mountain, would tend to show that Rainier is still a comparatively young mountain. With the exception of the projecting lips of the craters and the top of a subordinate summit a short distance to the northward, the mountain is solidly capped with ice all around; and it is this ice-cap which forms the grand central fountain whence all the twenty glaciers of Rainier flow, radiating in every direction.

The descent was accomplished without disaster, though several of the party had narrow escapes. One slipped and fell, and as he shot past me seemed to be going to certain death. So steep was the ice-slope no one could move to help him, but fortunately, keeping his presence of mind, he threw himself on his face and digging his alpenstock into the ice, gradually retarded his motion until he came to rest. Another broke through a slim bridge over a crevasse, but his momentum at the time carried him against the lower edge and only his alpenstock was lost in the abyss. Thus crippled by the loss of his staff, we had to lower him the rest of the way down the dome by means of the rope we carried. Falling rocks from the upper precipitous part of the ridge were also a source of danger, as they came whizzing past in successive volleys; but none told on us, and when we at length gained the gentle slopes of the lower ice-fields, we ran and slid at our ease, making fast, glad time, all care and danger past, and arrived at our beloved Cloud Camp before sundown.

We were rather weak from want of nourishment, and some suffered from sunburn, notwithstanding the partial protection of glasses and veils; otherwise, all were unscathed and well. The view we enjoyed from the summit could hardly be surpassed in sublimity and grandeur; but one feels far from home so high in the sky, so much so that one is inclined to guess that, apart from the acquisition of knowledge and the exhilaration of climbing, more pleasure is to be found at the foot of mountains than on their frozen tops. Doubly happy, however, is the man to whom lofty mountain-tops are within reach, for the lights that shine there illumine all that lies below.

21

The Physical and Climatic Characteristics of Oregon

OREGON is a large, rich, compact section of the west side of the continent, containing nearly a hundred thousand square miles of deep, wet evergreen woods, fertile valleys, icy mountains, and high, rolling, wind-swept plains, watered by the majestic Columbia River and its countless branches. It is bounded on the north by Washington, on the east by Idaho, on the south by California and Nevada, and on the west by the Pacific Ocean. It is a grand, hearty, wholesome, foodful wilderness and, like Washington, once a part of the Oregon Territory, abounds in bold, far-reaching contrasts as to scenery, climate, soil, and productions. Side by side there is drouth on a grand scale and overflowing moisture; flinty, sharply cut lava-beds, gloomy and forbidding, and smooth, flowery lawns; cool bogs, exquisitely plushy and soft, overshadowed by jagged crags barren as icebergs; forests seemingly boundless and plains with no tree in sight; presenting a wide range of conditions, but as a whole favorable to industry. Natural wealth of an available kind abounds nearly everywhere, inviting the farmer, the stockraiser, the lumberman, the fisherman, the manufacturer, and the miner, as well as the free walker in search of knowledge and wildness. The scenery is mostly of a comfortable, assuring kind, grand and inspiring without too much of that dreadful overpowering sublimity and exuberance which tend to discourage effort and cast people into inaction and superstition.

Ever since Oregon was first heard of in the romantic, adventurous, hunting, trapping Wild West days, it seems to have been regarded as the most attractive and promising of all the Pacific countries for farmers. While yet the whole region as well as the way to it was wild, ere a single road or bridge was built, undaunted by the trackless thousand-mile distances and scalping, cattle-stealing Indians, long trains of covered wagons began to crawl wearily westward, crossing how many plains, rivers, ridges, and mountains, fighting the painted savages and weariness and famine. Setting out from the frontier of the old West in the spring as soon as the grass would support their cattle, they pushed on up the Platte, making haste slowly, however, that they might not be caught in the storms of winter ere they reached the promised land. They crossed the Rocky Mountains to Fort Hall; thence followed down the Snake River for three or four hundred miles, their cattle limping and failing on the rough lava plains; swimming the streams too deep to be forded, making boats out of wagon-boxes for the women and children and goods, or where trees could be had, lashing together logs for rafts. Thence, crossing the Blue Mountains and the plains of the Columbia, they followed the river to the Dalles. Here winter would be upon them, and before a wagon-road was built across the Cascade Mountains the toil-worn emigrants would be compelled to leave their cattle and wagons until the following summer, and, in the mean time, with the assistance of the Hudson's Bay Company, make their way to the Willamette Valley on the river with rafts and boats.

How strange and remote these trying times have already become! They are now dim as if a thousand years had passed over them. Steamships and locomotives with magical influence have well-nigh abolished the old distances and dangers, and brought forward the New West into near and familiar companionship with the rest of the world.

Purely wild for unnumbered centuries, a paradise of oily, salmon-fed Indians, Oregon is now roughly settled in part and surveyed, its rivers and mountains-ranges, lakes, valleys, and plains have been traced and mapped in a general way, civilization is beginning to take root, towns are springing up and flourishing vigorously like a crop adapted to the soil, and the whole kindly wilderness lies invitingly near with all its wealth open and ripe for use.

In sailing along the Oregon coast one sees but few more signs of human occupation than did Juan de Fuca three centuries ago. The shore bluffs rise abruptly from the waves, forming a wall apparently unbroken, though many short rivers from the coast range of mountains and two from the interior have made narrow openings on their way to the sea. At the mouths of these rivers good harbors have been discovered for coasting vessels, which are of great importance to the lumbermen, dairymen, and farmers of the coast region. But little or nothing of these appear in general views, only a simple gray wall nearly straight, green along the top, and the forest stretching back into the mountains as far as the eye can reach.

Going ashore, we find few long reaches of sand where one may saunter, or meadows, save the brown and purple meadows of the sea, overgrown with slippery kelp, swashed and swirled in the restless breakers. The abruptness of the shore allows the massive waves that have come from far over the broad Pacific to get close to the bluffs ere they break, and the thundering shock shakes the rocks to their foundations. No calm comes to these shores. Even in the finest weather, when the ships off shore are becalmed and their sails hang loose against the mast, there is always a wreath of foam at the base of these bluffs. The breakers are ever in bloom and crystal brine is ever in the air.

A scramble along the Oregon sea-bluffs proves as richly exciting to lovers of wild beauty as heart could wish. Here are three hundred miles of pictures of rock and water in black and white, or gray and white, with more or less of green and yellow, purple and blue. The rocks, glistening in sunshine and foam, are never wholly dry—many of them marvels of wave-sculpture and most imposing in bulk and bearing, standing boldly forward, monuments of a thousand storms, types of permanence, holding the homes and places of refuge of multitudes of seafaring animals in their keeping, yet ever wasting away. How grand the songs of the waves about them, every wave a fine, hearty storm in itself, taking its rise on the breezy plains of the sea, perhaps thousands of miles away, traveling with majestic, slow-heaving deliberation, reaching the end of its journey, striking its blow, bursting into a mass of white and pink bloom, then falling spent and withered to give place to the next in the endless procession, thus keeping up the glorious show and glorious song through all times and seasons forever!

Terribly impressive as is this cliff and wave scenery when the skies are bright and kindly sunshine makes rainbows in the spray, it is doubly so in dark, stormy nights, when, crouching in some hollow on the top of some jutting headland, we may gaze and listen undisturbed in the heart of it. Perhaps now and then we may dimly see the tops of the highest breakers, looking ghostly in the gloom;

but when the water happens to be phosphorescent, as it oftentimes is, then both the sea and the rocks are visible, and the wild, exulting, up-dashing spray burns, every particle of it, and is combined into one glowing mass of white fire; while back in the woods and along the bluffs and crags of the shore the storm-wind roars, and the rain-floods, gathering strength and coming from far and near, rush wildly down every gulch to the sea, as if eager to join the waves in their grand, savage harmony; deep calling unto deep in the heart of the great, dark night, making a sight and a song unspeakably sublime and glorious.

In the pleasant weather of summer, after the rainy season is past and only occasional refreshing showers fall, washing the sky and bringing out the fragrance of the flowers and the evergreens, then one may enjoy a fine, free walk all the way across the State from the sea to the eastern boundary on the Snake River. Many a beautiful stream we should cross in such a walk, singing through forest and meadow and deep rocky gorge, and many a broad prairie and plain, mountain and valley, wild garden and desert, presenting landscape beauty on a grand scale and in a thousand forms, and new lessons without number, delightful to learn. Oregon has three mountain-ranges which run nearly parallel with the coast, the most influential of which, in every way, is the Cascade Range. It is about six thousand to seven thousand feet in average height, and divides the State into two main sections called eastern and western Oregon, corresponding with the main divisions of Washington; while these are again divided, but less perfectly, by the Blue Mountains and the Coast Range. The eastern section is about two hundred and thirty miles wide, and is made up in great part of the treeless plains of the Columbia, which are green and flowery in spring, but gray, dusty, hot, and forbidding in summer. Considerable areas, however, on these plains, as well as some of the valleys countersunk below the general surface along the banks of the streams, have proved fertile and produce large crops of wheat, barley, hay, and other products.

In general views the western section seems to be covered with one vast, evenly planted forest, with the exception of the few snow-clad peaks of the Cascade Range, these peaks being the only points in the landscape that rise above the timber-line. Nevertheless, embosomed in this forest and lying in the great trough between the Cascades and coast mountains, there are some of the best bread-bearing valleys to be found in the world. The largest of these are the Willamette, Umpqua, and Rogue River valleys. Inasmuch as a considerable portion of these main valleys was treeless, or nearly so, as well as surpassingly fertile, they were the first to attract settlers; and the Willamette, being at once the largest and nearest to tide water, was settled first of all, and now contains the greater portion of the population and wealth of the State.

The climate of this section, like the corresponding portion of Washington, is rather damp and sloppy throughout the winter months, but the summers are bright, ripening the wheat and allowing it to be garnered in good condition. Taken as a whole, the weather is bland and kindly, and like the forest trees the crops and cattle grow plump and sound in it. So also do the people; children ripen well and grow up with limbs of good size and fiber and, unless overworked in the woods, live to a good old age, hale and hearty.

But, like every other happy valley in the world, the sunshine of this one is not without its shadows. Malarial fevers are not unknown in some places, and untimely frosts and rains may at long intervals in some measure disappoint the hopes of the husband-man. Many a tale, good-natured or otherwise, is told concerning the overflowing abundance of the Oregon rains. Once an English traveler, as the story goes, went to a store to make some purchases and on leaving found that rain was falling; therefore not liking to get wet, he stepped back to wait till the shower was over. Seeing no signs of clearing, he soon became impatient and inquired of the storekeeper how long he thought the shower would be likely to last. Going to the door and looking wisely into the gray sky and noting the direction of the wind, the latter replied that he thought the shower would probably last about six months, an opinion that of course disgusted the fault-finding Briton with the "blawsted country," though in fact it is but little if at all wetter or cloudier than his own.

No climate seems the best for everybody. Many there be who waste their lives in a vain search for weather with which no fault may be found, keeping themselves and their families in constant motion, like floating seaweeds that never strike root, yielding compliance to every current of news concerning countries yet untried, believing that everywhere, anywhere, the sky is fairer and the grass grows greener than where they happen to be. Before the Oregon and California railroad was built, the overland journey between these states across the Siskiyou Mountains in the old-fashioned emigrant wagon was a long and tedious one. Nevertheless, every season dissatisfied climate-seekers, too wet and too dry, might be seen plodding along through the dust in the old " '49 style," making their way one half of them from California to Oregon, the other half from Oregon to California. The beautiful Sisson meadows at the base of Mount Shasta were a favorite halfway resting-place, where the weary cattle were turned out for a few days to gather strength for better climates, and it was curious to hear those perpetual pioneers comparing notes and seeking information around the camp-fires.

"Where are you from?" some Oregonian would ask.

"The Joaquin."

"It's dry there, ain't it?"

"Well, I should say so. No rain at all in summer and none to speak of in winter, and I'm dried out. I just told my wife I was on the move again, and I'm going to keep moving till I come to a country where it rains once in a while, like it does in every reg'lar white man's country; and that, I guess, will be Oregon, if the news be true."

"Yes, neighbor, you's heading in the right direction for rain," the Oregonian would say. "Keep right on to Yamhill and you'll soon be damp enough. It rains there more than twelve months in the year; at least, no saying but it will. I've just come from there, plumb drowned out, and I told my wife to jump into the wagon and we would start out and see if we couldn't find a dry day somewhere. Last fall the hay was out and the wood was out, and the cabin leaked, and I made up my mind to try California the first chance."

"Well, if you be a horned toad or coyote," the seeker of moisture would reply, "then maybe you can stand it. Just keep right on by the Alabama Settlement to Tulare and you can have my place on Big Dry Creek and welcome. You'll be drowned there mighty seldom. The wagon spokes and tires will rattle and tell you when you come to it."

"All right, partner, we'll swap square, you can have mine in

Characteristics of Oregon

Yamhill and the rain thrown in. Last August a painter sharp came along one day wanting to know the way to Willamette Falls, and I told him: 'Young man, just wait a little and you'll find falls enough without going to Oregon City after them. The whole dog-gone Noah's flood of a country will be a fall and melt and float away some day.'" And more to the same effect.

But no one need leave Oregon in search of fair weather. The wheat and cattle region of eastern Oregon and Washington on the upper Columbia plains is dry enough and dusty enough more than half the year. The truth is, most of these wanderers enjoy the freedom of gypsy life and seek not homes but camps. Having crossed the plains and reached the ocean, they can find no farther west within reach of wagons, and are therefore compelled now to go north and south between Mexico and Alaska, always glad to find an excuse for moving, stopping a few months or weeks here and there, the time being measured by the size of the camp-meadow, conditions of the grass, game, and other indications. Even their so-called settlements of a year or two, when they take up land and build cabins, are only another kind of camp, in no common sense homes. Never a tree is planted, nor do they plant themselves, but like good soldiers in time of war are ever ready to march. Their journey of life is indeed a journey with very matter-of-fact thorns in the way, though not wholly wanting in compensation.

One of the most influential of the motives that brought the early settlers to these shores, apart from that natural instinct to scatter and multiply which urges even sober salmon to climb the Rocky Mountains, was their desire to find a country at once fertile and winterless, where their flocks and herds could find pasture all the year, thus doing away with the long and tiresome period of haying and feeding necessary in the eastern and old western States and Territories. Cheap land and good land there was in abundance in Kansas, Nebraska, Minnesota, and Iowa; but there the labor of providing for animals of the farm was very great, and much of that labor was crowded together into a few summer months, while to keep cool in summers and warm in the icy winters was well-nigh impossible to poor farmers.

Along the coast and throughout the greater part of western Oregon in general, snow seldom falls on the lowlands to a greater depth than a few inches, and never lies long. Grass is green all winter. The average temperature for the year in the Willamette Valley is about 52°, the highest and lowest being about 100° and 20°, though occasionally a much lower temperature is reached.

The average rainfall is about fifty or fifty-five inches in the Willamette Valley, and along the coast seventy-five inches, or even more at some points—figures that bring many a dreary night and day to mind, however fine the effect on the great evergreen woods and the fields of the farmers. The rainy season begins in September or October and lasts until April or May. Then the whole country is solemnly soaked and poulticed with the gray, streaming clouds and fogs, night and day, with marvelous constancy. Towards the beginning and end of the season a good many bright days occur to break the pouring gloom, but whole months of rain, continuous, or nearly so, are not at all rare. Astronomers beneath these Oregon skies would have a dull time of it. Of all the year only about one fourth of the days are clear, while three fourths have more or less of fogs, clouds, or rain.

The fogs occur mostly in the fall and spring. They are grand, far-reaching affairs of two kinds, the black and the white, some of the latter being very beautiful, and the infinite delicacy and tenderness of their touch as they linger to caress the tall evergreens is most exquisite. On farms and highways and in streets of towns, where work has to be done, there is nothing picturesque or attractive in any obvious way about the gray, serious-faced rain-storms. Mud abounds. The rain seems dismal and heedless and gets in everybody's way. Every face is turned from it, and it has but few friends who recognize its boundless beneficence. But back in the untrodden woods where no axe has been lifted, where a deep, rich carpet of brown and golden mosses covers all the ground like a garment, pressing warmly about the feet of the trees and rising in thick folds softly and kindly over every fallen trunk, leaving no spot naked or uncared-for, there the rain is welcomed, and every drop that falls finds a place and use as sweet and pure as itself. An excursion into the woods when the rain harvest is at its height is a noble pleasure, and may be safely enjoyed at small expense, though very few care to seek it. Shelter is easily found beneath the great trees in some hollow out of the wind, and one need carry but little provision, none at all of a kind that a wetting would spoil. The colors of the woods are then at their best, and the mighty hosts of the forest, every needle tingling in the blast, wave and sing in glorious harmony.

> 'T were worth ten years of peaceful life, one glance at
> this array.

The snow that falls in the lowland woods is usually soft, and makes a fine show coming through the trees in large, feathery tufts, loading the branches of the firs and spruces and cedars and weighing them down against the trunks until they look slender and sharp as arrows, while a strange, muffled silence prevails, giving a peculiar solemnity to everything. But these lowland snowstorms and their effects quickly vanish; every crystal melts in a day or two, the bent branches rise again, and the rain resumes its sway.

While these gracious rains are searching the roots of the lowlands, corresponding snows are busy along the heights of the Cascade Mountains. Month after month, day and night the heavens shed their icy bloom in stormy, measureless abundance, filling the grand upper fountains of the rivers to last through the summer. Awful then is the silence that presses down over the mountain forests. All the smaller streams vanish from sight, hushed and obliterated. Young groves of spruce and pine are bowed down as by a gentle hand and put to rest, not again to see the light or move leaf or limb until the grand awakening of the springtime, while the larger animals and most of the birds seek food and shelter in the foothills on the borders of the valleys and plains.

The lofty volcanic peaks are yet more heavily snow-laden. To their upper zones no summer comes. They are white always. From the steep slopes of the summit the new-fallen snow, while yet dry and loose, descends in magnificent avalanches to feed the glaciers, making meanwhile the most glorious manifestations of power. Happy is the man who may get near them to see and hear. In some sheltered camp nest on the edge of the timber-line one may lie snug and warm, but after the long shuffle on snowshoes we may have to wait more than a month ere the heavens open and the grand show is unveiled. In the mean time, bread may be scarce, unless with careful forecast a sufficient supply has been provided and securely placed during the summer. Nevertheless, to be thus deeply snowbound high in the sky is not without generous compensation for all the cost. And when we at length go down the long white slopes to the levels of civilization, the pains vanish like snow in sunshine, while the noble and exalting pleasures we have gained remain with us to enrich our lives forever.

The fate of the high-flying mountain snow-flowers is a fascinating study, though little may we see of their works and ways while their storms go on. The glinting, swirling swarms fairly thicken the blast, and all the air, as well as the rocks and trees, is as one smothering mass of bloom, through the midst of which at close intervals come the low, intense thunder-tones of the avalanches as they speed on their way to fill the vast fountain hollows. Here they seem at last to have found rest. But this rest is only apparent. Gradually the loose crystals by the pressure of their own weight are welded together into clear ice, and, as glaciers, march steadily, silently on, with invisible motion, in broad, deep currents, grinding their way with irresistible energy to the warmer lowlands, where they vanish in glad, rejoicing streams.

In the sober weather of Oregon lightning makes but little show. Those magnificent thunder-storms that so frequently adorn and glorify the sky of the Mississippi Valley are wanting here. Dull thunder and lightning may occasionally be seen and heard, but the imposing grandeur of great storms marching over the landscape with streaming banners and a network of fire is almost wholly unknown.

Crossing the Cascade Range, we pass from a green to a gray country, from a wilderness of trees to a wilderness of open plains, level or rolling or rising here and there into hills and short mountain spurs. Though well supplied with rivers in most of its main sections, it is generally dry. The annual rainfall is only from about five to fifteen inches, and the thin winter garment of snow seldom lasts more than a month or two, though the temperature in many places falls from five to twenty-five degrees below zero for a short time. That the snow is light over eastern Oregon, and the average temperature not intolerably severe, is shown by the fact that large droves of sheep, cattle, and horses live there through the winter without other food or shelter than they find for themselves on the open plains or down in the sunken valleys and gorges along the streams.

When we read of the mountain-ranges of Oregon and Washington with detailed descriptions of their old volcanoes towering snow-laden and glacier-laden above the clouds, one may be led to imagine that the country is far icier and whiter and more mountainous than it is. Only in winter are the Coast and Cascade mountains covered with snow. Then as seen from the main interior valleys they appear as comparatively low, bossy walls stretching along the horizon and making a magnificent display of their white wealth. The Coast Range in Oregon does not perhaps average more than three thousand feet in height. Its snow does not last long, most of its soil is fertile all the way to the summits, and the greater part of the range may at some time be brought under cultivation. The immense deposits on the great central uplift of the Cascade Range are mostly melted off before the middle of summer by the comparatively warm winds and rains from the coast, leaving only a few white spots on the highest ridges, where the depth from drifting has been greatest, or where the rate of waste has been diminished by specially favorable conditions as to exposure. Only the great volcanic cones are truly snow-clad all the year, and these are not numerous and make but a small portion of the general landscape.

As we approach Oregon from the coast in summer, no hint of snowy mountains can be seen, and it is only after we have sailed into the country by the Columbia, or climbed some one of the commanding summits, that the great white peaks send us greeting and make telling advertisements of themselves and of the country over which they rule. So, also, in coming to Oregon from the east the country by no means impresses one as being surpassingly mountainous, the abode of peaks and glaciers. Descending the spurs of the Rocky Mountains into the basin of the Columbia, we see hot, hundred-mile plains, roughened here and there by hills and ridges that look hazy and blue in the distance, until we have pushed well to the westward. Then one white point after another comes into sight to refresh the eye and the imagination; but they are yet a long way off, and have much to say only to those who know them or others of their kind. How grand they are, though insignificant-looking on the edge of the vast landscape! What noble woods they nourish, and emerald meadows and gardens! What springs and streams and waterfalls sing about them, and to what a multitude of happy creatures they give homes and food!

The principal mountains of the range are Mounts Pitt, Scott, and Thielson, Diamond Peak, the Three Sisters, Mounts Jefferson, Hood, St. Helen's, Adams, Ranier, Aix, and Baker. Of these the seven first named belong to Oregon, the others to Washington. They rise singly at irregular distances from one another along the main axis of the range or near it, with an elevation of from about eight thousand to fourteen thousand four hundred feet above the level of the sea. From few points in the valleys may more than three or four of them be seen, and of the more distant ones of these only the tops appear. Therefore, speaking generally, each of the lowland landscapes of the State contains only one grand snowy mountain.

The heights back of Portland command one of the best general views of the forests and also of the most famous of the great mountains both of Oregon and Washington. Mount Hood is in full view, with the summits of Mounts Jefferson, St. Helen's, Adams, and Rainier in the distance. The city of Portland is at our feet, covering a large area along both banks of the Willamette, and, with its fine streets, schools, churches, mills, shipping, parks, and gardens, makes a telling picture of busy, aspiring civilization in the midst of the green wilderness in which it is planted. The river is displayed to fine advantage in the foreground of our main view, sweeping in beautiful curves around rich, leafy islands, its banks fringed with willows.

A few miles beyond the Willamette flows the renowned Columbia, and the confluence of these two great rivers is at a point only about ten miles below the city. Beyond the Columbia extends the immense breadth of the forest, one dim, black, monotonous field, with only the sky, which one is glad to see is not forested, and the tops of the majestic old volcanoes to give diversity to the view. That sharp, white, broad-based pyramid on the south side of the Columbia, a few degrees to the south of east from where you stand, is the famous Mount Hood. The distance to it in a straight line is about fifty miles. Its upper slopes form the only bare ground, bare as to forests, in the landscape in that direction. It is the pride of Oregonians, and when it is visible is always pointed out to strangers as the glory of the country, the mountain of mountains. It is one of the grand series of extinct volcanoes extending from Lassen's Butte[1] to Mount Baker, a distance of about six hundred miles, which once flamed like gigantic watch-fires along the coast. Some of them have been active in recent times, but no considerable addition to the bulk of Mount Hood has been made for several centuries, as is shown by the amount of glacial denudation it has suffered. Its summit has been ground to a point, which gives it a rather thin, pinched appearance. It has a wide-flowing base, however, and is fairly well proportioned. Though it is eleven thousand feet high, it is too far off to make much show under ordinary conditions in so extensive a landscape. Through a great part of the summer it is invisible on account of smoke poured into the sky from burning woods, logging-camps, mills, etc., and in winter for weeks at a time, or even months, it is in the clouds. Only in spring and early summer and in what there may chance to be of bright weather in winter is it or any of its companions at all clear or telling. From the Cascades on the Columbia it may be seen at a distance of twenty miles or thereabouts, or from other points up and down the river, and with the magnificent foreground it is very impressive. It gives the supreme touch of grandeur to all the main Columbia views, rising at every turn, solitary, majestic, awe-inspiring, the ruling spirit of the landscape. But, like mountains everywhere, it varies greatly in impressiveness and apparent height at different times and seasons, not alone from differences as to the dimness or transparency of the air. Clear, or arrayed in clouds, it changes both in size and general expression. Now it looms up to an immense height and seems to draw near in tremendous grandeur and beauty,

[1]Lassen Peak on recent maps. [Editor.]

holding the eyes of every beholder in devout and awful interest. Next year or next day, or even in the same day, you return to the same point of view, perhaps to find that the glory has departed, as if the mountain had died and the poor dull, shrunken mass of rocks and ice had lost all power to charm.

Never shall I forget my first glorious view of Mount Hood one calm evening in July, though I had seen it many times before this. I was then sauntering with a friend across the new Willamette bridge between Portland and East Portland for the sake of the river views, which are here very fine in the tranquil summer weather. The scene on the water was a lively one. Boats of every description were gliding, glinting, drifting about at work or play, and we leaned over the rail from time to time, contemplating the gay throng. Several lines of ferry-boats were making regular trips at intervals of a few minutes, and river steamers were coming and going from the wharves, laden with all sorts of merchandise, raising long diverging swells that made all the light pleasure-craft bow and nod in hearty salutation as they passed. The crowd was being constantly increased by new arrivals from both shores, sailboats, rowboats, racing-shells, rafts, were loaded with gayly dressed people, and here and there some adventurous man or boy might be seen as a merry sailor on a single plank or spar, apparently as deep in enjoyment as were any on the water. It seemed as if all the town were coming to the river, renouncing the cares and toils of the day, determined to take the evening breeze into their pulses, and be cool and tranquil ere going to bed.

Absorbed in the happy scene, given up to dreamy, random observation of what lay immediately before me, I was not con-

Characteristics of Oregon

scious of anything occurring on the outer rim of the landscape. Forest, mountain, and sky were forgotten, when my companion suddenly directed my attention to the eastward, shouting, "Oh, look! look!" in so loud and excited a tone of voice that passers-by, saunterers like ourselves, were startled and looked over the bridge as if expecting to see some boat upset. Looking across the forest, over which the mellow light of the sunset was streaming, I soon discovered the source of my friend's excitement. There stood Mount Hood in all the glory of the alpenglow, looming immensely high, beaming with intelligence, and so impressive that one was overawed as if suddenly brought before some superior being newly arrived from the sky.

The atmosphere was somewhat hazy, but the mountain seemed neither near nor far. Its glaciers flashed in the divine light. The rugged, storm-worn ridges between them and the snowfields of the summit, these perhaps might have been traced as far as they were in sight, and the blending zones of color about the base. But so profound was the general impression, partial analysis did not come into play. The whole mountain appeared as one glorious manifestation of divine power, enthusiastic and benevolent, glowing like a countenance with ineffable repose and beauty, before which we could only gaze in devout and lowly admiration.

The far-famed Oregon forests cover all the western section of the State, the mountains as well as the lowlands, with the exception of a few gravelly spots and open spaces in the central portions of the great cultivated valleys. Beginning on the coast, where their outer ranks are drenched and buffeted by wind-driven scud from the sea, they press on in close, majestic ranks over the coast mountains, across the broad central valleys, and over the Cascade Range, broken and halted only by the few great peaks that rise like islands above the sea of evergreens.

In descending the eastern slopes of the Cascades the rich, abounding, triumphant exuberance of the trees is quickly subdued; they become smaller, grow wide apart, leaving dry spaces without moss covering or underbrush, and before the foot of the range is reached, fail altogether, stayed by the drouth of the interior almost as suddenly as on the western margin they are stayed by the sea. Here and there at wide intervals on the eastern plains patches of a small pine (*Pinus contorta*) are found, and a scattering growth of juniper, used by the settlers mostly for fence-posts and firewood. Along the stream-bottoms there is usually more or less of cottonwood and willow, which, though yielding inferior timber, is yet highly prized in this bare region. On the Blue Mountains there is pine, spruce, fir, and larch in abundance for every use, but beyond this range there is nothing that may be called a forest in the Columbia River basin, until we reach the spurs of the Rocky Mountains; and these Rocky Mountain forests are made up of trees which, compared with the giants of the Pacific Slope, are mere saplings.

22

The Forests of Oregon and
Their Inhabitants

LIKE the forests of Washington, already described, those of Oregon are in great part made up of the Douglas spruce,[1] or Oregon pine (*Abies Douglasii*). A large number of mills are at work upon this species, especially along the Columbia, but these as yet have made but little impression upon its dense masses, the mills here being small as compared with those of the Puget Sound region. The white cedar, or Port Orford cedar (*Cupressus Lawsoniana*, or *Chamœcyparis Lawsoniana*), is one of the most beautiful of the evergreens, and produces excellent lumber, considerable quantities of which are shipped to the San Francisco market. It is found mostly about Coos Bay, along the Coquille River, and on the northern slopes of the Siskiyou Mountains, and extends down the coast into California. The silver firs, the spruces, and the colossal arbor-vitæ, or white cedar[2] (*Thuja gigantea*), described in the chapter on Washington, are also found here in great beauty and perfection, the largest of these (*Picea grandis*, Loud.; *Abies grandis*, Lindl.) being confined mostly to the coast region, where it attains a height of three hundred feet, and a diameter of ten or twelve feet. Five or six species of pines are found in the State, the

[1]*Pseudotsuga taxifolia*. Brit. [Editor.]
[2]*Thuja plicata* Don. [Editor.]

most important of which, both as to lumber and as to the part they play in the general wealth and beauty of the forests, are the yellow and sugar pines (*Pinus ponderosa* and *P. Lambertiana*). The yellow pine is most abundant on the eastern slopes of the Cascades, forming there the main bulk of the forest in many places. It is also common along the borders of the open spaces in Willamette Valley. In the southern portion of the State the sugar pine, which is the king of all the pines and the glory of the Sierra forests, occurs in considerable abundance in the basins of the Umpqua and Rogue rivers, and it was in the Umpqua Hills that this noble tree was first discovered by the enthusiastic botanical explorer David Douglas, in the year 1826.

This is the Douglas for whom the noble Douglas spruce is named, and many a fair blooming plant also, which will serve to keep his memory fresh and sweet as long as beautiful trees and flowers are loved. The Indians of the lower Columbia River watched him with lively curiosity as he wandered about in the woods day after day, gazing intently on the ground or at the great trees, collecting specimens of everything he saw, but, unlike all the eager fur-gathering strangers they had hitherto seen, caring nothing about trade. And when at length they came to know him better, and saw that from year to year the growing things of the woods and prairies, meadows and plains, were his only object of pursuit, they called him the "Man of Grass," a title of which he was proud.

He was a Scotchman and first came to this coast in the spring of 1825 under the auspices of the London Horticultural Society, landing at the mouth of the Columbia after a long, dismal voyage of eight months and fourteen days. During this first season he chose Fort Vancouver, belonging to the Hudson's Bay Company, as his headquarters, and from there made excursions into the glorious wilderness in every direction, discovering many new species among the trees as well as among the rich underbrush and smaller herbaceous vegetation. It was while making a trip to Mount Hood this year that he discovered the two largest and most beautiful firs in the world (*Picea amabilis* and *P. nobilis*—now called *Abies*), and from the seeds which he then collected and sent home tall trees are now growing in Scotland.

In one of his trips that summer, in the lower Willamette Valley, he saw in an Indian's tobacco-pouch some of the seeds and scales of a new species of pine, which he learned were gathered from a large tree that grew far to the southward. Most of the following season was spent on the upper waters of the Columbia, and it was not until September that he returned to Fort Vancouver, about the time of the setting-in of the winter rains. Nevertheless, bearing in mind the great pine he had heard of, and the seeds of which he had seen, he made haste to set out on an excursion to the headwaters of the Willamette in search of it; and how he fared on this excursion and what dangers and hardships he endured is best told in his own journal, part of which I quote as follows:—

October 26th, 1826. Weather dull. Cold and cloudy. When my friends in England are made acquainted with my travels I fear they will think that I have told them nothing but my miseries. . . . I quitted my camp early in the morning to survey the neighboring country, leaving my guide to take charge of the horses until my return in the evening. About an hour's walk from the camp I met an Indian, who on perceiving me

instantly strung his bow, placed on his left arm a sleeve
of raccoon skin and stood on the defensive. Being quite
sure that conduct was prompted by fear and not by hostile intentions, the poor fellow having probably never
seen such a being as myself before, I laid my gun at my
feet on the ground and waved my hand for him to come
to me, which he did slowly and with great caution. I
then made him place his bow and quiver of arrows beside my gun, and striking a light gave him a smoke out
of my own pipe and a present of a few beads. With my
pencil I made a rough sketch of the cone and pine tree
which I wanted to obtain and drew his attention to it,
when he instantly pointed with his hand to the hills
fifteen or twenty miles distant towards the south; and
when I expressed my intention of going thither, cheer-
fully set about accompanying me. At midday I reached
my long-wished-for pines and lost no time in examining
them and endeavoring to collect specimens and seeds.
New and strange things seldom fail to make strong
impressions and are therefore frequently overrated; so
that, lest I should never see my friends in England to
inform them verbally of this most beautiful and immensely grand tree, I shall here state the dimensions of
the largest I could find among several that had been
blown down by the wind. At three feet from the ground
its circumference is fifty-seven feet, nine inches; at one
hundred and thirty-four feet, seventeen feet five inches;
the extreme length two hundred and forty-five
feet. . . . As it was impossible either to climb the tree

or hew it down, I endeavored to knock off the cones by firing at them with ball, when the report of my gun brought eight Indians, all of them painted with red earth, armed with bows, arrows, bone-tipped spears, and flint knives. They appeared anything but friendly. I explained to them what I wanted and they seemed satisfied and sat down to smoke; but presently I saw one of them string his bow and another sharpen his flint knife with a pair of wooden pincers and suspend it on the wrist of his right hand. Further testimony of their intentions was unnecessary. To save myself by flight was impossible, so without hesitation I stepped back about five paces, cocked my gun, drew one of the pistols out of my belt, and holding it in my left hand, the gun in my right, showed myself determined to fight for my life. As much as possible I endeavored to preserve my coolness, and thus we stood looking at one another without making any movement or uttering a word for perhaps ten minutes, when one at last, who seemed to be the leader, gave a sign that they wished for some tobacco; this I signified they should have if they fetched a quantity of cones. They went off immediately in search of them, and no sooner were they all out of sight than I picked up my three cones and some twigs of the trees and made the quickest possible retreat, hurrying back to my camp, which I reached before dusk. The Indian who last undertook to be my guide to the trees I sent off before gaining my encampment, lest he should betray me. How irksome is the darkness of night to one under such circumstances. I cannot speak a word to my guide, nor have I a book to divert my thoughts, which are continually occupied with the dread lest the hostile Indians should trace me hither and make an attack. I now write lying on the grass with my gun cocked beside me, and penning these lines by the light of my *Columbian candle*, namely, an ignited piece of rosin-wood.

Douglas named this magnificent species *Pinus Lambertiana*, in honor of his friend Dr. Lambert, of London. This is the noblest pine thus far discovered in the forests of the world, surpassing all others not only in size but in beauty and majesty. Oregon may well be proud that its discovery was made within her borders, and that, though it is far more abundant in California, she has the largest known specimens. In the Sierra the finest sugar pine forests lie at an elevation of about five thousand feet. In Oregon they occupy much lower ground, some of the trees being found but little above tide-water.

No lover of trees will ever forget his first meeting with the sugar pine. In most coniferous trees there is a sameness of form and expression which at length becomes wearisome to most people who travel far in the woods. But the sugar pines are as free from conventional forms as any of the oaks. No two are so much alike as to hide their individuality from any observer. Every tree is appreciated as a study in itself and proclaims in no uncertain terms the surpassing grandeur of the species. The branches, mostly near the summit, are sometimes nearly forty feet long, feathered richly all around with short, leafy branchlets, and tasselled with cones a foot and a half long. And when these superb arms are outspread, radiating in every direction, an immense crown-like mass is formed which, poised on the noble shaft and filled with sunshine, is one of the grandest forest objects conceivable. But though so wild and unconventional when full-grown, the sugar pine is a remarkably regular tree in youth, a strict follower of coniferous fashions, slim, erect, tapering, symmetrical, every branch in place. At the age of fifty or sixty years this shy, fashionable form begins to give way. Special branches are thrust out away from the general outlines of the trees and bent down with cones. Henceforth it becomes more and more original and independent in style, pushes boldly aloft into the winds and sunshine, growing ever more stately and beautiful, a joy and inspiration to every beholder.

Unfortunately, the sugar pine makes excellent lumber. It is too good to live, and is already passing rapidly away before the woodman's axe. Surely out of all the abounding forest-wealth of Oregon a few specimens might be spared to the world, not as dead lumber, but as living trees. A park of moderate extent might be set apart and protected for public use forever, containing at least a few hundreds of each of these noble pines, spruces, and firs. Happy will be the men who, having the power and the love and benevolent forecast to do this, will do it. They will not be forgotten. The trees and their lovers will sing their praises, and generations yet unborn will rise up and call them blessed.

Dotting the prairies and fringing the edges of the great evergreen forests we find a considerable number of hardwood trees, such as the oak, maple, ash, alder, laurel, madrone, flowering dogwood, wild cherry, and wild apple. The white oak (*Quercus Garryana*) is the most important of the Oregon oaks as a timber tree, but not nearly so beautiful as Kellogg's oak (*Q. Kelloggii*). The former is found mostly along the Columbia River, particularly about the Dalles, and a considerable quantity of useful lumber is made from it and sold, sometimes for eastern white oak, to wagon-makers. Kellogg's oak is a magnificent tree and does much for the picturesque beauty of the Umpqua and Rogue River valleys where it abounds. It is also found in all the Yosemite valleys of the Sierra, and its acorns form an important part of the food of the Digger Indians. In the Siskiyou Mountains there is a live oak (*Q. chrysolepsis*), wide-spreading and very picturesque in form, but not very common. It extends southward along the western flank of the Sierra and is there more abundant and much larger than in Oregon, oftentimes five to eight feet in diameter.

The maples are the same as those in Washington, already described, but I have not seen any maple groves here equal in extent or in the size of the trees to those on the Snoqualmie River.

The Oregon ash is now rare along the stream-banks of western Oregon, and it grows to a good size and furnishes lumber that is for some purposes equal to the white ash of the Western States.

Nuttall's flowering dogwood makes a brave display with its wealth of showy involucres in the spring along cool streams. Specimens of the flowers may be found measuring eight inches in diameter.

The wild cherry (*Prunus emarginata*, var. *mollis*) is a small, handsome tree seldom more than a foot in diameter at the base. It makes valuable lumber and its black, astringent fruit furnishes a rich resource as food for the birds. A smaller form is common in the Sierra, the fruit of which is eagerly eaten by the Indians and hunters in time of need.

The wild apple (*Pyrus rivularis*) is a fine, hearty, handsome little tree that grows well in rich, cool soil along streams and on the edges of beaver-meadows from California through Oregon and Washington to southeastern Alaska. In Oregon it forms dense, tangled thickets, some of them almost impenetrable. The largest trunks are nearly a foot in diameter. When in bloom it makes a fine show with its abundant clusters of flowers, which are white and fragrant. The fruit is very small and savagely acid. It is wholesome, however, and is eaten by birds, bears, Indians, and many other adventurers, great and small.

Passing from beneath the shadows of the woods where the trees grow close and high, we step into charming wild gardens full of lilies, orchids, heathworts, roses, etc., with colors so gay and forming such sumptuous masses of bloom, they make the gardens of civilization, however lovingly cared for, seem pathetic and silly. Around the great fire-mountains, above the forests and beneath the snow, there is a flowery zone of marvelous beauty planted with anemones, erythroniums, daisies, bryanthus, kalmia, vaccinium, cassiope, saxifrages, etc., forming one continuous garden fifty or sixty miles in circumference, and so deep and luxuriant and closely woven it seems as if Nature, glad to find an opening, were economizing space and trying to see how many of her bright-eyed darlings she can get together in one mountain wreath.

Along the slopes of the Cascades, where the woods are less dense, especially about the headwaters of the Willamette, there are miles of rhododendron, making glorious outbursts of purple bloom, and down on the prairies in rich, damp hollows the blue-flowered camassia grows in such profusion that at a little distance its dense masses appear as beautiful blue lakes imbedded in the green, flowery plains; while all about the streams and the lakes and the beaver-meadows and the margins of the deep woods there is a magnificent tangle of gaultheria and huckleberry bushes with their myriads of pink bells, reinforced with hazel, cornel, rubus of many species, wild plum, cherry, and crab apple; besides thousands of charming bloomers to be found in all sorts of places throughout the wilderness whose mere names are refreshing, such as linnæa, menziesia, pyrola, chimaphila, brodiæa, smilacina, fritillaria, calochortus, trillium, clintonia, veratrum, cypripedium, goodyera, spiranthes, habenaria, and the rare and lovely "Hider of the North," *Calypso borealis*, to find which is alone a sufficient object for a journey into the wilderness. And besides these there is a charming underworld of ferns and mosses flourishing gloriously beneath all the woods.

Everybody loves wild woods and flowers more or less. Seeds of all these Oregon evergreens and of many of the flowering shrubs and plants have been sent to almost every country under the sun, and they are now growing in carefully tended parks and gardens. And now that the ways of approach are open one would expect to find these woods and gardens full of admiring visitors reveling in their beauty like bees in a clover-field. Yet few care to visit them. A portion of the bark of one of the California trees, the mere dead skin, excited the wondering attention of thousands when it was set up in the Crystal Palace in London, as did also a few peeled spars, the shafts of mere saplings from Oregon or Washington. Could one of these great silver firs or sugar pines three hundred feet high have been transplanted entire to that exhibition, how enthusiastic would have been the praises accorded to it!

Nevertheless, the countless hosts waving at home beneath

their own sky, beside their own noble rivers and mountains, and standing on a flower-enameled carpet of mosses thousands of square miles in extent, attract but little attention. Most travelers content themselves with what they may chance to see from car windows, hotel verandas, or the deck of a steamer on the lower Columbia—clinging to the battered highways like drowning sailors to a life-raft. When an excursion into the woods is proposed, all sorts of exaggerated or imaginary dangers are conjured up, filling the kindly, soothing wilderness with colds, fevers, Indians, bears, snakes, bugs, impassable rivers, and jungles of brush, to which is always added quick and sure starvation.

As to starvation, the woods are full of food, and a supply of bread may easily be carried for habit's sake, and replenished now and then at outlying farms and camps. The Indians are seldom found in the woods, being confined mainly to the banks of the rivers, where the greater part of their food is obtained. Moreover, the most of them have been either buried since the settlement of the country or civilized into comparative innocence, industry, or harmless laziness. There are bears in the woods, but not in such numbers nor of such unspeakable ferocity as town-dwellers imagine, nor do bears spend their lives in going about the country like the devil, seeking whom they may devour. Oregon bears, like most others, have no liking for man either as meat or as society; and while some may be curious at times to see what manner of creature he is, most of them have learned to shun people as deadly enemies. They have been poisoned, trapped, and shot at until they have become shy, and it is no longer easy to make their acquaintance. Indeed, since the settlement of the country, notwithstanding far the greater portion is yet wild, it is difficult to find any of the larger animals that once were numerous and comparatively familiar, such as the bear, wolf, panther, lynx, deer, elk, and antelope.

As early as 1843, while the settlers numbered only a few thousands, and before any sort of government had been organized, they came together and held what they called "a wolf meeting," at which a committee was appointed to devise means for the destruction of wild animals destructive to tame ones, which committee in due time begged to report as follows:—

> It being admitted by all that bears, wolves, panthers, etc., are destructive to the useful animals owned by the settlers of this colony, your committee would submit the following resolutions as the sense of this meeting, by which the community may be governed in carrying on a defensive and destructive war on all such animals:—
>
> Resolved, 1st.—That we deem it expedient for the community to take immediate measures for the destruction of all wolves, panthers and bears, and such other animals as are known to be destructive to cattle, horses, sheep and hogs.
>
> 2d.—That a bounty of fifty cents be paid for the destruction of a small wolf, $3.00 for a large wolf, $1.50 for a lynx, $2.00 for a bear and $5.00 for a panther.

This center of destruction was in the Willamette Valley. But for many years prior to the beginning of the operations of the "Wolf Organization" the Hudson's Bay Company had established forts and trading-stations over all the country, wherever fur-gathering

Indians could be found, and vast numbers of these animals were killed. Their destruction has since gone on at an accelerated rate from year to year as the settlements have been extended, so that in some cases it is difficult to obtain specimens enough for the use of naturalists. But even before any of these settlements were made, and before the coming of the Hudson's Bay Company, there was very little danger to be met in passing through this wilderness as far as animals were concerned, and but little of any kind as compared with the dangers encountered in crowded houses and streets.

When Lewis and Clark made their famous trip across the continent in 1804–05, when all the Rocky Mountain region was wild, as well as the Pacific Slope, they did not lose a single man by wild animals, nor, though frequently attacked, especially by the grizzlies of the Rocky Mountains, were any of them wounded seriously. Captain Clark was bitten on the hand by a wolf as he lay asleep; that was one bite among more than a hundred men while traveling through eight to nine thousand miles of savage wilderness. They could hardly have been so fortunate had they stayed at home. They wintered on the edge of the Clatsop plains, on the south side of the Columbia River near its mouth. In the woods on that side they found game abundant, especially elk, and with the aid of the friendly Indians who furnished salmon and "wapatoo" (the tubers of *Sagittaria variabilis*), they were in no danger of starving.

But on the return trip in the spring they reached the base of the Rocky Mountains when the range was yet too heavily snow-laden to be crossed with horses. Therefore they had to wait some weeks. This was at the head of one of the northern branches of Snake River, and, their scanty stock of provisions being nearly exhausted, the whole party was compelled to live mostly on bears and dogs; deer, antelope, and elk, usually abundant, were now scarce because the region had been closely hunted over by the Indians before their arrival.

Lewis and Clark had killed a number of bears and saved the skins of the more interesting specimens, and the variations they found in size, color of the hair, etc., made great difficulty in classification. Wishing to get the opinion of the Chopumish Indians, near one of whose villages they were encamped, concerning the various species, the explorers unpacked their bundles and spread out for examination all the skins they had taken. The Indian hunters immediately classed the white, the deep and the pale grizzly red, the grizzly dark-brown—in short, all those with the extremities of the hair of a white or frosty color without regard to the color of the ground or foil—under the name of *hoh-host*. The Indians assured them that these were all of the same species as the white bear, that they associated together, had longer nails than the others, and never climbed trees. On the other hand, the black skins, those that were black with white hairs intermixed or with a white breast, the uniform bay, the brown, and the light reddish-brown, were classed under the name *yack-ah*, and were said to resemble each other in being smaller and having shorter nails, in climbing trees, and being so little vicious that they could be pursued with safety.

Lewis and Clark came to the conclusion that all those with white-tipped hair found by them in the basin of the Columbia belonged to the same species as the grizzlies of the upper Missouri; and that the black and reddish-brown, etc., of the Rocky Mountains belong to a second species equally distinct from the grizzly and the black bear of the Pacific Coast and the East, which never vary in color.

As much as possible should be made by the ordinary traveler of these descriptions, for he will be likely to see very little of any species for himself; not that bears no longer exist here, but because, being shy, they keep out of the way. In order to see them and learn their habits one must go softly and alone, lingering long in the fringing woods on the banks of the salmon streams, and in the small openings in the midst of thickets where berries are most abundant.

As for rattlesnakes, the other grand dread of town-dwellers when they leave beaten roads, there are two, or perhaps three, species of them in Oregon. But they are nowhere to be found in great numbers. In western Oregon they are hardly known at all. In all my walks in the Oregon forest I have never met a single specimen, though a few have been seen at long intervals.

When the country was first settled by the whites, fifty years ago, the elk roamed through the woods and over the plains to the east of the Cascades in immense numbers; now they are rarely seen except by experienced hunters who know their haunts in the deepest and most inaccessible solitudes to which they have been driven. So majestic an animal forms a tempting mark for the sportsman's rifle. Countless thousands have been killed for mere amusement and they already seem to be nearing extinction as rapidly as the buffalo. The antelope also is vanishing from the Columbia plains before the farmers and cattle-men. Whether the moose still lingers in Oregon or Washington I am unable to say.

On the highest mountains of the Cascade Range the wild goat

roams in comparative security, few of his enemies caring to go so far in pursuit and to hunt on ground so high and so dangerous. He is a brave, sturdy, shaggy mountaineer of an animal, enjoying the freedom and security of crumbling ridges and overhanging cliffs above the glaciers, oftentimes beyond the reach of the most daring hunter. They seem to be as much at home on the ice and snow-fields as on the crags, making their way in flocks from ridge to ridge on the great volcanic mountains by crossing the glaciers that lie between them, traveling in single file guided by an old experienced leader, like a party of climbers on the Alps. On these ice-journeys they pick their way through networks of crevasses and over bridges of snow with admirable skill, and the mountaineer may seldom do better in such places than to follow their trail, if he can. In the rich alpine gardens and meadows they find abundance of food, venturing sometimes well down in the prairie openings on the edge of the timber-line, but holding themselves ever alert and watchful, ready to flee to their highland castles at the faintest alarm. When their summer pastures are buried beneath the winter snows, they make haste to the lower ridges, seeking the wind-beaten crags and slopes where the snow cannot lie at any great depth, feeding at times on the leaves and twigs of bushes when grass is beyond reach.

The wild sheep is another admirable alpine rover, but comparatively rare in the Oregon mountains, choosing rather the drier ridges to the southward on the Cascades and to the eastward among the spurs of the Rocky Mountain chain.

Deer give beautiful animation to the forests, harmonizing finely in their color and movements with the gray and brown shafts of the trees and the swaying of the branches as they stand in groups at rest, or move gracefully and noiselessly over the mossy ground about the edges of beaver-meadows and flowery glades, daintily culling the leaves and tips of the mints and aromatic bushes on which they feed. There are three species, the black-tailed, white-tailed, and mule deer; the last being restricted in its range to the open woods and plains to the eastward of the Cascades. They are nowhere very numerous now, killing for food, for hides, or for mere wanton sport having well-nigh exterminated them in the more accessible regions, while elsewhere they are too often at the mercy of the wolves.

Gliding about in their shady forest homes, keeping well out of sight, there is a multitude of sleek fur-clad animals living and enjoying their clean, beautiful lives. How beautiful and interesting they are is about as difficult for busy mortals to find out as if their homes were beyond sight in the sky. Hence the stories of every wild hunter and trapper are eagerly listened to as being possibly true, or partly so, however thickly clothed in successive folds of exaggeration and fancy. Unsatisfying as these accounts must be, a tourist's frightened rush and scramble through the woods yields far less than the hunter's wildest stories, while in writing we can do but little more than to give a few names, as they come to mind,—beaver, squirrel, coon, fox, marten, fisher, otter, ermine, wildcat,—only this instead of full descriptions of the bright-eyed furry throng, their snug home nests, their fears and fights and loves, how they get their food, rear their young, escape their enemies, and keep themselves warm and well and exquisitely clean through all the pitiless weather.

For many years before the settlement of the country the fur of the beaver brought a high price, and therefore it was pursued with weariless ardor. Not even in the quest for gold has a more ruthless, desperate energy been developed. It was in those early beaver-days that the striking class of adventurers called "free trappers" made their appearance. Bold, enterprising men, eager to make money, and inclined at the same time to relish the license of a savage life, would set forth with a few traps and a gun and a hunting-knife, content at first to venture only a short distance up the beaver-streams nearest to the settlements, and where the Indians were not likely to molest them. There they would set their traps, while the buffalo, antelope, deer, etc., furnished a royal supply of food. In a few months their pack-animals would be laden with thousands of dollars' worth of fur.

Next season they would venture farther, and again farther, meanwhile growing rapidly wilder, getting acquainted with the Indian tribes, and usually marrying among them. Thenceforward no danger could stay them in their exciting pursuit. Wherever there were beaver they would go, however far or wild,—the wilder the better, provided their scalps could be saved. Oftentimes they were compelled to set their traps and visit them by night and lie hid during the day, when operating in the neighborhood of hostile Indians. Not then venturing to make a fire or shoot game, they lived on the raw flesh of the beaver, perhaps seasoned with wild cresses or berries. Then, returning to the trading-stations, they would spend their hard earnings in a few weeks of dissipation and "good time," and go again to the bears and beavers, until at length a bullet or arrow would end all. One after another would be missed by some friend or trader at the autumn rendezvous, reported killed by the Indians, and—forgotten. Some men of this class have, from superior skill or fortune, escaped every danger, lived to a good old age, and earned fame, and, by their knowledge of the topography of the vast West then unexplored, have been able to render important service to the country; but most of them laid their bones in the wilderness after a few short, keen seasons. So great were the perils that beset them, the average length of the life of a "free trapper" has been estimated at less than five years. From the Columbia waters beaver and beaver men have almost wholly passed away, and the men once so striking a part of the view have left scarcely the faintest sign of their existence. On the other hand, a thousand meadows on the mountains tell the story of the beavers, to remain fresh and green for many a century, monuments of their happy, industrious lives.

But there is a little airy, elfin animal in these woods, and in all the evergreen woods of the Pacific Coast, that is more influential and interesting than even the beaver. This is the Douglas squirrel (*Sciurus Douglasi*). Go where you will throughout all these noble forests, you everywhere find this little squirrel the master-existence. Though only a few inches long, so intense is his fiery vigor and restlessness, he stirs every grove with wild life, and makes himself more important than the great bears that shuffle through the berry tangles beneath him. Every tree feels the sting of his sharp feet. Nature has made him master-forester, and committed the greater part of the coniferous crops to his management. Probably over half of all the ripe cones of the spruces, firs, and pines are cut off and handled by this busy harvester. Most of them are stored away for food through the winter and spring, but a part are pushed into shallow pits and covered loosely, where some of the seeds are no doubt left to germinate and grow up. All the tree squirrels are more or less birdlike in voice and movements, but the Douglas is preëminently so, possessing every squirrelish attribute, fully developed and concentrated. He is the squirrel of squirrels, flashing from branch to branch of his favorite evergreens, crisp and glossy and sound as a sunbeam. He stirs the leaves like a rustling breeze, darting across openings in arrowy lines, launching in curves, glinting deftly from side to side in sudden zigzags, and swirling in giddy loops and spirals around the trunks, now on his haunches, now on his head, yet ever graceful and performing all his feats of strength and skill without apparent effort. One never tires of this bright spark of life, the brave little voice crying in the wilderness. His varied, piney gossip is as savory to the air as balsam to the palate. Some of his notes are almost flutelike in softness, while others prick and tingle like thistles. He is the mockingbird of squirrels, barking like a dog, screaming like a hawk, whistling like a blackbird or linnet, while in bluff, audacious noisiness he is a jay. A small thing, but filling and animating all the woods.

Nor is there any lack of wings, notwithstanding few are to be seen on short, noisy rambles. The ousel sweetens the shady glens and cañons where waterfalls abound, and every grove or forest, however silent it may seem when we chance to pay it a hasty visit, has its singers,—thrushes, linnets, warblers,—while hummingbirds glint and hover about the fringing masses of bloom around stream and meadow openings. But few of these will show themselves or sing their songs to those who are ever in haste and getting lost, going in gangs formidable in color and accoutrements, laughing, hallooing, breaking limbs off the trees as they pass, awkwardly struggling through briery thickets, entangled like blue-bottles in spider-webs, and stopping from time to time to fire off their guns and pistols for the sake of the echoes, thus frightening all the life about them for miles. It is this class of hunters and travelers who report that there are "no birds in the woods or game animals of any kind larger than mosquitoes."

Besides the singing-birds mentioned above, the handsome Oregon grouse may be found in the thick woods, also the dusky grouse and Franklin's grouse, and in some places the beautiful mountain partridge, or quail. The white-tailed ptarmigan lives on the lofty snow peaks above the timber, and the prairie-chicken and sage-cock on the broad Columbia plains from the Cascade Range back to the foothills of the Rocky Mountains. The bald eagle is very common along the Columbia River, or wherever fish, especially salmon, are plentiful, while swans, herons, cranes, pelicans, geese, ducks of many species, and water-birds in general abound in the lake region, on the main streams, and along the coast, stirring the waters and sky into fine, lively pictures, greatly to the delight of wandering lovers of wildness.

23

The Rivers of Oregon

TURNING from the woods and their inhabitants to the rivers, we find that while the former are rarely seen by travelers beyond the immediate borders of the settlements, the great river of Oregon draws crowds of visitors, and is never without enthusiastic admirers to sound its praises. Every summer since the completion of the first overland railroad, tourists have been coming to it in ever increasing numbers, showing that in general estimation the Columbia is one of the chief attractions of the Pacific Coast. And well it deserves the admiration so heartily bestowed upon it. The beauty and majesty of its waters, and the variety and grandeur of the scenery through which it flows, lead many to regard it as the most interesting of all the great rivers of the continent, notwithstanding the claims of the other members of the family to which it belongs and which nobody can measure—the Fraser, McKenzie, Saskatchewan, the Missouri, Yellowstone, Platte, and the Colorado, with their glacier and geyser fountains, their famous cañons, lakes, forests, and vast flowery prairies and plains. These great rivers and the Columbia are intimately related. All draw their upper waters from the same high fountains on the broad, rugged uplift of the Rocky Mountains, their branches interlacing like the branches of trees. They sing their first songs together on the heights; then, collecting their tributaries, they set out on their grand journey to the Atlantic, Pacific, or Arctic Ocean.

The Rivers of Oregon

The Columbia, viewed as one from the sea to the mountains, is like a rugged, broad-topped, picturesque old oak about six hundred miles long and nearly a thousand miles wide measured across the spread of its upper branches, the main limbs gnarled and swollen with lakes and lakelike expansions, while innumerable smaller lakes shine like fruit among the smaller branches. The main trunk extends back through the Coast and Cascade mountains in a general easterly direction for three hundred miles, when it divides abruptly into two grand branches which bend off to the northeastward and southeastward.

The south branch, the longer of the two, called the Snake, or Lewis, River, extends into the Rocky Mountains as far as the Yellowstone National Park, where its head tributaries interlace with those of the Colorado, Missouri, and Yellowstone. The north branch, still called the Columbia, extends through Washington far into British territory, its highest tributaries reaching back through long parallel spurs of the Rockies between and beyond the headwaters of the Fraser, Athabasca, and Saskatchewan. Each of these main branches, dividing again and again, spreads a network of channels over the vast complicated mass of the great range throughout a section nearly a thousand miles in length, searching every fountain, however small or great, and gathering a glorious harvest of crystal water to be rolled through forest and plain in one majestic flood to the sea, reinforced on the way by tributaries that drain the Blue Mountains and more than two hundred miles of the Cascade and Coast ranges. Though less than half as long as the Mississippi, it is said to carry as much water. The amount of its discharge at different seasons, however, has never been exactly measured, but in time of flood its current is sufficiently massive and powerful to penetrate the sea to a distance of fifty or sixty miles from shore, its waters being easily recognized by the difference in color and by the drift of leaves, berries, pine cones, branches, and trunks of trees that they carry.

That so large a river as the Columbia, making a telling current so far from shore, should remain undiscovered while one exploring expedition after another sailed past seems remarkable, even after due allowance is made for the cloudy weather that prevails hereabouts and the broad fence of breakers drawn across the bar. During the last few centuries, when the maps of the world were in great part blank, the search for new worlds was a fashionable business, and when such large game was no longer to be found, islands lying unclaimed in the great oceans, inhabited by useful and profitable people to be converted or enslaved, became attractive objects; also new ways to India, seas, straits, El Dorados, fountains of youth, and rivers that flowed over golden sands.

Those early explorers and adventurers were mostly brave, enterprising, and, after their fashion, pious men. In their clumsy sailing-vessels they dared to go where no chart or lighthouse showed the way, where the set of the currents, the location of sunken outlying rocks and shoals, were all unknown, facing fate and weather, undaunted however dark the signs, heaving the lead and thrashing the men to their duty and trusting to Providence. When a new shore was found on which they could land, they said their prayers with superb audacity, fought the natives if they cared to fight, erected crosses, and took possession in the names of their sovereigns, establishing claims, such as they were, to everything in sight and beyond, to be quarreled for and battled for, and passed from hand to hand in treaties and settlements made during the intermissions of war.

The branch of the river that bears the name of Columbia all the way to its head takes its rise in two lakes about ten miles in length that lie between the Selkirk and main ranges of the Rocky Mountains in British Columbia, about eighty miles beyond the boundary-line. They are called the Upper and Lower Columbia Lakes. Issuing from these, the young river holds a nearly straight course for a hundred and seventy miles in a northwesterly direction to a plain called "Boat Encampment," receiving many beautiful affluents by the way from the Selkirk and main ranges, among which are the Beaver-Foot, Blackberry, Spill-e-Mee-Chene, and Gold rivers. At Boat Encampment it receives two large tributaries, the Canoe River from the northwest, a stream about a hundred and twenty miles long; and the Whirlpool River from the north, about a hundred and forty miles in length.

The Whirlpool River takes its rise near the summit of the main axis of the range on the fifty-fourth parallel, and is the northmost of all the Columbia waters. About thirty miles above its confluence with the Columbia it flows through a lake called the Punch-Bowl, and thence it passes between Mounts Hooker and Brown, said to be fifteen thousand and sixteen thousand feet high, making magnificent scenery; though the height of the mountains thereabouts has been considerably over-estimated. From Boat Encampment the river, now a large, clear stream, said to be nearly a third of a mile in width, doubles back on its original course and flows southward as far as its confluence with the Spokane in Washington, a distance of nearly three hundred miles in a direct line, most of the way through a wild, rocky, picturesque mass of mountains, charmingly forested with pine and spruce—though the trees seem strangely small, like second growth saplings, to one familiar with the western forests of Washington, Oregon, and California.

About forty-five miles below Boat Encampment are the Upper Dalles, or Dalles de Mort, and thirty miles farther the Lower Dalles, where the river makes a magnificent uproar and interrupts navigation. About thirty miles below the Lower Dalles the river expands into Upper Arrow Lake, a beautiful sheet of water forty miles long and five miles wide, straight as an arrow and with the beautiful forests of the Selkirk Range rising from its east shore, and those of the Gold Range from the west. At the foot of the lake are the Narrows, a few miles in length, and after these rapids are passed, the river enters Lower Arrow Lake, which is like the Upper Arrow, but is even longer and not so straight.

A short distance below the Lower Arrow the Columbia receives the Kootenay River, the largest affluent thus far on its course and said to be navigable for small steamers for a hundred and fifty miles. It is an exceedingly crooked stream, heading beyond the upper Columbia lakes, and, in its mazy course, flowing to all points of the compass, it seems lost and baffled in the tangle of mountain spurs and ridges it drains. Measured around its loops and bends, it is probably more than five hundred miles in length. It is also rich in lakes, the largest, Kootenay Lake, being upwards of seventy miles in length with an average width of five miles. A short distance below the confluence of the Kootenay, near the boundary-line between Washington and British Columbia, another large stream comes in from the east, Clarke's Fork, or the Flathead River. Its upper sources are near those of the Missouri and South Saskatchewan, and in its course it flows through two large and beautiful lakes, the Flathead and the Pend d'Oreille. All the lakes we have noticed thus far would make charming places of summer resort; but Pend d'Oreille, besides being surpassingly beautiful, has the advantage of being easily accessible, since it is on the main line of the Northern Pacific Railroad in the Territory of Idaho. In the purity of its waters it reminds one of Tahoe, while its many picturesque islands crowned with evergreens, and its winding shores forming an endless variety of bays and promontories lavishly crowded with spirey spruce and cedar, recall some of the best of the island scenery of Alaska.

About thirty-five miles below the mouth of Clark's Fork the Columbia is joined by the Ne-whoi-al-pit-ku River from the northwest. Here too are the great Chaudière, or Kettle, Falls on the main river, with a total descent of about fifty feet. Fifty miles farther down, the Spokane River, a clear, dashing stream, comes in from the east. It is about one hundred and twenty miles long, and takes its rise in the beautiful Lake Cœur d'Alène, in Idaho, which receives the drainage of nearly a hundred miles of the western slopes of the Bitter Root Mountains, through the St. Joseph and Cœur d'Alène rivers. The lake is about twenty miles long, set in the midst of charming scenery, and, like Pend d'Oreille, is easy of access and is already attracting attention as a summer place for enjoyment, rest, and health.

The famous Spokane Falls are in Washington, about thirty miles below the lake, where the river is outspread and divided and makes a grand descent from a level basaltic plateau, giving rise to one of the most beautiful as well as one of the greatest and most available of water-powers in the State. The city of the same name is built on the plateau along both sides of the series of cascades and falls, which, rushing and sounding through the midst, give singular beauty and animation. The young city is also rushing and booming. It is founded on a rock, leveled and prepared for it, and its streets require no grading or paving. As a power to whirl the machinery of a great city and at the same time to train the people to a love of the sublime and beautiful as displayed in living water, the Spokane Falls are unrivalled, at least as far as my observation has reached. Nowhere else have I seen such lessons given by a river in the streets of a city, such a glad, exulting, abounding outgush, crisp and clear from the mountains, dividing, falling, displaying its wealth, calling aloud in the midst of the busy throng, and making glorious offerings for every use of utility or adornment.

From the mouth of the Spokane the Columbia, now out of the woods, flows to the westward with a broad, stately current for a hundred and twenty miles to receive the Okinagan, a large, generous tributary a hundred and sixty miles long, coming from the north and drawing some of its waters from the Cascade Range. More than half its course is through a chain of lakes, the largest of which at the head of the river is over sixty miles in length. From its confluence with the Okinagan the river pursues a southerly course for a hundred and fifty miles, most of the way through a dreary, treeless, parched plain to meet the great south fork. The Lewis, or Snake, River is nearly a thousand miles long and drains nearly the whole of Idaho, a territory rich in scenery, gold mines, flowery, grassy valleys, and deserts, while some of the highest tributaries reach into Wyoming, Utah, and Nevada. Throughout a great part of its course it is countersunk in a black lava plain and shut in by mural precipices a thousand feet high, gloomy, forbidding, and unapproachable, although the gloominess of its cañon is relieved in some manner by its many falls and springs, some of the springs being large enough to appear as the outlets of subterranean rivers. They gush out from the faces of the sheer black walls and descend foaming with brave roar and beauty to swell the flood below.

From where the river skirts the base of the Blue Mountains its surroundings are less forbidding. Much of the country is fertile, but its cañon is everywhere deep and almost inaccessible. Steamers make their way up as far as Lewiston, a hundred and fifty miles, and receive cargoes of wheat at different points through chutes that extend down from the tops of the bluffs. But though the Hudson's Bay Company navigated the north fork to its sources, they depended altogether on pack-animals for the transportation of supplies and furs between the Columbia and Fort Hall on the head of the south fork, which shows how desperately unmanageable a river it must be.

A few miles above the mouth of the Snake the Yakima, which drains a considerable portion of the Cascade Range, enters from the northwest. It is about a hundred and fifty miles long, but carries comparatively little water, a great part of what it sets out with from the base of the mountains being consumed in irrigated fields and meadows in passing through the settlements along its course, and by evaporation on the parched desert plains. The grand flood of the Columbia, now from half a mile to a mile wide, sweeps on to the westward, holding a nearly direct course until it reaches the mouth of the Willamette, where it turns to the northward and flows fifty miles along the main valley between the Coast and Cascade ranges ere it again resumes its westward course to the sea. In all its course from the mouth of the Yakima to the sea, a distance of three hundred miles, the only considerable affluent from the northward is the Cowlitz, which heads in the glaciers of Mount Rainier.

From the south and east it receives the Walla-Walla and Umatilla, rather short and dreary-looking streams, though the plains they pass through have proved fertile, and their upper tributaries in the Blue Mountains, shaded and tall pines, firs, spruces, and the beautiful Oregon larch (*Larix brevifolia*), lead into a delightful region. The John Day River also heads in the Blue Mountains, and flows into the Columbia sixty miles below the mouth of the Umatilla. Its valley is in great part fertile, and is noted for the interesting fossils discovered in it by Professor Condon in sections cut by the river through the overlying lava-beds.

The Deschutes River comes in from the south about twenty miles below the John Day. It is a large, boisterous stream, draining the eastern slope of the Cascade Range for nearly two hundred miles, and from the great number of falls on the main trunk, as well as on its many mountain tributaries, well deserves its name. It enters the Columbia with a grand roar of falls and rapids, and at times seems almost to rival the main stream in the volume of water it carries. Near the mouth of the Deschutes are the Falls of the Columbia, where the river passes a rough bar of lava. The descent is not great, but the immense volume of water makes a grand display. During the flood-season the falls are obliterated and skillful boatmen pass over them in safety; while the Dalles, some six or eight miles below, may be passed during low water but are utterly impassable in flood-time. At the Dalles the vast river is jammed together into a long, narrow slot of unknown depth cut sheer down in the basalt.

The Rivers of Oregon

This slot, or trough, is about a mile and a half long and about sixty yards wide at the narrowest place. At ordinary times the river seems to be set on edge and runs swiftly but without much noisy surging with a descent of about twenty feet to the mile. But when the snow is melting on the mountains the river rises here sixty feet, or even more during extraordinary freshets, and spreads out over a great breadth of massive rocks through which have been cut several other gorges running parallel with the one usually occupied. All these inferior gorges now come into use, and the huge, roaring torrent, still rising and spreading, at length overwhelms the high jagged rock walls between them, making a tremendous display of chafing, surging, shattered currents, counter-currents, and hollow whirls that no words can be made to describe. A few miles below the Dalles the storm-tossed river gets itself together again, looks like water, becomes silent, and with stately, tranquil deliberation goes on its way, out of the gray region of sage and sand into the Oregon woods. Thirty-five or forty miles below the Dalles are the Cascades of the Columbia, where the river in passing through the mountains makes another magnificent display of foaming, surging rapids, which form the first obstruction to navigation from the ocean, a hundred and twenty miles distant. This obstruction is to be overcome by locks, which are now being made.

Between the Dalles and the Cascades the river is like a lake a mile or two wide, lying in a valley, or cañon, about three thousand feet deep. The walls of the cañon lean well back in most places, and leave here and there small strips, or bays, of level ground along the water's edge. But towards the Cascades, and for some distance below them, the immediate banks are guarded by walls of columnar basalt, which are worn in many places into a great variety of bold and picturesque forms, such as the Castle Rock, the Rooster Rock, the Pillars of Hercules, Cape Horn, etc., while back of these rise the sublime mountain-walls, forest-crowned and fringed more or less from top to base with pine, spruce, and shaggy underbrush, especially in the narrow gorges and ravines, where innumerable small streams come dancing and drifting down, misty and white, to join the mighty river. Many of these falls on both sides of the cañon of the Columbia are far larger and more interesting in every way than would be guessed from the slight glimpses one gets of them while sailing past on the river, or from the car windows. The Multnomah Falls are particularly interesting, and occupy fern-lined gorges of marvelous beauty in the basalt. They are said to be about eight hundred feet in height and, at times of high water when the mountain snows are melting, are well worthy of a place beside the famous falls of the Yosemite Valley.

According to an Indian tradition, the river of the Cascades once flowed through the basalt beneath a natural bridge that was broken down during a mountain war, when the old volcanoes, Hood and St. Helen's, on opposite sides of the river, hurled rocks at each other, thus forming a dam. That the river has been dammed here to some extent, and within a comparatively short period, seems probable, to say the least, since great numbers of submerged trees standing erect may be found along both shores, while, as we have seen, the whole river for thirty miles above the Cascades looks like a lake or mill-pond. On the other hand, it is held by some that the submerged groves were carried into their places by immense landslides.

Much of interest in this connection must necessarily be omitted for want of space. About forty miles below the Cascades the river receives the Willamette, the last of its great tributaries. It is navigable for ocean vessels as far as Portland, ten miles above its mouth, and for river steamers a hundred miles farther. The Falls of the Willamette are fifteen miles above Portland, where the river, coming out of dense woods, breaks its way across a bar of black basalt and falls forty feet in a passion of snowy foam, showing to fine advantage against its background of evergreens.

Of the fertility and beauty of the Willamette all the world has heard. It lies between the Cascade and Coast ranges, and is bounded on the south by the Calapooya Mountains, a cross-spur that separates it from the valley of the Umpqua.

It was here the first settlements for agriculture were made and a provisional government organized, while the settlers, isolated in the far wilderness, numbered only a few thousand and were laboring under the opposition of the British Government and the Hudson's Bay Company. Eager desire in the acquisition of territory on the part of these pioneer state-builders was more truly boundless than the wilderness they were in, and their unconscionable patriotism was equaled only by their belligerence. For here, while negotiations were pending for the location of the northern boundary, originated the celebrated "Fifty-four forty or fight," about as reasonable a war-cry as the "North Pole or fight." Yet sad was the day that brought the news of the signing of the treaty fixing their boundary along the forty-ninth parallel, thus leaving the little land-hungry settlement only a mere quarter-million of miles!

As the Willamette is one of the most foodful of valleys, so is the Columbia one of the most foodful of rivers. During the fisher's harvest-time salmon from the sea come in countless millions, urging their way against falls, rapids, and shallows, up into the very heart of the Rocky Mountains, supplying everybody by the way with most bountiful masses of delicious food, weighing from twenty to eighty pounds each, plump and smooth like loaves of bread ready for the oven. The supply seemed inexhaustible, as well it might. Large quantities were used by the Indians as fuel, and by the Hudson's Bay people as manure for their gardens at the forts. Used, wasted, canned and sent in shiploads to all the world, a grand harvest was reaped every year while nobody sowed. Of late, however, the salmon crop has begun to fail, and millions of young fry are now sown like wheat in the river every year, from hatching-establishments belonging to the Government.

All of the Oregon waters that win their way to the sea are tributary to the Columbia, save the short streams of the immediate coast, and the Umpqua and Rogue rivers in southern Oregon. These both head in the Cascade Mountains and find their way to the sea through gaps in the Coast Range, and both drain large and fertile and beautiful valleys. Rogue River Valley is peculiarly attractive. With a fine climate, and kindly, productive soil, the scenery is delightful. About the main, central open portion of the basin, dotted with picturesque groves of oak, there are many smaller valleys charmingly environed, the whole surrounded in the distance by the Siskiyou, Coast, Umpqua, and Cascade mountains. Besides the cereals nearly every sort of fruit flourishes here, and large areas are being devoted to peach, apricot, nectarine, and vine culture. To me it seems above all others the garden valley of Oregon and the most delightful place for a home. On the eastern rim of the valley, in the Cascade Mountains, about sixty miles from Medford in a direct line, is the remarkable Crater Lake, usually regarded as the one grand wonder of the region. It lies in a deep, sheer-walled basin about seven thousand feet above the level of the sea, supposed to be the crater of an extinct volcano.

Oregon as it is to-day is a very young country, though most of it seems old. Contemplating the Columbia sweeping from forest to forest, across plain and desert, one is led to say of it, as did Byron of the ocean,—

Such as Creation's dawn beheld, thou rollest now.

How ancient appear the crumbling basaltic monuments along its banks, and the gray plains to the east of the Cascades! Nevertheless, the river as well as its basin in anything like their present condition are comparatively but of yesterday. Looming no further back in the geological records than the Tertiary Period, the Oregon of that time looks altogether strange in the few suggestive glimpses we may get of it—forests in which palm trees wave their royal crowns, and strange animals roaming beneath them or about the reedy margins of lakes, the oreodon, the lophiodon, and several extinct species of the horse, the camel, and other animals.

Then came the fire period with its darkening showers of ashes and cinders and its vast floods of molten lava, making quite another Oregon from the fair and fertile land of the preceding era. And again, while yet the volcanic fires show signs of action in the smoke and flame of the higher mountains, the whole region passes under the dominion of ice, and from the frost and darkness and death of the Glacial Period, Oregon has but recently emerged to the kindly warmth and life of to-day.

24

The Grand Cañon of the Colorado

HAPPY nowadays is the tourist, with earth's wonders, new and old, spread invitingly open before him, and a host of able workers as his slaves making everything easy, padding plush about him, grading roads for him, boring tunnels, moving hills out of his way, eager, like the Devil, to show him all the kingdoms of the world and their glory and foolishness, spiritualizing travel for him with lightning and steam, abolishing space and time and almost everything else. Little children and tender, pulpy people, as well as storm-seasoned explorers, may now go almost everywhere in smooth comfort, cross oceans and deserts scarce accessible to fishes and birds, and, dragged by steel horses, go up high mountains, riding gloriously beneath starry showers of sparks, ascending like Elijah in a whirlwind and chariot of fire.

First of the wonders of the great West to be brought within reach of the tourist were the Yosemite and the Big Trees, on the completion of the first transcontinental railway; next came the Yellowstone and icy Alaska, by the northern roads; and last the Grand Cañon of the Colorado, which, naturally the hardest to reach, has now become, by a branch of the Santa Fé, the most accessible of all.

Of course, with this wonderful extension of steel ways through our wildness there is loss as well as gain. Nearly all railroads are bordered by belts of desolation. The finest wilderness perishes as if stricken with pestilence. Bird and beast people, if not the dryads, are frightened from the groves. Too often the groves also vanish, leaving nothing but ashes. Fortunately, nature has a few big places beyond man's power to spoil—the ocean, the two icy ends of the globe, and the Grand Cañon.

When I first heard of the Santa Fé trains running to the edge of the Grand Cañon of Arizona, I was troubled with thoughts of the disenchantment likely to follow. But last winter, when I saw those trains crawling along through the pines of the Coconino Forest and close up to the brink of the chasm at Bright Angel, I was glad to discover that in the presence of such stupendous scenery they are nothing. The locomotives and trains are mere beetles and caterpillars, and the noise they make is as little disturbing as the hooting of an owl in the lonely woods.

In a dry, hot, monotonous forested plateau, seemingly boundless, you come suddenly and without warning upon the abrupt edge of a gigantic sunken landscape of the wildest, most multitudinous features, and those features, sharp and angular, are made out of flat beds of limestone and sandstone forming a spiry, jagged, gloriously colored mountain-range countersunk in a level gray plain. It is a hard job to sketch it even in scrawniest outline; and, try as I may, not in the least sparing myself, I cannot tell the hundredth part of the wonders of its features—the side-cañons, gorges, alcoves, cloisters, and amphitheaters of vast sweep and depth, carved in its magnificent walls; the throng of great architectural rocks it contains resembling castles, cathedrals, temples, and palaces, towered and spired and painted, some of them nearly a mile high, yet beneath one's feet. All this, however, is less difficult than to give any idea of the impression of wild, primeval beauty and power one receives in merely gazing from its brink. The view down the gulf of color and over the rim of its wonderful wall, more than any other view I know, leads us to think of our earth as a star with stars swimming in light, every radiant spire pointing the way to the heavens.

But it is impossible to conceive what the cañon is, or what impression it makes, from descriptions or pictures, however good. Naturally it is untellable even to those who have seen something perhaps a little like it on a small scale in this same plateau region. One's most extravagant expectations are indefinitely surpassed, though one expects much from what is said of it as "the biggest chasm on earth"—"so big is it that all other big things—Yosemite, the Yellowstone, the Pyramids, Chicago—all would be lost if tumbled into it." Naturally enough, illustrations as to size are sought for among other cañons like or unlike it, with the common result of worse confounding confusion. The prudent keep silence. It was once said that the "Grand Cañon could put a dozen Yosemites in its vest pocket."

The justly famous Grand Cañon of the Yellowstone is, like the Colorado, gorgeously colored and abruptly countersunk in a plateau, and both are mainly the work of water. But the Colorado's cañon is more than a thousand times larger, and as a score or two of new buildings of ordinary size would not appreciably change the general view of a great city, so hundreds of Yellowstones might be eroded in the sides of the Colorado Cañon without noticeably augmenting its size or the richness of its sculpture.

But it is not true that the great Yosemite rocks would be thus lost or hidden. Nothing of their kind in the world, so far as I know, rivals El Capitan and Tissiack, much less dwarfs or in any way belittles them. None of the sandstone or limestone precipices of the cañon that I have seen or heard of approaches in smooth, flawless strength and grandeur the granite face of El Capitan or the Tenaya side of Cloud's Rest. These colossal cliffs, types of permanence, are about three thousand and six thousand feet high; those of the cañon that are sheer are about half as high, and are types of fleeting change; while glorious-domed Tissiack, noblest of mountain buildings, far from being overshadowed or lost in this rosy, spiry cañon company, would draw every eye, and, in serene majesty, "aboon them a'" she would take her place—castle, temple, palace, or tower. Nevertheless a noted writer, comparing the Grand Cañon in a general way with the glacial Yosemite, says: "And the Yosemite—ah, the lovely Yosemite! Dumped down into the wilderness of gorges and mountains, it would take a guide who knew of its existence a long time to find it." This is striking, and shows up well above the levels of commonplace description; but it is confusing, and has the fatal fault of not being true. As well try to describe an eagle by putting a lark in it. "And, the lark—ah, the lovely lark! Dumped down the red, royal gorge of the eagle, it would be hard to find." Each in its own place is better, singing at heaven's gate, and sailing the sky with the clouds.

Every feature of Nature's big face is beautiful,—height and hollow, wrinkle, furrow, and line,—and this is the main masterfurrow of its kind on our continent, incomparably greater and more impressive than any other yet discovered, or likely to be discovered, now that all the great rivers have been traced to their heads.

The Colorado River rises in the heart of the continent on the dividing ranges and ridges between the two oceans, drains thousands of snowy mountains through narrow or spacious valleys, and thence through cañons of every color, sheer-walled and deep, all of which seem to be represented in this one grand cañon of cañons.

It is very hard to give anything like an adequate conception of its size; much more of its color, its vast wall-sculpture, the wealth of ornate architectural buildings that fill it, or, most of all, the tremendous impression it makes. According to Major Powell, it is about two hundred and seventeen miles long, from five to fifteen miles wide from rim to rim, and from about five thousand to six thousand feet deep. So tremendous a chasm would be one of the world's greatest wonders even if, like ordinary cañons cut in sedimentary rocks, it were empty and its walls were simple. But instead of being plain, the walls are so deeply and elaborately carved into all sorts of recesses—alcoves, cirques, amphitheaters, and side-cañons—that, were you to trace the rim closely around on both sides, your journey would be nearly a thousand miles long. Into all these recesses the level, continuous beds of rock in ledges and benches, with their various colors, run like broad ribbons, marvelously beautiful and effective even at a distance of ten or twelve miles. And the vast space these glorious walls inclose, instead of being empty, is crowded with gigantic architectural rock-forms gorgeously colored and adorned with towers and spires like works of art.

Looking down from this level plateau, we are more impressed with a feeling of being on the top of everything than when looking from the summit of a mountain. From side to side of the vast gulf, temples, palaces, towers, and spires come soaring up in thick array half a mile or nearly a mile above their sunken, hidden bases, some to a level with our standpoint, but none higher. And in the inspiring morning light all are so fresh and rosy-looking that they seem new-born; as if, like the quick-growing crimson snow-plants of the California woods, they had just sprung up, hatched by the warm, brooding, motherly weather.

In trying to describe the great pines and sequoias of the Sierra, I have often thought that if one of these trees could be set by itself in some city park, its grandeur might there be impressively realized; while in its home forests, where all magnitudes are great, the weary, satiated traveler sees none of them truly. It is so with these majestic rock structures.

Though mere residual masses of the plateau, they are dowered with the grandeur and repose of mountains, together with the finely chiseled carving and modeling of man's temples and palaces, and often, to a considerable extent, with their symmetry. Some, closely observed, look like ruins; but even these stand plumb and true, and show architectural forms loaded with lines strictly regular and decorative, and all are arrayed in colors that storms and time seem only to brighten. They are not placed in regular rows in line with the river, but "a' through ither," as the Scotch say, in lavish, exuberant crowds, as if nature in wildest extravagance held her bravest structures as common as gravel-piles. Yonder stands a spiry cathedral nearly five thousand feet in height, nobly symmetrical, with sheer buttressed walls and arched doors and windows, as richly finished and decorated with sculptures as the great rock temples of India or Egypt. Beside it rises a huge castle with arched gateway, turrets, watch-towers, ramparts, etc., and to right and left palaces, obelisks, and pyramids fairly fill the gulf, all colossal and all lavishly painted and carved. Here and there a flat-topped structure may be seen, or one imperfectly domed; but the prevailing style is ornate Gothic, with many hints of Egyptian and Indian.

Throughout this vast extent of wild architecture—nature's own capital city—there seem to be no ordinary dwellings. All look like grand and important public structures, except perhaps some of the lower pyramids, broad-based and sharp-pointed, covered with down-flowing talus like loosely set tents with hollow, sagging sides. The roofs often have disintegrated rocks heaped and draggled over them, but in the main the masonry is firm and laid in regular courses, as if done by square and rule.

Nevertheless they are ever changing: their tops are now a dome, now a flat table or a spire, as harder or softer strata are reached in their slow degradation, while the sides, with all their fine moldings, are being steadily undermined and eaten away. But no essential change in style or color is thus effected. From century to century they stand the same. What seems confusion among the rough earthquake-shaken crags nearest one comes to order as soon as the main plan of the various structures appears. Every building, however complicated and laden with ornamental lines, is at one with itself and every one of its neighbors, for the same characteristic controlling belts of color and solid strata extend with wonderful constancy for very great distances, and pass through and give style to thousands of separate structures, however their smaller characters may vary.

Of all the various kinds of ornamental work displayed—carving, tracery on cliff-faces, moldings, arches, pinnacles—none is more admirably effective or charms more than the webs of rain-channeled taluses. Marvelously extensive, without the slightest appearance of waste or excess, they cover roofs and dome-tops and the base of every cliff, belt each spire and pyramid and massy, towering temple, and in beautiful continuous lines go sweeping along the great walls in and out around all the intricate system of side-cañons, amphitheaters, cirques, and scallops into which they are sculptured. From one point hundreds of miles of this fairy embroidery may be traced. It is all so fine and orderly that it would seem that not only had the clouds and streams been kept harmoniously busy in the making of it, but that every raindrop sent like a bullet to a mark had been the subject of a separate thought, so sure is the outcome of beauty through the stormy centuries. Surely nowhere else are there illustrations so striking of the natural beauty of desolation and death, so many of nature's own mountain buildings wasting in glory of high desert air—going to dust. See how steadfast in beauty they all are in their going. Look again and again how the rough, dusty boulders and sand of disintegration from the upper ledges wreathe in beauty the next and next below with these wonderful taluses, and how the colors are finer the faster the waste. We oftentimes see Nature giving beauty for ashes—as in the flowers of a prairie after fire—but here the very dust and ashes are beautiful.

Gazing across the mighty chasm, we at last discover that it is not its great depth nor length, nor yet these wonderful buildings, that most impresses us. It is its immense width, sharply defined by precipitous walls plunging suddenly down from a flat plain, declaring in terms instantly apprehended that the vast gulf is a gash in the once unbroken plateau, made by slow, orderly erosion and removal of huge beds of rocks. Other valleys of erosion are as great—in all their dimensions some are greater—but none of these produces an effect on the imagination at once so quick and profound, coming without study, given at a glance. Therefore by far the greatest and most influential feature of this view from Bright Angel or any other of the cañon views is the opposite wall. Of the one beneath our feet we see only fragmentary sections in cirques and amphitheaters and on the sides of the out-jutting promontories between them, while the other, though far distant, is beheld in all its glory of color and noble proportions—the one supreme beauty and wonder to which the eye is ever turning. For while charming with its beauty it tells the story of the stupendous erosion of the cañon—the foundation of the unspeakable impression made on everybody. It seems a gigantic statement for even nature to make, all in one mighty stone word, apprehended at once like a burst of light, celestial color its natural vesture, coming in glory to mind and heart as to a home prepared for it from the very beginning. Wildness so godful, cosmic, primeval, bestows a new sense of earth's beauty and size. Not even from high mountains does the world seem so wide, so like a star in glory of light on its way through the heavens.

I have observed scenery-hunters of all sorts getting first views of yosemites, glaciers, White Mountain ranges, etc. Mixed with the enthusiasm which such scenery naturally excites, there is often weak gushing, and many splutter aloud like little waterfalls. Here, for a few moments at least, there is silence, and all are in dead earnest, as if awed and hushed by an earthquake—perhaps until the cook cries "Breakfast!" or the stable-boy "Horses are ready!" Then the poor unfortunates, slaves of regular habits, turn quickly away, gasping and muttering as if wondering where they had been and what had enchanted them.

The Grand Cañon

Roads have been made from Bright Angel Hotel through the Coconino Forest to the ends of outstanding promontories, commanding extensive views up and down the cañon. The nearest of them, three or four miles east and west, are McNeil's Point and Rowe's Point; the latter, besides commanding the eternally interesting cañon, gives wide-sweeping views southeast and west over the dark forest roof to the San Francisco and Mount Trumbull volcanoes—the bluest of mountains over the blackest of level woods.

Instead of thus riding in dust with the crowd, more will be gained by going quietly afoot along the rim at different times of day and night, free to observe the vegetation, the fossils in the rocks, the seams beneath overhanging ledges once inhabited by Indians, and to watch the stupendous scenery in the changing lights and shadows, clouds, showers, and storms. One need not go hunting the so-called "points of interest." The verge anywhere, everywhere, is a point of interest beyond one's wildest dreams.

As yet, few of the promontories or throng of mountain buildings in the cañon are named. Nor among such exuberance of forms are names thought of by the bewildered, hurried tourist. He would be as likely to think of names for waves in a storm. The Eastern and Western Cloisters, Hindu Amphitheater, Cape Royal, Powell's Plateau, Grand View Point, Point Sublime, Bissell and Moran Points, the Temple of Set, Vishnu's Temple, Shiva's Temple, Twin Temples, Tower of Babel, Hance's Column—these fairly good names given by Dutton, Holmes, Moran, and others are scattered over a large stretch of the cañon wilderness.

All the cañon rock-beds are lavishly painted, except a few neutral bars and the granite notch at the bottom occupied by the river, which makes but little sign. It is a vast wilderness of rocks in a sea of light, colored and glowing like oak and maple woods in autumn, when the sun-gold is richest. I have just said that it is impossible to learn what the cañon is like from descriptions and pictures. Powell's and Dutton's descriptions present magnificent views not only of the cañon but of all the grand region round about it; and Holmes's drawings, accompanying Dutton's report, are wonderfully good. Surely faithful and loving skill can go no farther in putting the multitudinous decorated forms on paper. But the *colors*, the living, rejoicing *colors*, chanting morning and evening in chorus to heaven! Whose brush or pencil, however lovingly inspired, can give us these? And if paint is of no effect, what hope lies in pen-work? Only this: some may be incited by it to go and see for themselves.

No other range of mountainous rock-work of anything like the same extent have I seen that is so strangely, boldly, lavishly colored. The famous Yellowstone Cañon below the falls comes to mind; but, wonderful as it is, and well deserved as is its fame, compared with this it is only a bright rainbow ribbon at the roots of the pines. Each of the series of level, continuous beds of carboniferous rocks of the cañon has, as we have seen, its own characteristic color. The summit limestone-beds are pale yellow; next below these are the beautiful rose-colored cross-bedded sandstones; next there are a thousand feet of brilliant red sandstones; and below these the red wall limestones, over two thousand feet thick, rich massy red, the greatest and most influential of the series, and forming the main color-fountain. Between these are many neutral-tinted beds. The prevailing colors are wonderfully deep and clear, changing and blending with varying intensity from hour to hour, day to day, season to season; throbbing, wavering, glowing, responding to every passing cloud or storm, a world of color in itself, now burning in separate rainbow bars streaked and blotched with shade, now glowing in one smooth, all-pervading ethereal radiance like the alpenglow, uniting the rocky world with the heavens.

The dawn, as in all the pure, dry desert country is ineffably beautiful; and when the first level sunbeams sting the domes and spires, with what a burst of power the big, wild days begin! The dead and the living, rocks and hearts alike, awake and sing the new-old song of creation. All the massy headlands and salient angles of the walls, and the multitudinous temples and palaces, seem to catch the light at once, and cast thick black shadows athwart hollow and gorge, bringing out details as well as the main massive features of the architecture; while all the rocks, as if wild with life, throb and quiver and glow in the glorious sunburst, rejoicing. Every rock temple then becomes a temple of music; every spire and pinnacle an angel of light and song, shouting color hallelujahs.

As the day draws to a close, shadows, wondrous, black, and thick, like those of the morning, fill up the wall hollows, while the glowing rocks, their rough angles burned off, seem soft and hot to the heart as they stand submerged in purple haze, which now fills the cañon like a sea. Still deeper, richer, more divine grow the great walls and temples, until in the supreme flaming glory of sunset the whole cañon is transfigured, as if all the life and light of centuries of sunshine stored up and condensed in the rocks was now being poured forth as from one glorious fountain, flooding both earth and sky.

Strange to say, in the full white effulgence of the midday hours the bright colors grow dim and terrestrial in common gray haze; and the rocks, after the manner of mountains, seem to crouch and drowse and shrink to less than half their real stature, and have nothing to say to one, as if not at home. But it is fine to see how quickly they come to life and grow radiant and communicative as soon as a band of white clouds come floating by. As if shouting for joy, they seem to spring up to meet them in hearty salutation, eager to touch them and beg their blessings. It is just in the midst of these dull midday hours that the cañon clouds are born.

A good storm-cloud full of lightning and rain on its way to its work on a sunny desert day is a glorious object. Across the cañon, opposite the hotel, is a little tributary of the Colorado called Bright Angel Creek. A fountain-cloud still better deserves the name "Angel of the Desert Wells"—clad in bright plumage, carrying cool shade and living water to countless animals and plants ready to perish, noble in form and gesture, seeming able for anything, pouring life-giving, wonder-working floods from its alabaster fountains, as if some sky-lake had broken. To every gulch and gorge on its favorite ground is given a passionate torrent, roaring, replying to the rejoicing lightning—stones, tons in weight, hurrying away as if frightened, showing something of the way Grand Cañon work is done. Most of the fertile summer clouds of the cañon are of this sort, massive, swelling cumuli, growing rapidly, displaying delicious tones of purple and gray in the hollows of their sun-beaten houses, showering favored areas of the heated landscape, and vanishing in an hour or two. Some, busy and thoughtful-looking, glide with beautiful motion along the middle of the cañon in flocks, turning aside here and there, lingering as if studying the needs of particular spots, exploring side-cañons, peering into hol-

The Grand Cañon

lows like birds seeking nest-places, or hovering aloft on outspread wings. They scan all the red wilderness, dispensing their blessings of cool shadows and rain where the need is the greatest, refreshing the rocks, their offspring as well as the vegetation, continuing their sculpture, deepening gorges and sharpening peaks. Sometimes, blending all together, they weave a ceiling from rim to rim, perhaps opening a window here and there for sunshine to stream through, suddenly lighting some palace or temple and making it flare in the rain as if on fire.

Sometimes, as one sits gazing from a high, jutting promontory, the sky all clear, showing not the slightest wisp or penciling, a bright band of cumuli will appear suddenly, coming up the cañon in single file, as if tracing a well-known trail, passing in review, each in turn darting its lances and dropping its shower, making a row of little vertical rivers in the air above the big brown one. Others seem to grow from mere points, and fly high above the cañon, yet following its course for a long time, noiseless, as if hunting, then suddenly darting lightning at unseen marks, and hurrying on. Or they loiter here and there as if idle, like laborers out of work, waiting to be hired.

Half a dozen or more showers may oftentimes be seen falling at once, while far the greater part of the sky is in sunshine, and not a raindrop comes nigh one. These thundershowers from as many separate clouds, looking like wisps of long hair, may vary greatly in effects. The pale, faint streaks are showers that fail to reach the ground, being evaporated on the way down through the dry, thirsty air, like streams in deserts. Many, on the other hand, which in the distance seem insignificant, are really heavy rain, however local; these are the gray wisps well zigzagged with lightning. The darker

[261]

ones are torrent rain, which on broad, steep slopes of favorable conformation give rise to so-called "cloud-bursts"; and wonderful is the commotion they cause. The gorges and gulches below them, usually dry, break out in loud uproar, with a sudden downrush of muddy, boulder-laden floods. Down they all go in one simultaneous gush, roaring like lions rudely awakened, each of the tawny brood actually kicking up a dust at the first onset.

During the winter months snow falls over all the high plateau, usually to a considerable depth, whitening the rim and the roofs of the cañon buildings. But last winter, when I arrived at Bright Angel in the middle of January, there was no snow in sight, and the ground was dry, greatly to my disappointment, for I had made the trip mainly to see the cañon in its winter garb. Soothingly I was informed that this was an exceptional season, and that the good snow might arrive at any time. After waiting a few days, I gladly hailed a broad-browed cloud coming grandly on from the west in big promising blackness, very unlike the white sailors of the summer skies. Under the lee of a rim-ledge, with another snow-lover, I watched its movements as it took possession of the cañon and all the adjacent region in sight. Trailing its gray fringes over the spiry tops of the great temples and towers, it gradually settled lower, embracing them all with ineffable kindness and gentleness of touch, and fondled the little cedars and pines as they quivered eagerly in the wind like young birds begging their mothers to feed them. The first flakes and crystals began to fly about noon, sweeping straight up the middle of the cañon, and swirling in magnificent eddies along the sides. Gradually the hearty swarms closed their ranks, and all the cañon was lost in gray gloom except a short section of the wall and a few trees beside us, which looked glad with snow in their needles and about their feet as they leaned out over the gulf. Suddenly the storm opened with magical effect to the north over the cañon of Bright Angel Creek, inclosing a sunlit mass of the cañon architecture, spanned by great white concentric arches of cloud like the bows of a silvery aurora. Above these and a little back of them was a series of upboiling purple clouds, and high above all, in the background, a range of noble cumuli towered aloft like snow-laden mountains, their pure pearl bosses flooded with sunshine. The whole noble picture, calmly glowing, was framed in thick gray gloom, which soon closed over it; and the storm went on, opening and closing until night covered all.

Two days later, when we were on a jutting point about eighteen miles east of Bright Angel and one thousand feet higher, we enjoyed another storm of equal glory as to cloud effects, though only a few inches of snow fell. Before the storm began we had a magnificent view of this grander upper part of the cañon and also of the Coconino Forest and the Painted Desert. The march of the clouds with their storm banners flying over this sublime landscape was unspeakably glorious, and so also was the breaking up of the storm next morning—the mingling of silver-capped rock, sunshine, and cloud.

Most tourists make out to be in a hurry even here; therefore their days or hours would be best spent on the promontories nearest the hotel. Yet a surprising number go down the Bright Angel Trail to the brink of the inner gloomy granite gorge overlooking the river. Deep cañons attract like high mountains; the deeper they are, the more surely we are drawn into them. On foot, of course, there is no danger whatever, and, with ordinary precautions, but little on animals. In comfortable tourist faith, unthinking, unfearing, down go men, women, and children on whatever is offered, horse, mule, or burro, as if saying with Jean Paul, "fear nothing but fear"—not without reason, for these cañon trails down the stairways of the gods are less dangerous than they seem, less dangerous than home stairs. The guides are cautious, and so are the experienced, much-enduring beasts. The scrawniest Rosinantes and wizened-rat mules cling hard to the rocks endwise or sidewise, like lizards or ants. From terrace to terrace, climate to climate, down one creeps in sun and shade, through gorge and gully and grassy ravine, and, after a long scramble on foot, at last beneath the mighty cliffs one comes to the grand, roaring river.

To the mountaineer the depth of the cañon, from five thousand to six thousand feet, will not seem so very wonderful, for he has often explored others that are about as deep. But the most experienced will be awestruck by the vast extent of strange, countersunk scenery, the multitude of huge rock monuments of painted masonry built up in regular courses towering above, beneath, and round about him. By the Bright Angel Trail the last fifteen hundred feet of the descent to the river has to be made afoot down the gorge of Indian Garden Creek. Most of the visitors do not like this part, and are content to stop at the end of the horse-trail and look down on the dull-brown flood from the edge of the Indian Garden Plateau. By the new Hance Trail, excepting a few daringly steep spots, you can ride all the way to the river, where there is a good spacious camp-ground in a mesquite grove. This trail, built by brave Hance, begins on the highest part of the rim, eight thousand feet above the sea, a thousand feet higher than the head of Bright Angel Trail, and the descent is a little over six thousand feet, through a wonderful variety of climate and life. Often late in the fall, when frosty winds are blowing and snow is flying at one end of the trail, tender plants are blooming in balmy summer weather at the other. The trip down and up can be made afoot easily in a day. In this way one is free to observe the scenery and vegetation, instead of merely clinging to his animal and watching its steps. But all who have time should go prepared to camp awhile on the river-bank, to rest and learn something about the plants and animals and the mighty flood roaring past. In cool, shady amphitheaters at the head of the trail there are groves of white silver fir and Douglas spruce, with ferns and saxifrages that recall snowy mountains; below these, yellow pine, nut pine, juniper, hop-hornbeam, ash, maple, holly-leaved berberis, cowania, spiræa, dwarf oak, and other small shrubs and trees. In dry gulches and on taluses and sun-beaten crags are sparsely scattered yuccas, cactuses, agave, etc. Where springs gush from the rocks there are willow thickets, grassy flats, and bright, flowery gardens, and in the hottest recesses the delicate abronia, mesquite, woody compositæ, and arborescent cactuses.

The most striking and characteristic part of this widely varied vegetation are the cactaceæ—strange, leafless, old-fashioned plants with beautiful flowers and fruit, in every way able and admirable. While grimly defending themselves with innumerable barbed spears, they offer both food and drink to man and beast. Their juicy globes and disks and fluted cylindrical columns are almost the only desert wells that never go dry, and they always seem to rejoice the more and grow plumper and juicier the hotter the sunshine and sand. Some are spherical, like rolled-up porcupines, crouching in rock-hollows beneath a mist of gray lances, unmoved by the wildest winds. Others, standing as erect as bushes and trees or tall branchless pillars crowned with magnificent flowers, their prickly armor sparkling, look boldly abroad over the glaring desert, making the strangest forests ever seen or dreamed of. *Cereus gigan-teus*, the grim chief of the desert tribe, is often thirty or forty feet high in southern Arizona. Several species of tree yuccas in the same deserts, laden in early spring with superb white lilies, form forests hardly less wonderful, though here they grow singly or in small lonely groves. The low, almost stemless *Yucca baccata*, with beautiful lily flowers and sweet banana-like fruit, prized by the Indians, is common along the cañon-rim, growing on lean, rocky soil beneath mountain-mahogany, nut pines, and junipers, beside dense flowery mats of *Spiræa cæspitosa* and the beautiful pinnate-leaved *Spiræa millefolia*. The nut pine (*Pinus edulis*) scattered along the upper slopes and roofs of the cañon buildings, is the principal tree of the strange dwarf Coconino Forest. It is a pictur-esque stub of a pine about twenty-five feet high, usually with dead, lichened limbs thrust through its rounded head, and grows on crags and fissured rock tables, braving heat and frost, snow and drought, and continuing patiently, faithfully fruitful for centuries. Indians and insects and almost every desert bird and beast come to it to be fed.

To civilized people from corn and cattle and wheat-field countries the cañon at first sight seems as uninhabitable as a glacier crevasse, utterly silent and barren. Nevertheless it is the home of a multitude of our fellow-mortals, men as well as animals and plants. Centuries ago it was inhabited by tribes of Indians, who, long before Columbus saw America, built thousands of stone houses in its crags, and large ones, some of them several stories high, with hundreds of rooms, on the mesas of the adjacent re-gions. Their cliff-dwellings, almost numberless, are still to be seen in the cañon, scattered along both sides from top to bottom and throughout its entire length, built of stone and mortar in seams and fissures like swallows' nests, or on isolated ridges and peaks. The ruins of larger buildings are found on open spots by the river, but most of them aloft on the brink of the wildest, giddiest precipices, sites evidently chosen for safety from enemies, and seemingly accessible only to the birds of the air. Many caves were also used as dwelling-places, as were mere seams on cliff-fronts formed by unequal weathering and with or without outer or side walls; and some of them were covered with colored pictures of animals. The most interesting of these cliff-dwellings had pathetic little ribbon-like strips of garden on narrow terraces, where irrigating-water could be carried to them—most romantic of sky-gardens, but eloquent of hard times.

In recesses along the river and on the first plateau flats above its gorge were fields and gardens of considerable size, where irrigating-ditches may still be traced. Some of these ancient gardens are still cultivated by Indians, descendants of cliff-dwellers, who raise corn, squashes, melons, potatoes, etc., to reinforce the produce of the many wild food-furnishing plants—nuts, beans, berries, yucca and cactus fruits, grass and sunflower seeds, etc.—and the flesh of animals—deer, rabbits, lizards, etc. The cañon Indians I have met here seem to be living much as did their ancestors, though not now driven into rock-dens. They are able, erect men, with commanding eyes, which nothing that they wish to see can escape. They are never in a hurry, have a strikingly measured, deliberate, bearish manner of moving the limbs and turning the head, are capable of enduring weather, thirst, hunger, and over-abundance, and are blessed with stomachs which triumph over everything the wilderness may offer. Evidently their lives are not bitter.

The largest of the cañon animals one is likely to see is the wild sheep, or Rocky Mountain bighorn, a most admirable beast, with limbs that never fail, at home on the most nerve-trying precipices, acquainted with all the springs and passes and broken-down jumpable places in the sheer ribbon cliffs, bounding from crag to crag in easy grace and confidence of strength, his great horns held high above his shoulders, wild red blood beating and hissing through every fiber of him like the wind through a quivering mountain pine.

Deer also are occasionally met in the cañon, making their way to the river when the wells of the plateau are dry. Along the short spring streams beavers are still busy, as is shown by the cottonwood and willow timber they have cut and peeled, found in all the river drift-heaps. In the most barren cliffs and gulches there dwell a multitude of lesser animals, well-dressed, clear-eyed, happy little beasts—wood rats, kangaroo rats, gophers, wood mice, skunks, rabbits, bob-cats, and many others, gathering food, or dozing in their sun-warmed dens. Lizards, too, of every kind and color are here enjoying life on the hot cliffs, and making the brightest of them brighter.

Nor is there any lack of feathered people. The golden eagle may be seen, and the osprey, hawks, jays, hummingbirds, the mourning dove, and cheery familiar singers—the black-headed grosbeak, robin, bluebird, Townsend's thrush, and many warblers, sailing the sky and enlivening the rocks and bushes through all the cañon wilderness.

Here at Hance's river-camp or a few miles above it brave Powell and his brave men passed their first night in the cañon on their adventurous voyage of discovery thirty-three[1] years ago. They faced a thousand dangers, open or hidden, now in their boats gladly sliding down swift, smooth reaches, now rolled over and over in back-combing surges of rough, roaring cataracts, sucked under in eddies, swimming like beavers, tossed and beaten like castaway drift—stout-hearted, undaunted, doing their work through it all. After a month of this they floated smoothly out of the dark, gloomy, roaring abyss into light and safety two hundred miles below. As the flood rushes past us, heavy-laden with desert mud, we naturally think of its sources, its countless silvery branches outspread on thousands of snowy mountains along the crest of the continent, and the life of them, the beauty of them, their history and romance. Its topmost springs are far north and east in Wyoming and Colorado, on the snowy Wind River, Front, Park, and Sawatch ranges, dividing the two ocean waters, and the Elk, Wahsatch, Uinta, and innumerable spurs streaked with streams, made famous by early explorers and hunters. It is a river of rivers—the Du Chesne, San Rafael, Yampa, Dolores, Gunnison, Cochetopa, Uncompahgre, Eagle, and Roaring rivers, the Green and the Grand, and scores of others with branches innumerable, as mad and glad a band as ever sang on mountains, descending in glory of foam and spray from snow-banks and glaciers through their rocky moraine-dammed, beaver-dammed channels. Then, all emerging from dark balsam and pine woods and coming together, they meander through wide, sunny park valleys, and at length enter the

---

[1]Muir wrote this description in 1902; Major J. W. Powell made his descent through the cañon, with small boats, in 1869. [Editor.]

great plateau and flow in deep cañons, the beginning of the system culminating in this grand cañon of cañons.

Our warm cañon camp is also a good place to give a thought to the glaciers which still exist at the heads of the highest tributaries. Some of them are of considerable size, especially those on the Wind River and Sawatch ranges in Wyoming and Colorado. They are remnants of a vast system of glaciers which recently covered the upper part of the Colorado basin, sculptured its peaks, ridges, and valleys to their present forms, and extended far out over the plateau region—how far I cannot now say. It appears, therefore, that, however old the main trunk of the Colorado may be, all its widespread upper branches and the landscapes they flow through are new-born, scarce at all changed as yet in any important feature since they first came to light at the close of the Glacial Period.

The so-called Grand Colorado Plateau, of which the Grand Cañon is only one of the well-proportioned features, extends with a breadth of hundreds of miles from the flanks of the Wahsatch and Park mountains to the south of the San Francisco Peaks. Immediately to the north of the deepest part of the cañon it rises in a series of subordinate plateaus, diversified with green meadows, marshes, bogs, ponds, forests, and grovy park valleys, a favorite Indian hunting-ground, inhabited by elk, deer, beaver, etc. But far the greater part of the plateau is good sound desert, rocky, sandy, or fluffy with loose ashes and dust, dissected in some places into a labyrinth of stream-channel chasms like cracks in a dry clay-bed, or the narrow slit crevasses of glaciers—blackened with lava-flows, dotted with volcanoes and beautiful buttes, and lined with long continuous escarpments—a vast bed of sediments of an ancient sea-bottom, still nearly as level as when first laid down after being heaved into the sky a mile or two high.

Walking quietly about in the alleys and byways of the Grand Cañon city, we learn something of the way it was made; and all must admire effects so great from means apparently so simple; rain striking light hammer-blows or heavier in streams, with many rest Sundays; soft air and light, gentle sappers and miners, toiling forever; the big river sawing the plateau asunder, carrying away the eroded and ground waste, and exposing the edges of the strata to the weather; rain torrents sawing cross-streets and alleys, exposing the strata in the same way in hundreds of sections, the softer, less resisting beds weathering and receding faster, thus undermining the harder beds, which fall, not only in small weathered particles, but in heavy sheer-cleaving masses, assisted down from time to time by kindly earthquakes, rain torrents rushing the fallen material to the river, keeping the wall rocks constantly exposed. Thus the cañon grows wider and deeper. So also do the side-cañons and amphitheaters, while secondary gorges and cirques gradually isolate masses of the promontories, forming new buildings, all of which are being weathered and pulled and shaken down while being built, showing destruction and creation as one. We see the proudest temples and palaces in stateliest attitudes, wearing their sheets of detritus as royal robes, shedding off showers of red and yellow stones like trees in autumn shedding their leaves, going to dust like beautiful days to night, proclaiming as with the tongues of angels the natural beauty of death.

Every building is seen to be a remnant of once continuous beds of sediments,—sand and slime on the floor of an ancient sea, and filled with the remains of animals,—and every particle of the

sandstones and limestones of these wonderful structures to be derived from other landscapes, weathered and rolled and ground in
the storms and streams of other ages. And when we examine the
escarpments, hills, buttes, and other monumental masses of the
plateau on either side of the cañon, we discover that an amount of
material has been carried off in the general denudation of the region compared with which even that carried away in the making
of the Grand Cañon is as nothing. Thus each wonder in sight
becomes a window through which other wonders come to view. In
no other part of this continent are the wonders of geology, the
records of the world's auld lang syne, more widely opened, or displayed in higher piles. The whole cañon is a mine of fossils, in
which five thousand feet of horizontal strata are exposed in regular
succession over more than a thousand square miles of wall-space,
and on the adjacent plateau region there is another series of beds
twice as thick, forming a grand geological library—a collection of
stone books covering thousands of miles of shelving, tier on tier,
conveniently arranged for the student. And with what wonderful
scriptures are their pages filled—myriad forms of successive floras
and faunas, lavishly illustrated with colored drawings, carrying us
back into the midst of the life of a past infinitely remote. And as we
go on and on, studying this old, old life in the light of the life
beating warmly about us, we enrich and lengthen our own.

Index

Adams, Mount, 207
Aix, Mount, 207
Alliums, 95
Animals. *See also* Antelope; Bears; Deer;
 Squirrels; Wild goats; Wild sheep
 of Nevada, 130
 of Puget Sound, 177–78
 of San Gabriel Mountains, 103–4,
  106–7
 of Shasta region, 27–28, 59, 64–65
Antelope, of Shasta region, 64
Arbor vitae (*Thuja gigantea*), 165, 213
Arc Dome, 133
Ash Creek glacier, 69
Aspens, in Nevada, 127
Athabasca River, 235
Augusta Range, 131–32
Austin, Nevada, 140

Baker, Mount, 151, 155, 159, 207, 209
Bears
 at Mount Shasta, 27–28
 in Oregon, 223–24, 226–27
Beaver-Foot River, 237
Big Smoky Valley, Nevada, 112, 140–41
Big Spring, Shasta region, 34
Birds, in Oregon, 232–33
Bitter Root Mountains, 239
Black Butte, Shasta region, 47
Blackberry River, 237
Blue Mountains, 194, 197, 235, 241, 242
Bremer, Mount, 64–65
Bremer Meadows, 65
Bright Angel, Grand Cañon, 249, 262
Bright Angel Creek, Grand Cañon, 260,
 263
Bright Angel Hotel, Grand Cañon, 257
Bright Angel Trail, Grand Cañon, 263–64

British Columbia, 151–54
Brown, Mount, 237

Calochortus (*Calochortus Nuttallii*), 95–
 96
Camp of the Clouds, Mount Rainier, 188,
 192
Canadian Railroad, 182
Canby, General, 67
Canoe River, 237
Carbon River, 182
Carson and Humboldt Sink, 125
Carson River, 112, 115
Cascade Range, 147, 246
 Columbia River and, 235, 240, 242
 described, 197–98
 Deschutes River and, 242
 elk of, 228
 flowers of, 221–22
 forests of, 212, 214
 settling of, 173
 snows at, 204–5, 206–7
 views of, from Mount Rainier, 190–91
 Washington State divided by, 146
 wild goat of, 227–28
 wild sheep of, 228
 Yakima River and, 241
Castle Lake, Shasta region, 34
Caves, of western Sierra Nevada, 63
Cedars, 166–67, 213
Chaparral, of San Gabriel Mountains, 108
Chaudière Falls, 239
Chehalis River, 172
Cherry Creek, Nevada, 142
Chico, California, 72
City Creek, Utah, 76, 77, 83
Clark, William, 225–27
Cloud's Rest, Yosemite, 14, 15, 16, 19

Index

Coast Range, 197, 206, 235
Cochetopa River, 269
Coconino Forest, 249, 257, 263
Coeur d'Alène, Lake, 239
Coeur d'Alène River, 239
Colorado River, 234, 235. *See also* Grand
    Cañon
    branches of, 269–70
    origin of, 251–52, 269
Columbia River, 209, 225, 231
    branches and tributaries, 234–47
    confluence with Willamette River, 208
    early explorers and, 236–7
    plains of, 197–8, 207, 225
Congar, Doctor, 98
Coos Bay, Oregon, 213
Coquille River, 213
Coulterville, California, 12
Cowlitz River, 172, 189
Crater Lake, 246–47
Cypresses, of Washington, 165, 166–67

Dana, Mount, 18
DeBarth Shorb, J., 99
Deer
    in Grand Cañon, 268
    in Oregon, 228–29
Deschutes River, 242
Diamond Peak, 207
Dolores River, 269
Douglas, David, 214–18
    firs discovered by, 215
    pine discovered by, 215–19
    journal quotations, 215–18
Du Chesne River, 269
Dutton, Clarence, 257, 258

Eagle River, 269
Eaton Basin, San Gabriel Mountains, 106
Eaton Cañon, San Gabriel Mountains,
    104
Eaton Creek, San Gabriel Mountains, 105
Eberhardt mine, Nevada, 143
Egan Range, 142
El Capitan, 250–51
Elk Flat, Shasta region, 58

Elk River, 269
Elliot Bay, Washington, 180
Emigrant Road, Shasta region, 58–59
Erythroniums (*Erythronium grandiflora*),
    92–94
Esquimalt, British Columbia, 151, 152
Eureka, Nevada, 141, 143

"Fall, The," San Gabriel Mountains, 105–
    6
Fall River, 72
Fay, Jerome, 42, 51, 52, 55
Feather River, 72
Firs, 165–66, 213, 215
Flathead Lake, 239
Flathead River, 238
Flattery, Cape, 150
Flowers
    liliaceous, of Utah, 93–94, 95–96
    of Oregon, 221–22
    of Salt Lake City, 76–77
    of San Gabriel Mountains, 103, 107–8
    of Shasta region, 61
    of Utah, 76–77, 92–93, 95–96
    of Victoria, British Columbia, 153
Forests
    of Mount Rainier, 188
    of Oregon, 149, 211–12, 213–33
    of Puget Sound, 147–48
    of Sierra Nevada, 163–64, 218
    of Washington, 147–48, 162–76, 188
Fort Crook, 72
Fort Douglas, 76
Fort Hall, 194, 241
Fort Vancouver, 214–15
Foxtail pine, 125–27, 128
Fraser River, 182, 234, 235
Fritillaria (*Fritillaria atropurpurea*), 92–
    94, 95–96
Front Range, 269

Glaciers
    of Nevada, 131–38
    of Oquirrh Range, 75
    of Shasta region, 59, 62–63, 69, 73
    of Sierra Nevada, 131–38

Index

of Wahsatch Mountains, 75
of Yosemite Valley, 18, 19
Goats, wild, of Cascade Range, 227–28
Golden Gate Range, 125, 134
Gold prospectors, in Nevada, 141–44
Gold Range, 238
Gold River, 237
Grand Cañon, 248–72
  deer of, 268
  impressions of, 249–72
  Indians of, 266–68
  named rock forms of, 257
  Santa Fé railroad to, 248–49
  vegetation of, 265–66
  wildlife of, 268
Grand Colorado Plateau, 270–71
Grand River, 269
Granite Mountain, 118–19
Great Basin, 110, 118, 137, 144, 163
  glacial traces in, 131–38
Great Salt Lake, 86–89, 116
  beneficial effects of swimming in, 88–89
Great Salt Lake Basin, 75
Green River, 269
Green River Hot Springs, 182
Gunnison River, 269

Half Dome (Tissiak), 13, 250–51
Hamilton, Nevada, 140
Hance Trail, Grand Cañon, 264
Homebuilding, in California, 100, 101
Hood, Mount, 207, 208–11, 215, 244
Hooker, Mount, 237
"Hop Ranch," Washington, 182–83
Hops, 182–83
Hot Creek Mountains, 125, 133–34
Huckleberry Valley, Shasta region, 38, 58, 71
Hudson's Bay Company, 154, 155, 194, 214–15, 224–25, 241, 245

Illilouette glacier, Yosemite, 18, 19
Independence Lake, 37
Indian Garden Creek, Grand Cañon, 264

Indians
  berries used by, 171
  of Grand Cañon, 266–68
  of McCloud River, 29
  Modoc, 29–30, 67, 68
  of Oregon, 195, 214, 215–18, 223
  pine-nuts harvested by, 121–23, 124
  Pitt River, 38
  of Washington, 171, 172, 178, 183
  of Yosemite, 67

Jefferson, Mount, 37, 132, 207, 208
John Day River, 242
Jordan River, 82, 85, 95
Jordan Valley, Utah, 76, 82
Juan de Fuca Strait, 147, 148, 149–50

Kaweah River, 63
Kettle Falls, 239
Klamath Lakes, 29, 37, 65
Kootenay River, 238

Lake Point, Great Salt Lake, 86–89
Lakes. See names of lakes, e.g., Washington, Lake
Lassen's Butte, 38, 48, 72, 73
Latter-Day Saints, of Salt Lake City, 76, 77, 78–80, 82, 83–84, 95
  children, 80
  practices of, 79–80
  women, 78–79, 96
Lewis, Meriwether, 225–27
Lewis River. See Snake River
Liliaceous flowers, of Utah, 92, 93–94, 95–96
Logging, in Washington, 173–76
Los Angeles, 97–98
Lower Arrow Lake, 238
Lower Columbia Lake, 237
Lyell, Mount, 18
Lyell glacier, Yosemite, 18

McCloud glacier, 69
McCloud River, 28–29, 34, 38, 63, 70–71
  salmon-hatching establishment at, 41
  spring of, 70–71, 72

Index

McKenzie River, 234
McNeil's Point, Grand Cañon, 257
Madroña, 167
Maples
  of Oregon, 219, 220
  of Washington 167, 168–69
Medford, Oregon, 246
Menzies, Archibald, 165
Merced River, 67
Mining towns, dead, 139–45
Mirror Lake, Yosemite, 13, 18
Missouri River, 234, 235, 238
Modoc Indians, 29–30, 67, 68
Modoc Lava Beds, 48, 64, 65–67, 69
Modoc War, 64
Monito Valley, Nevada, 132
Moriah, Mount, 118
Mormons. *See* Latter-Day Saints
Mount Shasta. *See* Shasta, Mount
Mountaineers, 31–32
Muir's Peak, 62
Multnomah Falls, 244

Nevada, 110–45
  animals of, 130
  dead mining towns in, 139–45
  farm products of, 112, 113, 114–15
  farmers of, 113–14
  farms of, 110–16
  forests of, 117–30
  glaciers of, 131–38
  timber belt, 124–30
  water resources of, for ranches, 111–13
Nevada Falls, 184
Ne-whoi-al-pit-ku River, 239
Nisqually Cañon, 187
Nisqually River, 187, 189
North Dome, 129–30
Northern Pacific Railroad, 180, 182, 239
Nut pine (*Pinus Fremontiana*), 119, 120–23

Oaks, 167–68, 219–20
Okinagan River, 240
Olympic Mountains, 150–51, 156

Oquirrh Range, 75, 81, 83, 86
  ascent of, 91–96
  forests of, 94
  liliaceous flowers of, 92–93, 95–96
Orange groves, San Gabriel Valley, 98–99
Oregon, 193–247
  climate of, 197–207
  coast of, 140, 195–97
  flowers of, 221–22
  forests of, 211–12, 213–33
  Indians of, 214, 215–18, 223
  physical characteristics of, 193–212
  rivers of, 234–47 (*see also names of rivers*)
  settlers' routes to, 194, 199–201
  travelers to, 223
  wildlife of, 223–33
Oregon and California Railroad, 199

Pacific Slope, 212, 225
Painted Desert, 263
Park Range, 269
Pasadena, California, 98, 101
Pend d'Oreille Lake, 239
Pine-nuts, 130. *See also* Nut pine
  Indians and, 121–23, 124
Pines
  foxtail, 125–27, 128
  nut (*Pinus Fremontiana*), 119, 120–23
  Oregon (*Abies Douglasii*), 213
  sugar (*Pinus Lambertiana*), 214, 215–18
  white (*Pinus flexilis*), 125
  yellow (*Pinus ponderosa*), 166, 214
Pitt, Mount, 37, 207
Pitt River, 72–73
Platte River, 234
Pluto's Cave, Shasta region, 63
Port Townsend, 155, 156–58
Port Townsend Bay, 156
Portland and Tacoma Railroad, 171
Portland, Oregon, 208, 210
Powell, John Wesley, 257, 258, 268–69
Puget Sound, 146–61, 162, 173
  animals of, 177–78
  forests of, 147–48

Index

peoples of, 180–81
towns of, 179–85
weather of, 161
Punch-Bowl Lake, 237

Railroads
 Canadian, 182
 logging, 173
 Northern Pacific, 180, 182, 239
 Oregon and California, 199
 Portland and Tacoma, 171
 Santa Fé, 248–49
 Seattle, Lake-Shore and Eastern, 186
 Western Utah, 86–87
Rainier, Mount, 149, 159, 207
 ascent of, from south side, 186–92
 descent of, 191–92
 forests of, 188
 height of, 186
 views from summit of, 190–91
Redding, California, 40
Reese River Valley, Nevada, 112, 115
Rhett Lake, 37
Rivers. *See also names of rivers*
 of Oregon, 234–47
 of Shasta region, 70–73
 of Sierra Nevada, 69–70
 tracing, 72
Roaring River, 269
Rocky Mountains, 225
 forests of, 212
 rivers originating in, 234
Rogue River, 246
Rogue River Valley, 198, 246
Rowe's Point, Grand Cañon, 257

Sacramento River, 38, 61–62
St. Elias, Mount, 151
St. Helen's, Mount, 159, 207, 208, 244
Salt Lake. *See* Great Salt Lake
Salt Lake City, 75–80, 83, 86
 flowers of, 76–77
 Latter-Day Saints of, 76, 77, 78–80,
  83–84
 physical appearance of, 75–78

surrounding commons, 77
surrounding mountains, 75–76, 84, 87
trees of, 78
San Antonio, Mount, 107
San Bernardino Mountains, 164
San Francisco Peaks, 257, 270
San Gabriel Mountains, 103–9, 164
 animals of, 103–4, 106–7
 flowers of, 103, 107–8
 inaccessibility of, 103
 physical appearance of, 103–4
 plant life, 108–9
San Gabriel Valley, 97–102
 climate of, 102
 homebuilding in, 100
 orange groves, 98–100
 settlers, 100–102
San Juan Island, 155–56
San Pasqual Rancho, 101
San Rafael River, 269
Santa Fé Railroad, 248–49
Santa Monica, California, 97
Saskatchewan River, 234, 235
Sawatch Range, 269, 270
Schellbourne, Nevada, 141–42
Scott, Mount, 37–38, 207
Seattle, 175, 179, 180, 181–82
Seattle, Lake-Shore and Eastern Railroad,
 186
Selkirk Range, 237, 238
Shasta, Mount, 2, 20–74, 199–200
 Alpine Zone, 22–23
 animal life at, 27–28, 59, 64–65
 bees at, 26–27
 bogs of, 61–62
 Chaparral Zone, 21–22, 56–57
 Cinder Cone, 38
 Fir Zone, 22
 flowers of, 26
 forests of, 38, 66, 71, 73
 glaciers of, 23–24, 59, 62–63, 69, 73
 highest point, 20
 human inhabitants of, 28–35
 need for preservation of, 74
 north side, 30–31

Index

rambles around base of, 58–74
rivers of, 70–73
stormy night on summit, 40–55
in summer, 20–39
summit, 36–37
tourists at, 34–35
volcanic craters, 23, 38–39
wild sheep of, 2–11
Shasta Pass, 63
Shasta River, 38, 70
Shasta Valley, 29, 38, 48, 58, 64
Sheep, 115
Sheep, wild
fleece of, 2–8
of Grand Cañon, 268
of Nevada, 130
of Oregon, 228
of Shasta region, 2–11, 30, 39, 46–47,
64–65
of Washington, 172
Sheep Rock, Shasta region, 39, 63–64, 69
Shermantown, Nevada, 140
Sierra Nevada, 113, 135
caves of, 63
dead mining towns of, 139–44
eastern flank of, 115, 117
forests of, 163–64, 218
glaciers of, 131–38
rivers of, 69–70
Siskiyou Mountains, 37–38, 199, 213
Sisson, 35, 41, 47, 56, 57, 63
Sisson meadows, 199
Smith, Sydney, 34
Snake Range, 124, 134–35
Jeff Davis group of, 134–35
Snake River, 194, 225, 235, 240–41
Snoqualmie Falls, 184–85
Snoqualmie River, 164, 169, 182–85
Soda Springs, Mount Rainier, 187
Soda Springs, Mount Shasta, 34
South Dome, 15–16, 19
South glacier, Yosemite, 18
South Saskatchewan River, 239
Spill-e-Mee-Chene River, 237
Spokane, Washington, 239–40

Spokane Falls, 239, 240
Spokane River, 237, 240
Spruce
Douglas (*Pseudotsuga Douglasii*), 128,
162–64, 185, 213, 214, 265
Hemlock, 165
Rocky Mountain, 128–29
white ("Sitka pine"), 164–65
Squak, Lake, 171, 184
Squaw Valley, Shasta region, 58
Squirrel, Douglas (*Sciurus Douglasi*)
at Mount Shasta, 46
in Oregon forests, 231–32
Strawberry Meadows, Shasta region, 25,
34
Strawberry Valley, Shasta region, 21, 38,
57, 61, 72
Sugar pine (*Pinus Lambertiana*), 218–19
Swansea, Nevada, 140

Tacoma, Washington, 171, 175, 179–80
Tenaya Cañon, 13, 14–18
Tenaya Creek, 17
Tenaya Falls, 13
Tenaya Lake, 17–18, 19
Thielson, Mount, 207
Three Sisters, 37, 207
Tissiak (Half Dome), 13, 250–51
Toquima Range, 132
Toyabe Range, 115, 131–32, 133, 140
Treasure Hill, Nevada, 140, 143
Trinity Mountains, 38
Troy Range, 127, 129
Truckee River, 112
Trumball, Mount, 257
Tule Lake, 65–66, 68–69
Turlock, California, 12

Uinta River, 269
Umatilla River, 242
Umpqua River, 246
Umpqua Valley, 198
Uncompahgre River, 269
Upper Arrow Lake, 238
Upper Columbia Lake, 237, 238

Index

Utah. *See also* Great Salt Lake; Salt Lake
  City
  climate, 116
  flowers of, 90–93, 95–96
  storm in, 81–85
Utah Lake, 95

Van Bremer brothers, 65
Vancouver, George, 158–60, 165
Vancouver, Washington, 182
Vancouver Island, British Columbia, 151,
  167
Victoria, British Columbia, 151–54, 182

Wahsatch Mountains, 75, 81, 84, 130,
  163
Wahsatch River, 269
Walker River, 112, 115
Walla-Walla River, 242
Washington, 146–92
  forests of, 162–76
  Indians of, 178, 183
  lakes of, 170–71
  logging in, 173–76, 177–78
  settlers of, 173–74
  spruces of, 185
Washington, Lake, 184
Wassuck Range, 131–32
Water resources, of Nevada, 111–13
Watkins, Lake, 18
Watkins, Mount, 16
Western Utah Railroad, 86–87
Wheeler's Peak, 118, 128–30

Whidbey Island, 158
Whirlpool River, 237
White Pine Hills, 143
White Pine Range, 125, 128, 134
Whitney Glacier, 35, 44, 47, 51, 62–63
Whitney, Mount, 20
Wild goats, of Cascade Range, 227–28
Wild sheep
  fleece of, 2–8
  of Grand Cañon, 268
  of Nevada, 130
  of Oregon, 228
  of Shasta region, 2–11, 30, 39, 46–47,
    64–65
  of Washington, 172
Willamette River, 208, 215, 221, 241,
  245–46
Willamette Valley, 173, 194, 198, 202,
  214, 224
Wind River Range, 269, 270

Yakima River, 241
Yampa River, 269
Yellowstone, 235, 248
  Grand Cañon of, 250
Yellowstone River, 234, 235
Yelm Prairie, 187
Yosemite Indians, 67
Yosemite Valley, 12–18, 67, 248, 250–51
  glaciers, 18, 19
  Tenaya region, 13–18
Young, Brigham, 83–84
Young, Lily, 96